Using Computers in Linguistics

A Practical Guide

Computing has had a dramatic impact on the discipline of linguistics and is shaping the way we conceptualize both linguistics and language.

Using Computers in Linguistics provides a practical introduction to recent developments in linguistic computing and offers specific guidance to the linguist or language professional who wishes to take advantage of them.

The book is divided into eight chapters, each of which is written by an expert in the field. The contributions focus on different aspects of the interaction of computing and linguistics: the Internet, software for field-work and teaching linguistics, Unix utilities, the availability of electronic texts, new methodologies in natural language processing, and the development of the CELLAR computing environment for linguistic analysis.

Features include:

- a glossary of technical terms, including acronyms
- chapter appendices which list and review relevant resources, such as books, software, URLs
- more extensive and regularly updated appendices of resources on the World Wide Web:
  http://www.lsa.umich.edu/ling/jlawler/routledge

Using Computers in Linguistics will be indispensable for anyone interested in linguistics.

John M. Lawler is associate professor of linguistics at the University of Michigan and director of its undergraduate program in linguistics.

Helen Aristar Dry is professor of linguistics at Eastern Michigan University, and is co-founder and moderator of The LINGUIST List, a 9000-member electronic discussion forum for academic linguists.

Using Computers in Linguistics

A Practical Guide

Edited by John M. Lawler and
Helen Aristar Dry

London and New York

First published 1998
by Routledge
11 New Fetter Lane, London EC4P 4EE

Simultaneously published in the USA and Canada
by Routledge
29 West 35th Street, New York, NY 10001

©1998 John M. Lawler and Helen Aristar Dry

Typeset in Plantin by Florencetype Ltd., Stoodleigh, Devon
Printed and bound in Great Britain by Biddles Ltd.,
Guildford and King's Lynn

British Library Cataloguing in Publication Data
A catalogue record for this book is available from the
British Library

Library of Congress Cataloguing in Publication Data
Using Computers in Linguistics: a practical guide/edited
by John M. Lawler and Helen Aristar Dry.
p. cm.
Includes bibliographical references (p.) and index.
1. Computational linguistics. I   Lawler, John M., 1942– .
II.   Dry, Helen Aristar, 1946– .
P98.U767   1998
410′.285–dc21   97–23787
                                                      CIP

ISBN 0–415–16793–0 (pbk)
ISBN 0–415–16792–2 (hbk)

This book is dedicated to the editors' parents:
Ida Maye Smith Dry
Harold Franklin Dry
Agnita Margaret Engler Lawler
and to the memory of
Edward Michael Lawler (1914–54),
who would have liked both computing and linguistics

Contents

List of figures

List of contributors

Evan L. Antworth has worked with the Summer Institute of Linguistics for 19 years, including seven years of work in the Philippines. Since the early 1980s he has worked with field linguists as a consultant in the area of using microcomputers to do linguistic field work. In 1989 he began work in the Academic Computing Department of SIL in Dallas, Texas where he is now associate editor of the department's series *Occasional Publications in Academic Computing*. He has collaborated on several software development projects of interest to linguists, including writing a book on PC-KIMMO, SIL's implementation of Kimmo Koskenniemis' two-level model of morphology.

Anthony Rodriques Aristar is Associate Professor of Linguistics at Texas A&M University and co-moderator of The LINGUIST List, which he founded in 1989 when he was a Lecturer in Linguistics at the University of Western Australia. Previously he was the Chief Linguist of a natural language research group at Microelectronics and Computer Technology Corporation, where he developed the first fully functional Arabic morphological analyzer. His primary research interests are typology, morphology, and historical linguistics. His recent publications include "Binder Anaphors and the Diachrony of Case Displacement" in *Double Case-agreement by Suffixaufname*, ed. Franz Plank (Oxford University Press: 1994) and "On Diachronic Sources of Synchronic Pattern: An Investigation into the Origin of Linguistic Universals," *Language* 67: 1–33 (1991).

Helen Aristar Dry is Professor of Linguistics at Eastern Michigan University. She is co-founder and moderator, with Anthony Aristar, of The LINGUIST List, a 9000-member electronic discussion forum for academic linguists. She received her PhD in 1975 in English Language and Linguistics from the University of Texas at Austin; and her primary research interests are textlinguistics, linguistic stylistics, and discourse analysis. Her publications have appeared in *Style, Language and Style,*

Text, Journal of Literary Semantics, Studies in Anthropological Linguistics,
and others. Recently she has done considerable legal consulting on author-
ship identification, and her non-academic publications include several
articles on this topic.

James E. Hoard received his PhD in Linguistics from the University of
Washington, where he was a National Defense Foreign Language Fellow
and a Woodrow Wilson Dissertation Fellow. Dr. Hoard is currently the
Program Manager of the Natural Language Processing Program, Boeing
Information and Support Services, Research and Technology organiza-
tion. He is responsible for the program's long range research and
development plan and is the principal investigator of the Natural
Language Understanding project. Dr. Hoard is also an Affiliate Professor
at the University of Washington and teaches courses in computational
linguistics. Recent publications include "The Application of Natural
Phonology to Computerized Speech Understanding" (with R. Wojcik, in
B. Hurch and R. A. Rhodes (eds), *Natural Phonology: The State of the
Art, Trends in Linguistics, Studies and Monographs*, 92; 1996, pp. 121–131).

Susan Hockey is Professor in the Faculty of Arts at the University of
Alberta. She has been active in humanities computing since 1969. From
1975 to 1991 she was at Oxford University where her most recent position
was Director of the Computers in Teaching Initiative Centre for Textual
Studies and Director of the Office for Humanities Communication. From
1991 to 1997 she served as the first director of the Center for Electronic
Texts in the Humanities (CETH) at Princeton and Rutgers Universities,
where, together with Willard McCarty, she founded and directed the
CETH Seminar on Methods and Tools for Electronic Texts in the
Humanities. She is chair of the Association for Literary and Linguistic
Computing and a member (currently chair) of the Steering Committee
of the Text Encoding Initiative. Her experience in electronic texts includes
text archiving, concordance and retrieval software (development of the
Oxford Concordance Program), teaching literary and linguistic computing
(for 15 years), corpus design and development, cataloguing and documenting electronic texts. She is the author of two books, editor of three
collections of essays, and author of approximately thirty articles on various
aspects of text analysis computing.

John M. Lawler is Associate Professor of Linguistics at the University
of Michigan in Ann Arbor, where he is Director of the Undergraduate
Program in Linguistics, and teaches also in the Residential College. As
chair of the Linguistic Society of America's Computing Committee, he
organized the symposium and software exhibit that generated this volume.
After a BA in Mathematics and German, an MA thesis on *Some*

Applications of Computers to Linguistic Field Methods, and several years of teaching English as a Foreign Language, he received his PhD under George Lakoff and Robin T. Lakoff. He is a software author (*A World of Words, The Chomskybot*) and has been a consultant on computing organization and software development for industry and academia. A generalist by inclination, he has published on a broad spectrum of linguistic topics, including the semantics of generic reference, second-language learning, Acehnese syntax, metaphor, English lexical semantics, metalinguistics, negation and logic, sound symbolism, and popular English usage.

Henry Rogers, having received a PhD in Linguistics from Yale, is an Associate Professor of Linguistics, Anthropology, and Speech Pathology at the University of Toronto, and currently Associate Chair of Linguistics. He is the author of *Theoretical and Practical Phonetics,* the co-author of two software packages for teaching linguistics – Phthong and Arbourite, and the developer of a phonetic font family – IPAPhon. In 1994, he was the Acting Director of the Centre for Computing in the Humanities. His research interests are writing systems, phonetics, and Scots Gaelic; currently he is working on a book of the writing systems of northern South Asia.

Gary F. Simons is Director of the Academic Computing Department at the international headquarters of the Summer Institute of Linguistics in Dallas, Texas. In this capacity he has led a number of projects to develop software for field linguists, including the CELLAR project described in this volume. Prior to taking up this post in 1984, he did fieldwork with SIL in Papua New Guinea (1976) and the Solomon Islands (1977–1983). He was active in the committee that developed the Text Encoding Initiative's guidelines for text analysis and interpretation (1989–1994), and currently serves as a member of the TEI's Technical Review Committee. He received a PhD in general linguistics (with minor emphases in computer science and classics) from Cornell University in 1979.

J. Randolph Valentine is an Assistant Professor in Linguistics and American Indian studies at the University of Wisconsin–Madison. His research interests include the theory and practice of comprehensive grammatical documentation, especially as applied to Algonquian languages. He is also an avid student of Ojibwe ethnopoetics and stylistics, and seeks to develop a comprehensive approach to Ojibwe oral traditions, encompassing linguistic, antropological, folkloristic, and literary approaches. His work has involved extensive use of computer technology in the research and presentation of Algonquian languages.

The Natural Language Group at the MITRE Corporation in Bedford, Massachusetts has been investigating the properties of human language in text and interactive discourse for many years. The integrated approach of the group reflects the authors' diversity. The director of the group, **Dr. Lynette Hirschman**, holds a PhD in computational linguistics and is a leader in both the speech understanding and evaluation-based language processing communities. **Dr. Samuel Bayer** holds a PhD in theoretical linguistics, and currently coordinates MITRE's internal research effort in human-computer interaction. **Marc Vilain** leads MITRE's message understanding effort, and has contributed innovative research to the areas of corpus-based language processing, knowledge representation, and message understanding. **John Aberdeen** holds MA degrees in both linguistics and cognitive psychology and has made broad contributions to MITRE's message understanding work, both in primary development and technology transition. **David Palmer** holds an MS in computational linguistics and specializes in text segmentation, both at the word and sentence level. **John Burger** has both contributed to and led research in a wide range of areas related to language processing, including multimodal interaction, discourse understanding, and information retrieval. For a bibliography and more information, please visit the group's Web site at:

http://www.mitre.org/resources/centers/advanced_info/g04h/nl-index.html

Introduction

John M. Lawler and Helen Aristar Dry

0.1 COMPUTING AND LINGUISTICS

In the last decade computers have dramatically changed the professional life of the ordinary working linguist, altering the things we can do, the ways we can do them, and even the ways we can think about them. The change has been gradual, incremental, and largely experiential. But the handwriting is already on the screen – the rate of change is accelerating, and the end is not in sight.

The relations between computing and linguistics are in fact deeper and more interesting than mere technological change might suggest. Indeed, the advent of widespread access to computing power may well have had an effect on the discipline comparable to that of the early study of Native American languages. In the first half of this century, the experience of doing fieldwork on Native American languages shaped the concepts and methodologies of American Structuralism; now, in the second half of the century, the common experience of using computers is shaping the way we conceptualize both linguistics and language.

This is apparent, for example, in the metaphors we use. As is widely recognized, the metaphor of automatic data processing underlies and informs the goals and methodology of generative grammar. And, whatever the validity of this image as an intellectual or ideological basis for linguistic theory, it is unquestionably valid in representing the actual experience of doing linguistics today, as anyone who has studied both syntax and programming will attest.

Of course, one reason the computing metaphor works so well is that language truly is a form of software. Just as the human brain was the model for computer hardware, human language was the model for computer software – and we are now, after a decade of widespread, intensive experience with computers, in a position to recognize experientially what that means. The social, cultural, and intellectual activities of linguistics and computing (in academia, in hardware and software industries, and in various user communities) are woven of many of the same conceptual threads. The relations between linguistics and computing are not only metaphoric, but symmetrically so, and represent a natural and useful description of important aspects of both phenomena.

It is no wonder, then, that linguists were among the first scholars outside of the strictly technical fields to become generally computer-literate. Computational technologies offer linguists significant benefits, both at the individual and the disciplinary level. They can facilitate our individual research and teaching, allowing us to gather information more quickly, analyze large bodies of data more efficiently, and reach a more varied group of students through individualized teaching programs. At the same time, they are reshaping the discipline, bringing to light new areas of research, new types of data, and new analytical tools.

This book is an attempt to help the ordinary working linguist take full advantage of these technological opportunities. It provides wide-ranging information on linguistic computing, in all the senses of that phrase; and it was written specifically for readers with some knowledge of language and linguistics, as well as some curiosity about computing. This description fits not only linguists *per se*, but also an expanding group of individuals who are not professional linguists, but who deal computationally with language: among others, programmers and analysts, library information specialists, and academic humanists engaged in the study of texts. We have tried to meet the needs of these readers, at the same time as we focus on computational information particularly relevant to linguistics. Section 0.2 enumerates some of the features which are designed to make the book accessible to a wide range of readers.

0.2 NEEDS

First and foremost, the contributors were asked to write in a non-technical style and to assume a minimum of computational knowledge on the part of their readers. Given the claims in Section 0.1 about the general computer literacy of the discipline, this request may seem to require explanation. But, in the first place, the book is intended for students as well as working linguists. And, in fact, as noted in Section 0.4, most of the chapters would be effective as classroom introductions to particular topics, or as supplementary background reading.

And, in the second place, our experience suggests that – however computer-literate linguists are as a group – few individual linguists outside the strictly computational subfields would lay claim to thorough understanding of the technologies they use or perfect confidence in learning new ones. Many feel that their computer knowledge is spotty rather than systematic, since often it was acquired "on the fly," in bits and pieces, under pressure of the need to solve a particular problem or per-form a specific task. Such linguists, we believe, may welcome overviews which "begin at the beginning," even on topics they already know something about.

Similarly, many linguists may welcome guidance on choosing or adapting linguistic software, even though they are experienced computer users. Computer technology is, of course, complex and rapidly changing, and the readily available commercial programs often turn out to be ill-suited to the needs of academics. As a result, most of us hesitate before embarking on learning a new piece of software or Internet functionality. After all, what we learn may soon be made obsolete by newer developments. And furthermore, it is difficult to tell, ahead of time, whether the benefits we will gain from the software will justify the effort involved in mastering it.

In such quandaries, we have received only minimal help from the software industry. Commercial developers rarely write software for academic purposes; and, as a result, there are few published evaluations to guide us in choosing software for teaching or research.

Commercial software development is, of course, a competitive business; and the particular economics of the industry almost insure that scholars will not be a primary market. Unlike many other industries, the software industry sustains development costs that far exceed manufacturing costs. Designing reliable software is a difficult, lengthy process; and it is also extremely expensive.[1] By contrast, the costs of duplicating the final deliverable programs are negligible. This means that software manufacturers must recoup what they spend on development by selling multiple copies of the finished product.

As a result, software development is driven by the perceived needs of businesses, which can and will pay high prices for multiple copies of programs, and which can and will upgrade their software regularly. Scholars, on the other hand, represent a small, specialized, and comparatively impoverished market. Those whose needs dovetail with the needs of business may be able to find useful commercial software. But those whose computing needs are more complex are usually disappointed. This group includes many linguists. And some of these have filled the gap by developing their own software, while others have learned to modify or enhance common software packages to suit their specialized purposes. Much of this "homegrown" software and many of the development tools could be useful to other linguists; so several of the overviews in this book also survey and evaluate relevant software.

0.3   PURPOSE AND PROVENANCE OF THE BOOK

This book sprang from a single event, a colloquium entitled "Computing and the Ordinary Working Linguist," which the editors organized for the 1992 meeting of the Linguistic Society of America in Philadelphia. John Lawler also organized the first annual LSA software exhibit for that meeting. Together these two events drew the attention of many linguists to the role of computing in their professional lives; and there were requests for a printed followup. This book is the result: its topics and contributors include many from the original panel, although the two lists are not identical.

Besides this introduction, the book has eight chapters, each focused on a different aspect of the interaction of computing and linguistics. The topics are arranged roughly in the order of increasing specialization. The early chapters are thus more general, and in some cases more accessible, than the last. However, all are designed for a non-technical audience. To that end, the book includes a glossary of the special computing terms used in the various articles. Terms in the glossary appear in **bold italic** upon their first occurrence in a chapter. And, where relevant, chapter appendices provide annotated lists of selected print, software, and network resources to guide the reader in learning more about the topic. Fuller versions of these appendices are also available on the World Wide Web (see Section 0.5).

0.4   OVERVIEW OF THE CHAPTERS

Chapter 1, "The nature of linguistic data and the requirements of a computing environment for linguistic research" by Gary F. Simons, the Director of Computing in the Summer Institute of Linguistics, discusses language data and the special demands which it makes on computational resources. As Simons puts it:

1 The data are multilingual, so the computing environment must be able to keep track of what language each datum is in, and then display and process it accordingly.
2 The data in text unfold sequentially, so the computing environment must be able to represent the text in proper sequence.
3 The data are hierarchically structured, so the computing environment must be able to build hierarchical structures of arbitrary depth.
4 The data are multidimensional, so the computing environment must be able to attach many kinds of analysis and interpretation to a single datum.
5 The data are highly integrated, so the computing environment must be able to store and follow associative links between related pieces of data.
6 While doing all of the above to model the information structure of the data correctly, the computing environment must be able to present conventionally formatted displays of the data.

This chapter prefigures most of the major themes that surface in the other chapters, and contains some discussion of the CELLAR prototype computing environment now under development by SIL. It should be read first, and in our opinion it should be required reading for anyone planning a research career in linguistics.

Chapter 2, "The Internet: an introduction" by Helen Aristar Dry of Eastern Michigan University and Anthony Rodrigues Aristar of Texas A&M University, the co-moderators of the LINGUIST List, is intended to be an Internet primer – it offers an overview of the workings of the Internet and prompts the reader to try out several basic Internet technologies. After a discussion of the immediate effects of the net on linguists, it describes the *protocol*s that make the Internet possible, discusses the software that implements features of the net like e-mail, *ftp*, *gopher*, and the *World Wide Web*, and concludes with instructions on constructing a Web page. The authors attempted to make the chapter clear enough to help new Internet users but also comprehensive enough to fill in gaps in the knowledge of "old hands." Linguists who make use of the Internet in their courses may find this a useful chapter to distribute to students at the beginning of the term.

Chapter 3, "Education," by Henry Rogers of the University of Toronto, an author of both linguistic teaching software (**Phthong**) and linguistics fonts (**Palphon**), explains the advantages and drawbacks of using software for teaching linguistics. It also offers tips on developing teaching software, useful to the many linguists who choose to create their own programs or customize existing software packages in order to better meet their needs. Besides a great deal of good advice, derived from experience, this chapter includes a complete, annotated survey of the currently available educational software for linguistics. It should therefore be very valuable to professors already committed to computer-aided instruction, as well as to those who have just begun looking for new ways to present linguistic material to their students.

Chapter 4, "Textual databases" by Susan Hockey of the University of Alberta, a major figure in the establishment of the Oxford Text Archive and the *Text Encoding Initiative*, is a discussion of the generation, maintenance, and study of large text *corpora*. The availability of data collections like the Brown and LOB corpora has dramatically changed many areas of language scholarship (see for example the chapter by Bayer *et al.* in this volume). This chapter describes what corpora are, where they can be accessed, how they are annotated, what the various types of markup communicate, and what software is available to manipulate them. SGML and the work of the Text Encoding Initiative are concisely explained; in sum, the article represents a succinct and authoritative overview useful to anyone wishing to use electronic texts in their teaching or research.

While Chapter 4 deals with getting and organizing textual data, Chapter 5, "The Unix language family" deals with what you can do with it once you've got it. This chapter, written by John M. Lawler of the University of Michigan, is an introduction to Unix, the most widely-used computer **operating system** for workstation-class machines. It is written in the form of a language sketch, à la Comrie (1987), on the assumption that linguists who are comfortable with complex technical subjects like case and aspect systems, complex clauses, and formal grammars will find the technical complexities of Unix more amenable if they are presented in familiar ways. Among other topics, it explains **regular expressions** (a formal specification of lexical strings for search-and-replace operations), **filter** programs, and **software tools**. Examples include simple **scripts** and **alias**es, and techniques for construction of lexical analysis tools from standard Unix programs. For experienced computer users who have yet to try creating programs, the chapter demystifies the construction of software tools. And it should be valuable to computer novices as well, since it shows what can be accomplished by ordinary linguists using only analytic thinking and the power of Unix.

In Chapter 6, "Software for doing field linguistics," Evan L. Antworth of the Summer Institute of Linguistics and J. Randolph Valentine of the University of Wisconsin-Madison discuss a basic problem for ordinary working linguists: how to use computers to advantage in organizing and analyzing linguistic data. Along the way, they give thoughtful and detailed answers to some perennial questions, like "What kind of computer should I buy?" and "What criteria should I use to judge software for linguistic use?" The chapter concludes with an annotated survey of available language analysis software, focusing on "readily available, low cost software products that run on personal computers, especially portable computers." This survey should be an important resource list for research linguists and their students, whether or not they ever do fieldwork.

The final two chapters deal with **Computational Linguistics** (CL), or **Natural Language Processing** (NLP), an area that is as much a part of Computer Science as of Linguistics, and that is *terra incognita* for many linguists, even those who regularly use computers. It is also an area that has significant commercial applications, and both chapters are written by computational linguists working in non-academic environments.

By design, they constitute a point-counterpoint discussion of the recent history and prospective future of the field of NLP. While the authors of both chapters agree on the importance of NLP and its eventual impact on linguistic theory, they represent two quite distinct viewpoints on the nature and practice of natural language processing, and its relation to traditional linguistics.

In Chapter 7, "Language understanding and the emerging alignment of linguistics and natural language processing," James E. Hoard of the Boeing Corporation suggests that NLP has already developed the technology necessary to produce commercial-quality products which can perform the following functions:

Grammar and style checking – Providing editorial critiques of vocabulary usage, grammar, and style – improving the quality of all sorts of writing – especially the readability of complex technical documents.

Machine translation – Translating texts, especially business and technical texts, from one natural language to another.

Information extraction – Analyzing the meaning of texts in detail, answering specific questions about text content. For many kinds of text (e.g., medical case histories) that are in a well-bounded domain, systems will extract information and put it into databases for statistical analyses.

Natural language interfaces – Understanding natural language commands and taking appropriate actions, providing a much freer interchange between people and computers.

Programming in English – Enabling the use of carefully controlled, yet ordinary, human language to program computers, largely eliminating much of the need for highly-specialized and arcane computer "languages."

Modeling and simulation – Enabling computer modeling and simulation of all manner of real-world activities and scenarios where symbolic information and symbolic reasoning are essential to success.

Hoard's discussion is based on a "top-down" model of language understanding, with syntactic, lexical, semantic, and pragmatic components, most of which are familiar enough to traditional linguists. He advances the thesis "that the need for language understanding to meet the goals of NLP will have a profound effect on the objectives of linguistics itself," outlines criteria for applying linguistic theory to the goals of language understanding, and concludes:

> The effect of NLP on academic linguistics will produce a profound enlargement in its scope and objectives and greatly influence the work of its practitioners. The shift will be . . . one that places the present focus on language description, including the concern for language acquisition and linguistic universals, within the much larger (and to my mind, much more interesting) context of language understanding.

This is a provocative article, and it has provoked a response from representatives of a radically different tradition in NLP, that of ***Corpus-Based Linguistics***. In Chapter 8, "Theoretical and computational linguistics: toward a mutual understanding," Samuel L. Bayer and his colleagues at Mitre Corporation point out that, since its inception,

> CL has alternated between defining itself in terms of and in opposition to mainstream theoretical linguistics. . . . Since the late 1980s, it seems that a growing group of CL practitioners has once more turned away from formal theory. In response to the demands imposed by the

analysis of large corpora of linguistic data, statistical techniques have been adopted in CL which emphasize shallow, robust accounts of linguistic phenomena at the expense of the detail and formal complexity of current theory.

This "bottom-up," data-driven, statistical model of NLP has had great recent success, which Bayer *et al.* describe in detail. Linguists have always known that natural language is significantly redundant, though this has often been seen more as a performance matter than something linguistics should deal with. What the results of Corpus-based NLP seem to show is that, on the contrary, this is an exploitable design feature of natural language, and with the advent of powerful means of statistical analysis of large corpora, a surprising amount of structure and meaning can be extracted from text without recourse to techniques grounded in linguistic theory. A crucial point made in this chapter is that:

> a large subset of language can be handled with relatively simple computational tools; a much smaller subset requires a radically more expensive approach; and an even smaller subset something more expensive still. This observation has profound effects on the analysis of large corpora: there is a premium on identifying those linguistic insights which are simplest, most general, least controversial, and most powerful, in order to exploit them to gain the broadest coverage for the least effort.

Those who have wondered what has been going on in NLP, and how it will eventually affect conventional linguistics, should find much of interest in these chapters.

0.5   CONCLUSION

The eight chapters, then, explore many different facets of the interaction between computers and linguistics. In approach, they range from "How to" chapters teaching basic skills to knowledgeable overviews of whole subdisciplines, such as NLP. Together, they offer a range of linguistically relevant computing information intended to address some of the needs noted in section 0.2, e.g., the need for:

Coherence – The initial chapters by Simons, and by Dry and Aristar, though very different in level and scope, both attempt to provide systematic explanations of topics which many linguists understand only partially.

Evaluation – Each chapter includes some evaluative material, intended to compensate for the scarcity of evaluations of academic software. But the chapters by Rogers, and by Antworth and Valentine are primarily concerned with surveying the programs available for language scholarship and education.

Development and application – The chapters by Rogers and Lawler offer advice on customizing existing software and creating new software, often on an *ad hoc* basis, to solve immediate problems in language analysis.

Knowledge of the discipline – The chapter by Hockey describes a new datasource which is having considerable impact on several linguistic subfields. And, finally, the last two chapters on NLP by Hoard, and by Bayer *et al.*, suggest ways the discipline may develop in response to the changing scholarly and economic environments. These three chapters acquaint the reader with the effect that computer technology is having on the evolution of the field.

We hope that the book will serve novice linguists as a primer at the same time as it serves others as a handbook and guide to resources. Any such guide dates rapidly, of course; but we have attempted to maintain the book's technological relevance as long as possible by:

- focusing on technology that is both mature enough to be useful, and likely, in our opinion, to continue growing in importance to linguistics
- addressing each topic at a sufficiently general level, so that the usefulness of the information is not tied to a specific implementation or environment
- posting each chapter's annotated resource list as an online appendix on the World Wide Web. The appendices appearing in the printed book represent only the most important and stable resources. On the Web pages, these have been augmented with additional listings and live links to current Internet resources. These Web pages will be regularly updated by the authors. They can be found at the URL: http://www.routledge.com/

In this way, we hope to take advantage of one of the new avenues of communication opened up to academics by Internet technology. We expect electronic communication to become ever more important to our discipline, since a field like linguistics is defined in the last analysis by who communicates with whom, and how they interact. There is now a totally new communicational topology in linguistic demography, due in large part to the widespread use of computers. We hope this book will be of use to those mapping out these new lands.

NOTE

1 A glance at Brooks (1995) provides ample evidence of the inherent difficulties and the expense.

The nature of linguistic data and the requirements of a computing environment for linguistic research

Gary F. Simons

The progress made in the last decade toward harnessing the power of electronic computers as a tool for the ordinary working linguist (OWL) has been phenomenal. As the eighties dawned, virtually no OWLs were using computers, but the personal computer revolution was just beginning and it was possible to foresee its impact on our discipline (Simons, 1980). Now, more than fifteen years later, the personal computer is commonplace; battery-powered laptops have even made computing a routine part of life for the field linguist. But despite widespread success at getting hardware into the hands of linguists, we have fallen short of realizing the full potential of computing for the OWL. Why is this? Because commercial software does not meet all the requirements of the linguist, and the linguistic community has not yet been able to develop all the software that will fill the gap.

Other chapters in this book (particularly the survey by Antworth and Valentine) document the software that is available to the OWL. There are many good tools that many linguists have put to good use, but I think it is fair to say that this body of tools, for the most part, remains inaccessible to the average OWL. There are two chief reasons for this. First, there is a friendliness gap – many programs are hard to use because they have one-of-a-kind user interfaces that have a steep learning curve and are easy to forget if not used regularly. The emergence of graphical user interface standards (such as for Windows and Macintosh) is doing much to solve this problem. Second, there is a semantic gap – many programs model data in terms of computationally convenient objects (like *file*s with *line*s and *character*s, or with *record*s and *field*s). They require the user to understand how these computational objects map onto the objects of the problem domain (like grammatical categories, lexical entries, and phonemes). In cases where programs do present a semantically transparent model of the problem domain, the programmer has typically had to build it from scratch using underlying objects like files, lines, and characters. While the results can be excellent, the process of developing such software is typically slow.

As we look to the future, better (and faster) progress in developing software for linguists is going to depend on using methods that better model the nature of the data we are trying to manipulate. The first five sections of this article discuss five essential characteristics of linguistic data which any successful software for the OWL must account for, namely that the data are multilingual, sequential, hierarchically structured, multi-dimensional, and highly integrated. The sixth section discusses a further requirement, namely that the software must maintain a distinction between the information in the data and the appearance it receives when it is formatted for display. The concluding section briefly describes a computing environment developed by the Summer Institute of Linguistics to meet these (and other) requirements for a foundation on which to build better software for the OWL.

1.1   THE MULTILINGUAL NATURE OF LINGUISTIC DATA

Every instance of textual information entered into a computer is expressing information in some language (whether natural or artificial). The data that linguists work with typically include information in many languages. In a document like a bilingual dictionary, the chunks of data switch back and forth between different languages. In other documents, the use of multiple languages may be nested, such as when an English text quotes a paragraph in German which discusses some Greek words. Such multilingualism is a fundamental property of the textual data with which OWLs work.

Many computerists have conceived of the multilingual data problem as a *special character*s problem. This approach considers the multi-lingualism problem to be solved when all the *character*s needed for writing the languages being worked with can be displayed both on the screen and in printed output. In the computer's way of implementing writing, each character (like a letter of the alphabet or a punctuation mark) is assigned to a *character code*; this is a number that is used to represent that character in the computer's memory. All the character codes that are defined to implement a particular way of writing form a *character set*. In the *ASCII* character set, for instance, capital *A* is assigned to code 65, capital *B* to 66, and so on.

In the MS-DOS environment it has been difficult to do much with special characters since the operating system views the world in terms of a single, predefined set of 256 characters. Linguists have had to resort to using character shape editors (see, for instance, Simons, 1989b) to define a customized character set that contains all the characters they need to use in a particular document. The limit of having only 256 possible characters is exacerbated by the fact that each combination of a *diacritic* with a *base character* must be treated as a single *composite character*. For instance, to correctly display a lowercase Greek alpha with no breathing, a smooth breathing, or a rough breathing, and with no accent, an acute accent, a grave accent, or a circumflex accent, one would need to define twelve different characters; only then can we display all the possible combinations of diacritics on a lowercase alpha.

The Windows and Macintosh environments have made a significant advance beyond this. Rather than a single character inventory, these operating systems provide a *font system*. Data in languages with different writing systems can be represented in different *font*s. This means that the total character inventory is not limited by the number of possible character codes. One could put Roman characters in one font, Greek characters in another font, and Arabic characters in still another. The same string of character codes can then be displayed as different characters on the screen, depending on which font is selected. By switching between fonts in the application software, the user can access and display as many characters as are needed.

The Macintosh font manager offers yet another advance in that it supports zero-width overstriking diacritics. An overstriking diacritic is a character that is superimposed on-the-fly over a separate base character (somewhat like a dead key on a conventional typewriter). It is possible to build thousands of composites dynamically from a single font of 255 characters. Thus, for instance, almost all the European languages with Roman-based writing systems can be rendered with the basic Macintosh extended character set. (The Windows font system still has no notion of a zero-width diacritic. An overstriking diacritic can be simulated, however, by creating an extremely narrow character that spills over onto the neighboring character it is meant to overstrike. This works quite satisfactorily on some systems, and can be a real mess on others. The outcome depends on how the screen driver for the particular hardware was implemented.)

The special-character approach encodes information in terms of its visual form. It says that if two characters look the same, they should be represented by the same character code, and conversely, if they look different, they should have different codes. In so doing it causes us both to underdifferentiate and to overdifferentiate important semantic (or functional) distinctions that are present in the encoded information. We underdifferentiate when we use the same character codes to represent words in different languages. For instance, the character sequence *die* represents rather different information when it encodes a German word as opposed to an English word.

We overdifferentiate when we use different character codes to represent contextual variants of the same letter in a single language. For instance, the lowercase sigma in Greek has one form if it is word initial or medial, and a second form if it is word final. An even more dramatic example is Arabic, in which nearly every letter of the alphabet appears in one of four variant forms depending on whether the context is word initial, word medial, word final, or freestanding. Another type of overdifferentiation occurs when single composite characters are used to represent the combination of base characters with diacritics that represent functionally independent information. For instance, in the example given above of using twelve different composite characters to encode the possible combinations of Greek lowercase alpha with breathing marks and accents, the single functional unit (namely, lowercase alpha) is represented by twelve different character codes. Similarly, the single functional unit of rough breathing would be represented in four of these character codes, and in two dozen others for the other six vowels.

To represent our data in a semantically transparent way, it is necessary to do two things. First, we must explicitly encode the language that each particular datum is in; this makes it possible to use the same character codes for different languages without any ambiguity or loss of information. (This also makes it possible to correctly perform the language-specific aspects of data processing that will be discussed shortly.) Second, we need to encode characters at a functional level and let the computer handle the details of generating the correct context-sensitive display of form.

It was Joseph Becker, in his seminal article "Multilingual Word Processing" (1984), who pointed out the need to distinguish form and function in the computer implementation of writing systems. He observed that character *encoding* should consistently represent the same information unit by the same character code. He then defined *rendering* as the process of converting the encoded information into the correct graphic form for display. He observed correctly that for any writing system, this conversion from functional elements to formal elements is defined by regular rules, and therefore the computer should perform this conversion automatically. Elsewhere I have described a formalism for dealing with this process (Simons, 1989a).

The writing system is the most visible aspect of language data; thus we tend to think first of graphic *rendering* when we think of multilingual computing. But the language a particular datum is in governs much more than just its rendering on the screen or in printed output; it governs many other aspects of data processing. One of these is keyboarding: a multilingual computing environment would know that part of the definition of a language is its conventions for keyboarding, and would automatically switch keyboard layouts based on the language of the datum under the system cursor.

Another language-dependent aspect of data processing is the *collating sequence* that defines the alphabetical order for sorted lists in the language. For instance, the character sequence *ll* comes between *li* and *lo* in English, but in Spanish it is a separate "letter" of the alphabet and occurs between *lu* and *ma*. Still other language-dependent aspects are rules for finding word boundaries, sentence boundaries, and possible hyphenation points. Then there are language-specific conventions for formatting times, dates, and numbers. As stated in the opening sentence of this section, "Every instance of textual information entered into a computer is expressing information in some language;" it is necessary for the computer to know which language each string of text is in, if it is going to be able to process the information correctly.

There are two recent developments in the computing industry which bode well for our prospects of having a truly multilingual computing environment. The first of these is the **Unicode** standard for character encoding (Unicode Consortium, 1996). The Unicode Consortium, comprised of representatives from some of the leading commercial software and hardware vendors, has developed a single set of character codes for all the characters of all the major writing systems of the world (including the International Phonetic Alphabet). This system uses two bytes (16 **bits**) to encode each character. Version 2.0 of Unicode defines codes for 38,885 distinct characters (derived from 25 different scripts). There are still many scripts that are not supported (especially ancient ones), but the standard does reserve an unallocated block of 6,400 character codes for "private use." A major aim of Unicode is to make it possible for computer users to exchange highly multilingual documents with full confidence that the recipient will be able to correctly display the text. The definition of the standard is quick to emphasize, however, that it is only a standard for the interchange of character codes. Unicode itself does not address the question of context-sensitive rendering nor of any of the language-dependent aspects of data processing. In fact, it is ironic that Unicode fails to account for the most fundamental thing one must know in order to process a stream of character data, namely, what language it is encoding. Unicode is not by itself a solution to the problem of multilingual computing, but the support promised by key vendors like Microsoft and Apple is likely to make it an important part of the solution.

The second recent development is the incorporation of the **World Script** component into version 7.1 of the Macintosh operating system (Ford and Guglielmo, 1992). Almost ten years ago, Apple developed an extension to their font manager called the script manager (Apple, 1988). It handled particularly difficult font problems like the huge character inventory of Japanese and the context-sensitive rendering of consonant shapes in Arabic. A script system, in conjunction with a package of "international utilities," is able to handle just about all the language-dependent aspects of data processing mentioned above (Davis, 1987). The script manager's greatest failing was that only one non-Roman script system could be installed in the operating system. World Script has changed this. It is now possible to install as many script systems as one needs. Nothing comparable is yet available for Windows users; at one time the trade press reported that Apple intended to port this technology to the Windows platform, but we are still waiting. As software developers make their programs take advantage of technology like this, adequately multilingual computing may become a widespread reality.

1.2   THE SEQUENTIAL NATURE OF LINGUISTIC DATA

The stream of speech is a succession of sound that unfolds in temporal sequence. Written text is similarly sequential in nature, as word follows word and sentence follows sentence. The order of the words and sentences is, of course, a significant part of the information in text, since changing the order of constituents can change the meaning of the text.

We almost take this aspect of text for granted since our text editors and word processors support it so transparently. They excel at modeling the sequential nature of text, but fall short in modeling the other aspects of the information structure discussed below in sections 3 through 5. In particular, word processors do not allow us to represent the multidimensional and highly integrated nature of text. These are the areas where database systems shine; it is thus appealing to consider using a database system to model textual information.

Ironically, when it comes to the sequential nature of text, database management systems are as weak as word processors are strong. The relational database model, which is the model embodied by most popular database systems, does not inherently support the notion of sequence at all. Relations are, by definition, unordered. That is, the rows (or records) in a data table are inherently unordered. If one wants to represent sequence in a database model, one must add a column (or field) to store explicit sequence numbers and then manipulate these values to put pieces in the right order. For instance, if a data table represented a text and its rows represented the sentences in the text, then the table would need a column to store the sequence number of the sentence. A view that printed the text would first have to sort the rows by sentence number. With just sentences this does not sound too bad, but if we want a richer model that includes paragraphs, sentences, words, and morphemes, then we end up needing four columns for recording position in sequence. When the data model becomes this complex, relational database report generators do not have built-in views that can display the data as a conventionally formatted text.

Though relational databases do not model sequence as transparently as word processors, it can in fact be done. For instance, Parunak (1982) presents an approach to modeling Biblical text in a relational database;

his model provides columns for book, chapter, verse, and word number. Stonebraker *et al.* (1983) have developed extensions to the relational database model that make it better able to cope with texts. The main innovation was to implement a new kind of relation, called an "ordered relation," which supports the notion that text is inherently sequential. Unfortunately, extensions like this have not become commonplace in commercially available database systems.

1.3   THE HIERARCHICAL NATURE OF LINGUISTIC DATA

The data we deal with as linguists are highly structured. This is true of the primary data we collect, as well as of the secondary and tertiary data we create to record our analyses and interpretations. One aspect of that structuring, namely hierarchy, is discussed in this section. Two other aspects, the multidimensionality and the interrelatedness of data elements, are discussed in the next two sections.

Hierarchy is a fundamental characteristic of data structures in linguistics. The notion of hierarchy is familiar in syntactic analysis where, for instance, a sentence may contain clauses which contain phrases which contain words. Similar hierarchical structuring can be observed at higher levels of text analysis, such as when a narrative is made up of episodes which are made up of paragraphs and so on. We see hierarchy in the structure of a lexicon when the lexicon is made up of entries which contain sense subentries which in turn contain things like definitions and examples. Even meanings, when they are represented as feature structures which allow embedded feature structures as feature values, exhibit hierarchical structure. The list of examples is almost limitless.

As fundamental as hierarchy is, it is ironic that the tools that are most accessible to personal computer users – word processors, spreadsheets, and database managers – do not really support it. There is little question about this assessment of spreadsheets; they simply provide a two-dimensional grid of cells in which to place simple data values. In the case of database management systems (like dBase or 4th Dimension) and even card filing systems (like AskSam or Hypercard), a programmer can construct hierarchical data structures, but such a task would be beyond the average user. This is because the inherent model of these systems is that data are organized as a flat collection of records or cards.

Even word processors do not do a good job at modeling hierarchy. They essentially treat textual data as a sequence of paragraphs. They typically support no structure below this. For instance, if a dictionary entry were represented as a paragraph, the typical word processor would have no way of modeling the hierarchical structure of elements (like headword, etymology, sense subentries, and examples) within the entry. Rather, word processors can only model the contents of a dictionary entry as a sequence of characters; it would be up to the user to impose the internal structure mentally. Going up the hierarchy from paragraph, word processors do a little better, but it is done by means of special paragraph types rather than by modeling true hierarchy. For instance, if a document has a structure of chapters, sections, and subsections, this is imposed by putting the title of each element in a heading paragraph of level 1, 2, or 3, respectively. Under some circumstances, such as in an outline view, the word processor can interpret these level numbers to manipulate the text in terms of its hierarchical structure.

A new generation of document processing systems with a data model that is adequate to handle the hierarchical structure in textual data is beginning to emerge. They are based on an information markup language called **SGML**, for Standard Generalized Markup Language (Goldfarb, 1990; Herwijnen, 1990; Cover, 1992). SGML is not a program; it is a data interchange standard. It specifies a method for representing textual data in **ASCII files** so that the data can be interchanged among programs and among users without losing any information. The information in focus is not just the stream of characters, but also detailed information about the structure of the text. In 1986 SGML was adopted by the leading body for international standards (ISO, 1986); since that time it has gained momentum in the computing industry to the extent that SGML compatibility is now beginning to appear in popular software products.

The basic model of SGML is a hierarchical one. It views textual data as being comprised of content **element**s which are of different types and which embed inside each other. For instance, the following is a sample of what a dictionary entry for the word *abacus* might look like in an SGML-conforming interchange format:

```
<entry>
   <headword>abacus</headword>
   <etymology>L. abacus, from Gr. abax</etymology>
   <paradigm>pl. -cuses, or -ci</paradigm>
   <sense n=1><pos>n</pos>
      <def>a frame with beads sliding back and forth
            on wires for doing arithmetic</def></sense>
   <sense n=2><pos>n</pos>
      <def>in architecture, a slab forming the top of
            the capital of a column</def></sense>
</entry>
```

Each element of the text is delimited by an opening **tag** and a matching closing tag. An opening tag consists of the name of the element type enclosed in angle brackets. The matching closing tag adds a slash after the left angle bracket. In this example, the *entry* element contains five elements: a *headword,* an *etymology, paradigm* information, and two *sense* subentries. Each *sense* element embeds two elements: a part of speech and a definition. The *sense* elements also use the **attribute** *n* to encode the number of the sense.

Rather than forcing the data to fit a built-in model of hierarchical structure (like a word processor does), SGML allows the model of data structure to be as rich and as deep as necessary. An SGML-conforming data file is tied to a user-definable Document Type Definition. The **DTD** lists all the element types allowed in the document, and specifies the allowed structure of each in terms of what other element types it can contain and in what order. Though the notation of a DTD may be daunting at first, the concept that lies behind it should be very familiar to a linguist. A DTD is really nothing more than a context-free grammar. The left-hand side of each rewriting rule names an element, and the right-hand side tells what elements are allowed to occur within it. For instance, consider the following rewrite rule for the structure of a book:

```
book - > front-matter body (back-matter)
```

That is, a book consists of front matter, followed by a body, optionally followed by back matter. The SGML notation for declaring this same rule in a DTD is as follows:

```
<!ELEMENT book - (front-matter, body, back-matter?) >
```

In addition to sequence and optionality, the pattern for the right-hand side (called the "content model" in SGML parlance) may also express alternation, repetition, and grouping. This formalism provides the power to describe very rich document structures and to do so precisely and unambiguously.

The DTD is a machine-readable document with a formal syntax prescribed by the SGML standard. This makes it possible for SGML-based application software to read the DTD and to understand the structure of the text being processed. Because the DTD is a plain ASCII file, it is also human readable and thus serves as formal documentation, showing other potential users of a data set how it is encoded.

Perhaps the greatest impact of a formal definition of possible document structure is that it helps to close the semantic gap between the user and the computer application. This is particularly true when the formal model of the structure matches the model in the minds of practitioners in the domain, and when the formal model uses the same names for the data element types that domain specialists would use to name the corresponding real-world objects. For instance, an SGML-based document editor starts up by reading in the DTD for the type of document the user wants to create (whether it be, for instance, the transcription of a conversation or a bilingual dictionary). The editor then helps the user by showing what element types are possible at any given point in the document. If the user attempts to create an invalid structure, the editor steps in and explains what would be valid at that point. The formal definition of structure can help close the semantic gap when data are processed, too. For instance, an information retrieval tool that knows the structure of the documents in its database can assist the user in formulating queries on that database.

The academic community has recognized the potential of SGML for modeling linguistic (and related) data. The Text Encoding Initiative (*TEI*) is a large-scale international project to develop SGML-based standards for encoding textual data, including its analysis and interpretation (Burnard, 1991). It has been sponsored jointly by the Association for Computers and the Humanities, the Association for Linguistic and Literary Computing, and the Association for Computational Linguistics and has involved scores of scholars working in a variety of subcommittees (Hockey, 1989–92a). Guidelines for the encoding of machine-readable texts have now been published (Sperberg-McQueen and Burnard, 1994) and are being followed by many projects. The TEI proposal for markup of linguistic analysis depends heavily on feature structures; see Langendoen and Simons (1995) for a description of the approach and a discussion of its rationale. See Section 4.2.1 of Hockey's chapter in this volume on "Text databases" for more discussion of SGML and TEI.

While the power of SGML to model the hierarchical structure in linguistic data takes us beyond what is possible in word processors, spreadsheets, and database managers, it still does not provide a complete solution. It falls short in the two aspects of linguistic data considered in the next two sections. The attributes of SGML elements cannot themselves store other elements; thus the multidimensional nature of complex data elements must be modeled as hierarchical containment. To model the network of relationships among elements (i.e., the integrated nature of linguistic data), SGML offers a pointing mechanism (through IDs and IDREFs in attribute values), but there is no semantic validation of pointers. Any pointer can point to any element; there is no mechanism for specifying constraints on pointer destinations in the DTD. Thus the only relationships between element types that can be formally declared in the DTD (and can thus be enforced by it) are sequential precedence and hierarchical inclusion.

1.4   THE MULTIDIMENSIONAL NATURE OF LINGUISTIC DATA

A conventional text editing program views text as a one-dimensional sequence of characters. A tool like an SGML-based editor adds a second dimension – namely, the hierarchical structure of the text. But from the perspective of a linguist, the stream of speech which we represent as a one-dimensional sequence of characters has form and meaning in many simultaneous dimensions (Simons, 1987). The speech signal itself simultaneously comprises articulatory segments, pitch, timing, and intensity. A given stretch of speech can be simultaneously viewed in terms of its phonetic interpretation, its phonemic interpretation, its morphophonemic interpretation, its morphemic interpretation, or its lexemic interpretation. We may view its structure from a phonological perspective in terms of syllables, stress groups, and pause groups, or from a grammatical perspective in terms of morphemes, words, phrases, clauses, sentences, and so on.

The meaning of the text also has many dimensions and levels. There is the phonological meaning of devices like alliteration and rhyme. There is the lexical meaning of the morphemes and of compounds and idioms which they form. There is the functional meaning carried by the constituents of a grammatical construction. In looking at the meaning of a whole utterance, there is the literal meaning versus the figurative, the denotative versus the connotative, the explicit versus the implicit. All of these dimensions, and more, lurk behind that one-dimensional sequence of characters which we have traditionally called "text."

There are already some programs designed for the OWL which handle this multidimensional view of text rather well, namely interlinear text processing systems like *IT* (Simons and Versaw, 1987; Simons and Thomson, 1988) and Shoebox (Davis and Wimbish, 1993). In these programs, the user defines the dimensions of analysis that are desired. The program then steps through the text helping the user to fill in appropriate annotations on morphemes, words, and sentences for all the dimensions. Another kind of program that is good at modeling the multidimensional nature of linguistic data is a database manager: when a database record is used to represent a single object of data, the many fields of the record can be used to represent the many dimensions of information that pertain to it.

While interlinear text processors and database managers handle the multidimensional nature of linguistic data well, they fall short by not supporting the full hierarchical nature of the data. To adequately model linguistic data, the OWL needs a system which has the fully general, user-definable hierarchy of elements (such as SGML offers) in which the elements may: (1) contain the smaller elements which are their parts, and (2) have a record-like structure of fields which can simultaneously store multiple dimensions of information concerning the elements.

1.5   THE HIGHLY INTEGRATED NATURE OF LINGUISTIC DATA

Sequentially ordered hierarchies of data elements with annotations in multiple dimensions are still not enough. Sequence and hierarchy, by themselves, imply that the only relationships between data elements are those inherent in their relative positions in sequence and in the hierarchy of parts within wholes. But for the data on which linguistic research is based, this only scratches the surface. Crosscutting the basic hierarchical organization of the elements is a complex network of associations between them.

For instance, the words that occur in a text are composed of morphemes. Those morphemes are defined and described in the lexicon (rather than in the text). The relationship between the surface word form and its underlying form as a string of lexical morphemes is described in the morphophonology. When a morpheme in an analyzed text is glossed to convey its sense of meaning, that gloss is really an attribute of one of the senses of meaning listed in the lexicon entry for that morpheme. The part-of-speech code for that use of the morpheme in the text is another attribute of that same lexical subentry. The part-of-speech code itself does not ultimately belong to the lexical entry. It is the grammar which enumerates and defines the possible parts of speech, and the use of a part-of-speech code in the lexicon is really a pointer to its description in the grammar. The examples which are given in the lexicon or the grammar relate back to the text from which they were taken. Cultural terms which are defined in the lexicon and cultural activities which are exemplified in texts relate to their full analysis and description in an ethnography. All the above are examples of how the different parts of a field linguist's database are conceptually integrated by direct links of association. Weber (1986) has discussed this network-like nature of the linguistic database in his description of a futuristic style of computer-based reference grammar.

This network of associations is part of the information structure that is inherent in the phenomena we study. To maximize the usefulness of computing in our research, our computational model of the data must match this inherent structure. Having direct links between related bits of information in the database has the obvious benefit of making it easy and fast to retrieve related information.

An even more fundamental benefit has to do with the integrity of the data and the quality of the resulting work. Because the information structures we deal with in research are networks of relationships, we can never make a hypothesis in one part of the database without affecting other hypotheses elsewhere in the database. Having the related information linked together makes it possible to immediately check the impact of a change in the database.

The addition of associative links to the data structure also makes it possible to achieve the virtue of *normalization,* a concept which is well known in relational database theory. In a fully normalized database, any given piece of information occurs only once. That piece of information is then used throughout the database by referring to the single instance rather than by making copies of it. If, instead, there are multiple copies of a given piece of information throughout a database, the ubiquitous problem known as "update anomaly" is sure to arise when that piece of information needs to be changed. An update anomaly occurs when some of the copies of a given piece of information get updated, while others are overlooked. The end result is a database that is inconsistent in the best case, or invalid in the worst. Smith (1985) gives a good explanation of a process by which the design of a relational database can be normalized.

A linguistic example may help to illustrate the importance of database normalization. Consider, for instance, a lexical database. One kind of associative link that occurs in a lexical database is cross-references from one entry to another. One piece of information that occurs in each entry is the spelling of its headword. If we were using a text editor to build and manage the database, we would be likely to make cross-references by typing the headword for the entry we want to reference. However, this violates the normalization principle since the spelling of the headword now occurs more than once in the database. If we were to change the spelling of the headword in its main entry, then all cross-references to it would break and refer to a nonexistent entry. Another example is part-of-speech labels. If the labels are typed out in every lexical entry, then one is almost certain to introduce inconsistencies over the life of the database. The ideal solution in both cases is to use a database system that truly supports the integrated nature of the data by allowing direct links between data items. The cross-reference would be stored as a pointer to another lexical entry; the part-of-speech would be stored as a pointer to a part-of-speech object in the grammar. The latter would be the only place in which the label for the part-of-speech is actually spelled out. When the analyst decides to change the spelling of the label, all references are simultaneously updated since they now point to a changed spelling. When the data are normalized like this, an update anomaly is not even possible.

1.6   THE SEPARATION OF INFORMATION FROM FORMAT

It is imperative that any system for manipulating linguistic data maintain the distinction between information and format. In printed media, we use variations in format to signal different kinds of information. For instance, in a dictionary entry, bold type might be used to indicate the headword, square brackets might delimit the etymology, while italics with a trailing period might mark the part-of-speech label. The bold type is not really the information – it is the fact that the emboldened form is the headword. Similarly, the square brackets (even though they are characters in the display) are not really part of the data; they simply indicate that the delimited information is the etymology.

Generalized markup (the *GM* in SGML) is the notion of marking up a document by identifying its information structure rather than its display format (Coombs, Renear, and DeRose, 1987). For instance, in a dictionary entry one should insert a markup tag to say, "The following is the headword" (as does the <headword> tag in the SGML example given above in section 1.3, rather than putting typesetting codes to say, "The following should be in 10 point bold Helvetica type." In the generalized markup approach, each different type of information is marked by a different markup tag, and then details of typesetting are specified in a separate document which is often called a *style sheet* (Johnson and Beach, 1988). The style sheet declares for each markup tag what formatting parameters are to be associated with the content of the marked up element when it is output for display.

The separation of content and structure from display formatting has many advantages. (1) It allows authors to defer formatting decisions. (2) It ensures that formatting of a given element type will be consistent throughout. (3) It makes it possible to change formats globally by changing only a single description in the style sheet. (4) It allows the same document to be formatted in a number of different styles for different publishers or purposes. (5) It makes documents portable between systems. And perhaps most important of all for our purposes, (6) it makes possible computerized analysis and retrieval based on structural information in the text.

The lure of WYSIWYG ("what you see is what you get") word processors for building a linguistic database (like a dictionary) must be avoided at all costs when "what you see is *all* you get." On the other hand, a database manager which allows one to model the information structure correctly, but cannot produce nicely formatted displays is not much use either. The OWL needs a hybrid system that combines the notion of generalized markup for faithfully storing the information structure of the data with the notion of style sheets that can transform the information into conventionally formatted displays.

1.7 TOWARD A COMPUTING ENVIRONMENT FOR LINGUISTIC RESEARCH

The above sections have discussed six requirements for a computing environment that manages linguistic data:

1 The data are multilingual, so the computing environment must be able to keep track of what language each datum is in, and then display and process it accordingly.

2 The data in text unfold sequentially, so the computing environment must be able to represent the text in proper sequence.

3 The data are hierarchically structured, so the computing environment must be able to build hierarchical structures of arbitrary depth.

4 The data are multidimensional, so the computing environment must be able to attach many kinds of analysis and interpretation to a single datum.

5 The data are highly integrated, so the computing environment must be able to store and follow associative links between related pieces of data.

6 While doing all of the above to model the information structure of the data correctly, the computing environment must be able to present conventionally formatted displays of the data.

It is possible to find software products that meet some of these requirements, but we are not aware of any that can meet them all. Consequently, the Summer Institute of Linguistics (through its Academic Computing Department) has embarked on a project to build such a computing environment for the OWL. We call it CELLAR – for Computing Environment for Linguistic, Literary, and Anthropological Research. This name reflects our belief that these requirements are not unique to linguists – virtually any scholar working with textual data will have the same requirements.

Fundamentally, CELLAR is an *object-oriented* database system (Rettig, Simons, and Thomson, 1993). Borgida (1985) gives a nice summary of the advantages of modeling information as objects. Zdonik and Maier (1990) offer more extensive readings. Booch (1994) and Coad and Yourdon (1991) teach the methodology that is used in analyzing a domain to build an object-oriented information model for it.

In CELLAR each data element is modeled as an *object*. Each object has a set of named *attribute*s which record the many dimensions of information about it (addressing requirement 4 above). An attribute value can be a basic object like a string, a number, a picture, or a sound; every string stores an indication of the language which it encodes (requirement 1; see Simons and Thomson (forthcoming) for a detailed discussion of CELLAR's multilingual component). An attribute can store a single value or a sequence of values (requirement 2). An attribute value can also be one or more complex objects which are the parts of the original object, thus modeling the hierarchical structure of the information (requirement 3). Or, an attribute value can be one or more pointers to objects stored elsewhere in the database to which the original object is related (requirement 5).

Each object is an instance of a general class. Each class is sanctioned by a user-definable "class definition" which describes what all instances of the class have in common. This includes definitions of all the attributes with constraints on what their values can be, definitions of virtual attributes which compute their values on-the-fly by performing queries on the database, definitions of parsers which know how to convert plain ASCII files into instances of the class, definitions of views which programmatically build formatted displays of instances of the class, and definitions of tools which provide graphical user interfaces for manipulating instances of the class. The latter two features address requirement 6; see Simons (1997) for a fuller discussion of this aspect of CELLAR.

CELLAR is really a tool for building tools. Programmers will be able to use CELLAR to build class definitions that model the content, format, and behavior of linguistic data objects. These models are the tools that OWLs will use. Because CELLAR's model of data inherently supports the very nature of linguistic data, the programmer can quickly build semantically transparent models of linguistic data. CELLAR was first released to the public in December 1995 as part of the product named LinguaLinks. LinguaLinks uses CELLAR to implement applications for phonological analysis, interlinear text analysis, lexical database management, and other tasks typically performed by field linguists. See SIL's home page on the Internet (http://www.sil.org) for the latest information concerning availability.

Chapter 2

The Internet: an introduction

Helen Aristar Dry and Anthony Rodrigues Aristar

2.1 INTRODUCTION

Most linguists make regular use of several Internet functions: e-mail, *ftp*, *telnet*, and WWW *browser*s. Indeed, these functions are beginning to be taken for granted as part of our professional lives. However, many of us do not know what the Internet actually is or how it works. This chapter attempts to remedy this. It is essentially an Internet primer. It offers basic information about the operation of eight Internet technologies, as well as a brief review of Internet history, emphasizing how the Internet has changed linguistics in just a few short years.

Before the advent of the Internet, there were essentially only two ways to learn what others in the field were doing. One was by reading published material or private letters. The other was by verbal communication, at a conference, at work, or over the phone. Since work in some linguistic subfields was likely to be out-of-date by the time it was published, and much current work was circulated in draft form, the research that many individual linguists were aware of was limited to that of the small subset of linguists with which they were in regular contact. Isolation from the central figures in the discipline meant isolation from current scholarship.

Furthermore, much linguistic infrastructure was what may be called "local." Jobs, conferences, and graduate programs were often advertised only within national boundaries. As a result, many universities hired only their own nationals; and many linguists attended only conferences which reflected the theories predominant in their own countries.

Then, in the late 1980s, a change began. What had once been a network which linked US government research computers – the *ARPA*net – began to be made more generally accessible. By 1990, it had changed into the Internet, which linked the computers at most universities and colleges. Accounts on these computers became available to university faculty and students. And linguistic information began to be commonly disseminated among individuals who had no other professional contact. In 1989 the first linguistic mailing list was established. Shortly thereafter linguistics archives began to be made accessible via *anonymous ftp*. And before long the Internet had effectively eroded the isolation of the "lone linguist."

If you were on the Internet, it mattered less and less whether you worked as the only linguist in a foreign languages department, whether you lived in Australia or San Francisco, whether you were part of a central network of linguists or part of no network at all. The Internet enabled you to find out what other linguists were saying. It also enabled you to have an impact on the discipline previously available only to those at prestigious universities: if you had something of interest to say, you could say it at an international forum without leaving home.

Today, information about conferences, fellowships, linguistics programs, and jobs is distributed within a much wider geographical area. And because a small local conference can be advertised as widely as a large one, organizers often find that the number of submissions has increased, with a commensurate increase in quality. Similarly, universities are experiencing increases in the number and diversity of job and fellowship applications. The Chair of Linguistics at a Scandinavian university recently told us that applications had increased threefold since they began advertising job openings on the electronic mailing list which we help to run. (This is the LINGUIST List, discussed in section 2.3.1.4 below. Inevitably, many of our generalizations about the Internet derive from our experience with this list.) Similarly, one of our own universities received 130 applications following a single job announcement on this list – the job was filled before it was ever announced on paper.

Information about individual research has also become more widely available, in part because of new technologies which put the distribution of information into the hands of individuals. Publishing a book or starting a large e-mail list requires the cooperation of a considerable number of people, from editors to university administrators. Setting up a *World Wide Web* page, however, requires little more than a personal computer, a modem or ethernet card, and software obtainable free from the Internet. World Wide Web technology, in short, allows linguists for the first time to take control of the means by which their ideas are disseminated, substantially decreasing the lag-time between the completion of a piece of work and its publication.[1]

Given the impact of Internet technologies on the discipline and on the individual linguist, it is useful for linguists to know how Internet technology functions, what Internet services are commonly available, and how these can be used to enhance research. This chapter attempts to provide some of this information, in a style accessible to beginners. Let us begin by looking at one of the fundamental metaphors which describes the operation of the net.

2.2   WHAT IS THE INTERNET?[2]

The metaphor upon which the Internet is based is the metaphor of a *protocol*. In human terms, a protocol is a way some interaction must be carried out. Likewise, a computer protocol specifies the way that two machines must interact. However, Internet protocols not only tell the machines how to transfer data, they also ensure that the pieces of data they send are well-formed (i.e., "grammatical"). Protocols are the *linguae francae* of the Internet: they specify both the grammar of the language and the pragmatics of the interaction.

Protocols became the core of Internet operations because of the physical limitations of the earliest nets. When the first incarnation of the Internet, the ARPAnet, was put in place, there were no completely reliable networks. What lay between your machine and the machine you wished to communicate with was an unpredictable mixture of cables, phone-lines, and satellite relay stations. It was never certain whether all of the bits in between the machines were going to work. Connectivity, then, could not be based upon one invariant path to a destination. It required that machines be able to select alternate paths. But alternate paths might lead to different types of machines. Thus it was also necessary to transfer data in a way that was only minimally dependent on the nature of the machines involved.

2.2.1   Internet Protocol

The solution was provided by the combination of the **Internet Protocol** (**IP**), and the **router**. The IP is simply a set of instructions which tells a machine (1) what form the data it transfers must have, (2) how to open a connection with another machine, (3) how to transfer data, and (4) how to close the connection. All data, IP says, must be sent in "packets." A packet is a chunk of data surrounded by what is called an "envelope." This is accompanying information which tells the forwarding machine the unique address of the machine the packet is being sent to. This address is a 32-bit number, a sequence of 32 **binary** values like:

```
10000011 00001011 00000011 00000011
```

This usually appears to human beings in the form of "dotted octet" notation. Dotted octet notation groups the 32 bits of the real address into 4 sets (or **byte**s) of 8 **bit**s. So, for example, the 32 bit address above is divided into 4 parts, each of which is interpreted as a single binary number:

```
10000011 = 131
00001011 = 18
00010111 = 23
00000011 = 3
```

Combining these numbers gives `131.18.23.3` in dotted octet notation. This is called the **IP number** of the machine.

2.2.2 Domain names

For the benefit of human beings, each Internet machine has not only a unique IP number, but also a unique name. These names are arranged in dotted "domains" which can be read right to left by machines. The rightmost domain always indicates a domain which is more general than the one to its left. Thus, if we find an address like `zippy.bangor.uk`, we know that "uk" – which is the domain name for the United Kingdom – is more general than "bangor" – which is the domain name for the University of Bangor in Wales – which in turn is more general than "zippy", which is the name of the machine at Bangor which is to receive the packet.

When human beings send a message to `zippy.bangor.uk`, this address has to be translated into an IP address. This mapping is done by software called a "resolver", which sends a request to a set of machines called **Domain Name Servers** (usually abbreviated **DNS**). These servers may not themselves know every IP number on the Internet, but they know how to find them by interrogating other name servers. They can then return a valid IP number to the resolver, so that the source machine can create envelopes for each of the packets making up the message.

2.2.3 Routers

After a machine breaks the data it is sending into packets and encloses each in an IP envelope, it sends them to a router. A router is simply a machine whose specialized job is finding paths for packets through the Internet. It looks for functional, uncongested paths to destinations, and sends packets along them. If some part of the network is unresponsive or overused, it finds other paths to the target machine.

One reason the Internet has been able to grow so fast has to do with Internet addressing and the way routers work. No router needs to know the address of every machine on the Internet, because the Internet is hierarchically organized into networks and sub-networks. The largest network is indicated by the first set of digits in the IP number.[3] The second set of digits indicates a subnet of the major network, and the third a subnet of the subnet. If a router, then, needs to send a packet to the IP number 164.76.28.2, all the router needs to know is how to send the packet to the 164 network. The router at 164 will know how to get packets to the subnet 76, and so on down to the machine numbered 2, which is the target machine.

A major advantage of this addressing system is that all IP number assignment can be handled locally. And, as a result, a new machine at any site can become part of the Internet freely and immediately. If subnet 76 is assigned to a university, for example, with subnet 28 being one of its LANs (Local Area Networks), a new university machine can be assigned the number 164.76.28.16 by the local system administrators, without applying to any outside authority. Because of the router system, no machine outside the university network needs to be informed of the new address. It just needs to be able to get the information when it needs it.

2.2.4   Transmission Control Protocol

The packet surrounded by the IP envelope usually contains, along with the data, some information added by another important Internet protocol, *TCP* (*Transmission Control Protocol*). TCP is necessary because IP only delivers packets. It does not ensure that they will arrive in the same order as they were sent. So different packets belonging to the same body of data may arrive at their destination by totally different routes, and at different times.

For many kinds of interactions this is not acceptable. If you make a remote log-in (e.g., to read your mail when away from home), you must interact with the remote machine in real time, and it must receive your commands in the order you send them. You cannot have the packets that contain those commands arriving out of order. This is where TCP comes in. TCP puts sequence numbers in the packets. These numbers allow the receiving machine to rearrange the packets back into their original order. They also allow it to tell if anything is missing. If only packets 1, 2, 3, and 5 arrive, the machine knows that packet 4 is missing and gets it retransmitted.

TCP also allows the specification of what are called *ports*, so that a particular set of packets will be sent to a particular port on a machine. These ports are not real physical ports, but rather instructions to the receiving machine about the way it is supposed to handle the incoming data.

Recipient Internet machines often run a piece of software called *Inetd*, which "listens" simultaneously for messages on several ports and, when data arrive, starts the software appropriate to the port. When a message is directed to port 25, for example, Inetd wakes up the mailer software. If a message arrives at port 23, it activates telnet software. If a message arrives at port 21, it activates ftp software, and so forth.

However, when many functions are run on the same machine, it becomes inefficient to activate them each through Inetd. To increase speed, software for each function can also be run as a *daemon*, a pre-activated program that is always ready to perform its task. World Wide

Web servers are usually daemons; they "listen" on port 80 and spawn a process whenever a message is directed to that port.

2.2.5 Clients and servers

The simplicity of the way the Internet works makes it very flexible. Almost all interactions between machines are based upon the protocols outlined above. If a machine installs a version of TCP/IP, it doesn't matter what platform it is, whether it's a Mac (where the protocol is called MacTCP or TCP/IP) or a DOS machine running Windows 3.1 (where it's usually called Winsock) or a big Sun 1000 server (where it's called TCP/IP); using this protocol, all these machines can function on the Internet.

However, some Internet operations require two additional pieces of software, one residing on the target machine and one residing on the home machine. These are called, respectively, the *server* and the *client*. TCP/IP ensures that machines can connect with each other and send packets of data, sequentially numbered, to the right ports. It does not ensure that the packets will contain the right kind of information. Servers are pieces of software which know how to access information of specific types, and clients are pieces of software that know how to request information from the appropriate servers.

Of the three basic functionalities created to use TCP/IP (electronic mail, ftp, and telnet), two of these, ftp and telnet, require client and server software. To telnet to another machine, for example, you must run a telnet client on your machine and contact a telnet server on the other end. Most large Internet machines run ftp and telnet servers as a matter of course, so that other Internet machines can ftp or telnet to them; and they also run telnet and ftp clients, so that their own users can initiate ftp or telnet sessions to remote machines.

As more and more personal machines become part of the Internet, more individuals are installing ftp or telnet clients on their own machines. And some are even installing servers, so that others can connect to the machine and retrieve information. Suppose, for example, that you create an extensive database of Klingon Battle Poetry (the most popular *genre* on the Klingon homeworld). To make this important resource available to the Internet community, you can simply put it on your local machine and install an appropriate server. If you install an ftp server that accesses your Klingon directory, for example, then anyone with an ftp client on their machine can log on and copy your *files* of battle poetry to their own disk.

2.3 BASIC INTERNET FUNCTIONS

Sections 2.3.1, 2.3.2, and 2.3.3 below treat electronic mail, ftp, and telnet, describing how to access these functions and giving some hints about their use. However, users familiar with these services may wish to skip ahead to Section 2.5, where we discuss the World Wide Web.

2.3.1   Electronic mail

By now everyone is familiar with e-mail. Indeed, it is e-mail and mailing lists which have been primarily responsible for the changes in information dissemination described in Section 2.1. However, e-mail does have limitations which make other types of transfer more practical for some kinds of files.

On the Internet, mail delivery usually uses a piece of software called an MTA (Mail Transport Agent) which sends data via SMTP (Simple Mail Transfer Protocol). On a Unix platform, the MTA is usually *sendmail,* and it can be accessed directly by typing sendmail at the root prompt. However, users normally don't do this; rather they interact with *sendmail* via a mail interface, or mailer. On a Unix platform, the default mailer is usually either *mail* or *mailx.*

If *mailx* is your default, you activate it when you type mail at your home prompt; and it allows you to, e.g., display a list of the headers of incoming mail by typing h, read messages by typing their numbers, and send mail by typing mail plus an e-mail address. *Mailx* is actually a multifunction mailer that will allow you to perform numerous other operations, such as activate an **editor** within an e-mail message, make **alias**es for frequently used addresses, or save and concatenate messages in files. However, *mailx* is not menu-oriented, so it is not particularly easy to learn; and, unless you use an editor to compose your e-mail messages, it is fairly unforgiving: it will not allow you to move back a **line** in order to correct a mistake; nor will it wrap lines for you. If you forget to add returns at the ends of your lines, your message may display correctly on the screen but, unless it is very short, you will not be able to send it.

For these reasons, many people prefer other mail interfaces like Pine or Elm. One of these is likely to be available on your mainframe account; and they are significantly easier to learn than *mailx,* since they are menu-driven.

Figure 2.1 below, for example, gives the screen which displays when we type pine at the home prompt.

Some people prefer their mailers to be even more user-friendly and to reside on their home machines. Some mailers like Eudora and the mailer that comes with Netscape (a World Wide Web browser described in Section 2.5.3) allow you to access your mail on a mainframe account without ever having to log on to the mainframe. You simply call up your mail client and tell it to "Get new messages" or "Check mail." The client then logs on to the mainframe for you and transfers your new mail to the machine on your desk.

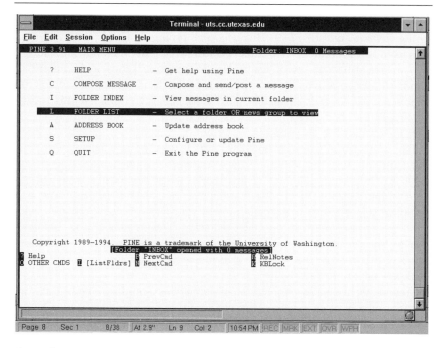

Figure 2.1   Initial screen of the Pine e-mail program

2.3.1.1   *The limitations of electronic mail*

Despite the utility of electronic mail in facilitating both discussion lists and personal correspondence, e-mail does have salient limitations for linguists. These limitations derive from two sources: the kind of encoding mail-messages require, and the way that fonts are handled on computers.

Normal mailers can handle only one kind of text, 7-bit US-*ASCII*. ASCII is a means of ***encoding characters*** that was designed in the bad old days when no one could imagine that anyone would wish to send a message in any character not used in English. ASCII cannot encode many of the characters used in European languages, let alone non-Latin characters and IPA (International Phonetic Alphabet). These are either lost or damaged in the mail transfer. You can't, therefore, simply put a word-processor file into a mail-message and expect it to arrive at the other end in a usable form. Almost all word-processors use non-ASCII characters.

Fonts are also a problem. When you type a letter into a word-processing system, what you're really doing is adding a code which is represented in a specified font as a particular ***glyph***. That same code will map to a totally different glyph in another font.

For example, when you type a p you add a code which is equivalent to the decimal number 112. But if you're typing in Hindi, 112 will map to a totally different glyph, since Hindi, which uses Devanagari script, also uses a different set of fonts. So, if someone sends a document in Hindi to someone who doesn't have a Hindi font, what will appear on their screen is a series of meaningless Latin characters. What this means for linguists is that any special fonts you might use – for example IPA – may be unreadable to your correspondents.

There are three ways around this difficulty. One is a permanent one: to change the way that fonts are encoded so that a particular code always maps to the same character in the same script no matter what font is used. This solution is on the horizon: it is called **Unicode**, and is a mapping scheme which assigns (or will ultimately assign) unique codes to all the symbols used in the representation of human language. Unicode mailers are already starting to appear, e.g. the Panglot mailer. When these come into common use, we can stop worrying about the fonts our recipients are using.

Meanwhile we have to tolerate less satisfying solutions. One is to use a utility which turns a text containing non-ASCII characters into a text which has only ASCII characters. The file can then be transmitted by mail to another machine where – hopefully – your recipients will have software which will turn the file back into its original non-ASCII version.

If you are on a Unix machine, the utility which turns non-ASCII to ASCII and back again is called **uuencode**. If you're on a Mac, the same functionality is served by **BinHex**. Word (and some other word-processing programs) can do something similar. You can save a word-processing file as **RTF** (**Rich Text Format**), which turns a word-processing file into 7-bit ASCII. If you save a file in RTF and send it via e-mail, your recipients can download it, remove the mail-header, and use Word to display it with its original formatting on their own computers.

However, if you use special fonts, such as an IPA font or an Arabic font, to write the file, you'll have to send the font along with the file unless your recipients already have it. Even then, unless your recipients are on the same platform, you can't be sure that the characters you typed will be the ones displayed on their machines. Although there are programs which translate fonts, e.g., Mac TrueType fonts into Windows TrueType fonts, these do not work flawlessly; often characters are lost.

There is another way to transmit non-ASCII files, one which is in many ways superior to the methods mentioned above, though it shares – and even compounds – some of its problems. This is to use mailers which can encode messages in **MIME**. Since MIME is becoming a more and more important way of sending mail, we will explore it in a little more detail here.

2.3.1.2 MIME

MIME, an acronym for "Multipurpose Internet Mail Extensions," is a protocol which allows mail messages with a very varied content to be exchanged successfully. With non-MIME mailers, you can't simply send a file in a word-processing format (such as Word or Word Perfect) and expect it to arrive undamaged at its destination, since only 7-bit US-ASCII and lines shorter than 1000 characters will survive the transfer. Images and audio files will also be damaged in transit.

MIME mailers are a partial solution to this problem. Such mailers include information in the messages which allows the recipient mailer to understand what kind of message it is receiving. And they allow you to include any kind of data in a mail message by encoding the message into the form mail messages must have, i.e. 7-bit US-ASCII with a line-length less than 1000 characters. The recipient mailer can then decode the message and return its contents to the original form.

Suppose, for example, you use a Mac and wish to send your friends your latest work on the syntax of Ngarindjin. You tell your MIME mailer to attach the file to your mail-message. The mailer encloses the message within lines (which are called *boundary-markers*), and sends it off to your friends. When they receive the message, their MIME mailers take note of the markers, which indicate the file type and the kind of decoding needed to turn the file back into its original form. If, for example, the message is a binhexed file, and if the recipient is also running a Mac, a MIME mailer will unbinhex it and save it as a file on the desktop. All your friend now needs to do is click on the file and read it.

With a MIME mailer you can even include sound files of Ngarindjin or picture files showing the ghost gum tree beneath which you collected your data. Your recipients may need to have special software on their machines in order to turn your files back into sound and/or pictures; but a fully MIME-compliant mailer will be able to tell them what kind of files they have received and what additional software is needed.

This does not mean that all difficulties disappear when a MIME mailer is used. There is still the problem of fonts. If you send someone a phonetic transcription of some data, the material will still be unreadable unless he or she has the same font you used for the transcription. What is more, like ordinary mailers, MIME mailers do not allow you to mix fonts easily in the same message. This means also that you can't use many different scripts in a single message, e.g. you can't have a message written in English which includes data in Thai script. However, with a MIME mailer you can at least write your message using a word-processing program and then add the word-processor file as an attachment to your MIME message. Most word-processing programs have no trouble handling different fonts in the same document; and this way you'll at least be able to send the information via e-mail.

However, if you use a MIME mailer you may encounter another problem as well: incompatibility with non-MIME mailers. Suppose someone who uses a MIME mailer sends a message to someone who does not have one. If the message uses only ASCII characters, the recipient will have no trouble reading it. Most people won't even notice that the message contains MIME headers. Thus a message such as the following, typed into a MIME mailer:

```
Hi, Penny! Congratulations on tenure!
```

will appear just as above. The only clue that a MIME mailer sent the message will be a line in the header which will say the following:

```
Content-Type: text/plain; charset="us-ascii"
```

But if the message was written in, say, Word, and then attached to the message, the result will be a message like the following, which is totally unreadable by a human being:

```
_============_-1349349553==_============
Content-Type: text/plain; charset="us-ascii"

_============_-1349349553==_============
Content-Type: application/msword;
name="congratulations.doc"
; x-mac-type="5736424E"
; x-mac-creator="4D535744"
Content-Disposition: attachment;
filename="congratulations.doc"
Content-Transfer-Encoding: base64

0M8R4KGxGuEAAAAAAAAAAAAAAAAAAAAOwADAP7/CQAGAAA
AAAAAAAAEAAAAgAAAAEAAAD+////AAAAAAAAAD////////////////
///////////. . . .
```

It's not enough, then, that you have a MIME mailer. The recipient has to have one too, or at least have software (such as *mpack*, *munpack*, or *Metamail*) which can convert what you have sent. Such software usually prompts the user to save the mail message as a file, which can then be transferred to the user's home computer and read using a word-processor.

At this writing, there are still many people using non-MIME mailers. If you use a MIME mailer, it's very likely that your attachments will be unreadable to some of your correspondents. So it is important that you know what kind of mailer you have.

Many people are using MIME mailers without knowing it, since some of the most user-friendly mailers are, in fact, MIME-compliant. Here we can not give a list of all MIME mailers for all platforms. But the following are the most common: Eudora, Pine, Elm, Netscape Mail, Explorer Mail. Most mailers included in the software packages of Internet providers are now also MIME-compatible.

Thus, though MIME is undoubtedly the wave of the future, the future is not quite with us yet. It may be a while before we can assume that every e-mail message we send will be easily read by every recipient.

2.3.1.3   E-mail addresses

In the early days of e-mail correspondence a recurring problem was that of finding an individual's e-mail address. Today most associations publish the e-mail addresses of members with their membership lists, so the directory of a linguistic society may be all you need. However, many universities and organizations are also simplifying addressing, so that it is becoming easier to make a good guess. They have compiled a mailer-accessible database of all the different e-mail addresses on site, so, if you know that someone works at, for example, the University of Texas, you can simply type your correspondent's name plus the university designation, e.g.:

```
Jane.Doe@utexas.edu
jdoe@utexas.edu
doe@utexas.edu
```

You no longer need to know the department name or machine name in order to reach a correspondent.

Another source of linguists' e-mail addresses is the Linguists' Nameserver at the address:

```
linguists@let.uva.nl
```

You ask this server for a linguist's address by sending it an e-mail message consisting of the **command**:

```
list SURNAME
```

This server has no connection with the e-mail discussion list called The LINGUIST List, but it is also possible to use The LINGUIST List to find an e-mail address (see section 2.3.1.4 below).

2.3.1.4   Mailing lists

As far as we know, the first electronic mailing list designed specifically for linguists was The LINGUIST List, started in 1989 at the University of Western Australia with 69 subscribers. By 1997, it had grown to over 9400 subscribers from 82 different countries, thereby offering a concrete illustration of the popularity and utility of mailing lists. The LINGUIST List has become a general clearinghouse for all kinds of information relating to the discipline, but it still remains a vehicle for the linguistic discussion it was founded to carry. It can be accessed at the e-mail address

linguist@linguistlist.org

or read at one of its World Wide Web sites. We give only the main LINGUIST site here. From it, you can find a site which may be nearer to you, and thus faster to access:

http://linguistlist.org/

You can use the search facility on the LINGUIST web site to find the e-mail address of another subscriber. Simply click on "Addresses" on the home page. Also, if you are a LINGUIST List subscriber, you can retrieve subscriber addresses by e-mail. Simply send the command

review linguist by name

to the LINGUIST listserv address:

listen@linguistlist.org

You will receive the names and e-mail addresses of all current subscribers. The file you receive is huge, however. So you should save the file immediately, without reading it (it will take 10 minutes to scroll across your screen as a mail message). Once you have saved the list as a file, you can use a search utility like *grep* to extract the name and address you want.

The LINGUIST List is also a good starting point from which to locate other linguistic resources on the World Wide Web. Every Web address which passes through LINGUIST is "captured" and added to its lists of datasources. The lists are extensive, since almost all linguistic Web addresses appear at some time in LINGUIST issues. In addition, LINGUIST now maintains the Virtual Library in linguistics, formerly at Brown University. Thus the LINGUIST homepage now offers access to the Web addresses of linguistic programs, software, corpora, mailing lists, fonts, conferences, jobs, personal pages of linguists, associations, journals, publishers, bibliographies, course syllabi, dictionaries, and sites dedicated to specific topics, e.g. sign language. (Most of the addresses in this article were retrieved from the LINGUIST website.)

There are numerous other mailing lists of interest to linguists, focussing on everything from the interface between archeology/prehistory and language (ARCLING. Server: listproc@anu.edu.au) to comparative linguistics in African Languages of the Sahel-Sahara zone (COMPARLIN-GAFRIC at listserv@unice.fr). Mailing lists frequently fade away, or change locations and contact persons. So if you are interested in joining a discussion list on a particular topic, it's a good idea to check one of the several regularly-updated lists of mailing lists, e.g.:

The List of Language Lists prepared by Bernard Comrie and Michael Everson:

```
http://www.indigo.ie/egt/langlist.html
```

The List of Mailing Lists kept by the LINGUIST list:

```
http://linguistlist.org/lists.html
```

Both of these are preceded by useful instructions on how to join a mailing list. Usually you can subscribe by sending to the list address a message consisting of the single line:

```
subscribe <listname> <firstname> <lastname>
```

List subscription is usually automated, and there are four software programs commonly used to maintain lists: Listserv, ListProc, Mailbase, and Majordomo. Interaction with the list server will differ slightly depending on what program the list uses.

2.3.2   File transfer protocol

Because of the limitations of e-mail, it is often practical to use *ftp* or *File Transfer Protocol* to transfer files between remote machines. If you are collaborating on a manuscript with a colleague, for example, you may well find it faster and more reliable to send your drafts back and forth using ftp rather than mail.

Ftp works as follows. If you wish to get a file from a remote machine, you must start an ftp client on your own machine, and tell it to access the target machine's ftp server. You do this, on most machines, by typing the following:

```
ftp machine-name
```

e.g.

```
ftp zippy.org
```

At this point you will be asked to type your login name, and your password. Usually you must already have an account, or know an account name and password, on the remote machine. However, some machines allow what is called *anonymous ftp* so that you can access files which have been made available to the public. These machines let you log in using anonymous as your login name and your e-mail address as the password.

After login, you will see a prompt like this:

```
ftp>
```

In order to find out what files are available on the remote system you can type one of two things: dir (for "directory") or ls (for "list"). Both will give you a directory of files, though ls will provide less information about them than `dir`. If you want to transfer a copy of one of these files to your home machine, you can type:

```
get filename
```

e.g.

```
get klingon.ode
```

If you want to get multiple files, then you use `mget`. For example, you might type the string:

```
mget *.ode
```

The remote machine will then transfer each file whose suffix is *.ode* to your machine, asking you each time whether you want the file. If you don't want to be asked, start ftp by typing `ftp  -i`. This could be a dangerous operation, since there are tens of thousands of Klingon odes, and you have just given the command to download all of them. But if you have lots of disk space, ftp is a fast and easy way to retrieve multiple files, or large files such as electronic texts or corpora.

If you want to put a file on a remote machine, you use `put` to copy a single file, and `mput` to copy multiple files. You can transfer even non-ASCII files this way, without having to uuencode, binhex or zip them. However, non-ASCII files must be sent using **binary transfer**. You set ftp to binary transfer by simply typing `binary`, e.g:

```
ftp>binary
```

Most ftp programs will reply as follows:

```
200 Type set to 1
```

If you want to transfer a word-processing file, or a font, or a piece of software, always set binary, or it will fail to work on the other end. After binary transfer is complete, you can reset ftp to ASCII transfer (also called *text* transfer) simply by typing `ASCII`, e.g.:

```
ftp>ASCII
```

And the ftp program will reply as follows:

```
200 Type set to A
```

However, you should probably make it a rule always to set binary for ftp. Certainly, if you don't know whether a file contains non-ASCII characters, you should transfer it as a binary file. To transfer an ASCII file as binary usually does no harm: it just takes slightly longer. The reverse, however, is not true. If you don't set binary, ftp will interpret anything you send as ASCII, deleting or mistranslating non-ASCII characters.

2.3.3 Telnet

It is often the case that you are on one machine but need to do some-thing on another. You might, for example, be visiting Los Angeles and need to read your mail on a machine in Chicago. If your Chicago machine allows remote logins (some do not, for security reasons), you can actu-ally interact with its processor just as if you were sitting at your own home terminal.

You do this by typing the function `telnet` followed by an argument which is your machine's full Internet name, e.g:

```
telnet trixi.uchicago.edu
```

The telnet software will respond with the following kind of message:

```
Trying . . .
Connected to trixi.uchicago.edu.
Escape character is '^]'.
SunOS UNIX 4.1 (trixi.uchicago.edu) (ttyp7)
login: <yourname>
Password: <yourpassword>
```

When you've typed your password, you'll be logged onto "trixi"; and everything should seem just like it is at home, although the commands you type may take somewhat longer to execute. What's actually happened, of course, is that you've opened a TCP/IP connection with the remote machine. And there is a great deal going on in the background. For example, telnet must be able to tell what kind of machine you're on, since a Mac, for example, will handle output to the screen differently from an IBM.

Telnet is useful for other purposes than simply reading mail from a remote terminal. Thousands of libraries across the world are accessible by telnet; when you log on to a remote library to find a citation or "read the shelves" to find new books, you are searching the card catalog by telnet. The Appendix to this chapter includes addresses at which you can find lists of libraries available via telnet.

There are also some linguistic databases which can be accessed in this way, e.g. the South Asia database at `columbianet.columbia.edu` (select the menu item called CLIO Plus), and the Australian Language & Literacy database at `lingua.cltr.uq.oz.au` (login as dbguest, pass-word NLLIA-db). Once logged on, you can search the database and display records by keying in commands, just as you would if the database were on your own machine. However, you can download copies of the records only in rather inconvenient ways, i.e., by having your machine record the whole telnet session as a file, or by telling your machine to Print Screen periodically.

2.4   FINDING INFORMATION ON THE INTERNET

The three functionalities we have discussed allow you to contact other machines and thus to retrieve information whose location you know. What they don't do, however, is help you find information. Finding information has, of course, always been a problem on the Internet, since there is no central index of available files or sites. And the problem is being exacerbated by the daily establishment of thousands of new World Wide Web pages. Whatever their information potential, Internet sites are valueless if no one knows they exist.

Three of the most important and earliest solutions to this problem were Archie, Gopher, and WAIS. As we shall see, the first two are now often accessed via Web browser interfaces, such as Netscape, Lynx, Explorer or Mosaic, whose primary protocol is *http* (*hypertext transfer protocol*). And both Archie and WAIS are becoming less and less useful as World Wide Web search facilities proliferate. However, they are still independently accessible on most mainframes and many workstations. So we describe them briefly in the sections which follow.

2.4.1   Archie

The most basic search system is called *Archie*, which is essentially a search facility for public ftp archives. Any such archive can register with Archie, and then keep what is called an *ls-lR* file, which is a recursive listing of all the files in that archive. Users may then use Archie to search all such registered files for substrings. Archie searches are very fast. For example, we searched on the string "linguist" and in approximately 3 seconds we received the information given as Figure 2.2.

In other words, Archie told us that if we ftp'd to any of the 4 hosts listed and changed the directory to the one specified after "Location," we would find a sub-directory there called "linguist." The string after "DIRECTORY," e.g., "drwxr-xr-x," tells us that "linguist" is a directory and that it is accessible to the public; the first "d" in the string indicates *directory* and the 3 "r's" in the string tell us that it is readable by user, group, and others. Note that Archie did not tell us what's in the directories it found. To see a list of available files when using ftp, you'll have to type dir, as described in 2.3.2 above.

Most large sites have an Archie client, which can talk to Archie servers, so that you can perform Archie searches from your command line when logged on to your mainframe account; you do this just by typing Archie followed by a search-term, as we did above. But you can also use e-mail for an Archie search, simply by sending an appropriate request to an Archie server. There is, for example, an Archie server at a machine called archie.internic.net. Here you use special commands. The command

```
Aristar{7}%>archie linguist
Host freebsd.cdrom.com

  Location: /.2/SimTel/msdos

    DIRECTORY drwxr-xr-x      1024 Aug 19 1994 linguist
Host ftp.clarkson.edu

  Location: /pub/simtel20-cdrom/msdos

    DIRECTORY dr-xr-xr-x      2048 Jan 14 1992 linguist
Host ftp.uga.edu

  Location: /pub/msdos/mirror

    DIRECTORY dr-xr-xr-x       512 Apr 7 1994 linguist
Host ftp.wustl.edu

  Location: /systems/ibmpc/msdos

    DIRECTORY drwxr-xr-x      8192 Dec 21 1993 linguist
```

Figure 2.2   Results of an Archie search

prog, for example, tells the Archie server to find any file containing your search-string. So if you send a message to the address:

archie@archie.internic.net

containing the search command:

prog linguist

you will, in due course, receive a message from that Archie server telling you the location of all the files which match that search-string.

Alternatively, if you have an ethernet connection or are running the kind of software that allows you to use a graphical browser on your personal machine, you may be able to install one of the more user-friendly Archie clients. A search on "linguist" via one of these clients, produced the screen given as Figure 2.3.

This helpful Archie client labels the search returns as hosts, directories, and files. It also allows you to see the size of the file and the date it was written, and to bring it down to your home machine simply by clicking on it with your mouse.

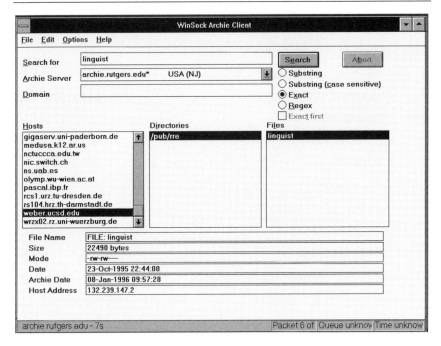

Figure 2.3 Archie search results displayed by a graphical Archie client

2.4.2   Gopher

Gopher is a system which complements Archie, in that it organizes data in a different way, and will thus enable you to find a different subset of the body of information. Archie searches through directory and file names (and in some instances through file descriptions) in order to determine whether a particular string is present. If it finds such a string, it returns a listing of the file. What this means, of course, is that there is no necessary relation between a file-name and its content. A file might be named "bubble-gum" and be a screensaver. So if you really are looking for files on bubble-gum, you're going to have to sift through files which are irrelevant to your search.

Gopher to some degree obviates this, because it is based on human-produced indices, and human beings (usually) know what their files contain. The way Gopher works is as follows. If a site has information, human beings group the files into categories and put them in files in a special form. They install a Gopher server which has access to the Gopher files and responds to Gopher clients by showing the categories in the form of a hierarchical set of menus. These menus typically include things like "libraries," which will allow you access to catalogs of on-line libraries, or local news. You can see such a menu in Figure 2.4:

```
          Internet Gopher Information Client v2.1.3
                Home Gopher server: gopher.tamu.edu

          ========== LOCAL INFORMATION ===========
-->▌ 2.  Browse by Subject/
     3.  Search TAMU Gophers - Veronica <?>
     4.  Electronic Phonebook <CSO>
     5.  Calendars/
     6.  Libraries/
     7.  Academic Departments/
     8.  Non-Academic Departments/
     9.  Student Organizations/
    10.  Texas A&M University System/
    11.  Hot Topics: New & Popular/
          ======= WORLD-WIDE INFORMATION =========
    13.  Gophers World-Wide/
    14.  Search All Gophers - Veronica/
    15.  Browse by Subject/
    16.  About Gopher & WWW/


Press ? for Help, ? to Quit                          Page: 1/1
```

Figure 2.4   Menu produced by a Gopher server

The particular set of menus you see varies according to the way your local Gopher server is set up. Since you can easily move to other Gophers, you can see their menu hierarchies as well. In Gopherspace, you can access any Gopher's menus, but what one site catalogs under one menu item might be catalogued under quite another at a different site. One site, for example, indexes Virginia Woolf's *To the Lighthouse* under literature, another under women's writing, a third under romance. And if you don't know what category something is catalogued under, you can't find it.

Gopher, however, has one utility which allows you to sidestep this problem. It's a utility which searches through file-names, just as Archie does, except that it searches inside Gopherspace. This utility is called Veronica, after the girlfriend of the comic-book character Archie, though it sometimes appears in Gopher menus under the anonymous menu-item "Search Titles in Gopherspace." With this utility you can often find what you want rather more easily than by browsing menus. But, of course, as with Archie, you can't rely on the title of a file to have any connection to its content.

Like many Archie clients, Gopher will not only allow you to find the files you want, it will also go get them for you as well. If, for example, you want the on-line version of *To the Lighthouse* you discovered through Veronica, a simple command will have Gopher initiate an ftp session to that site and download a copy onto your disk. Gopher will also initiate telnet sessions if that is the appropriate action. Suppose, for example, you find through Gopher a genetics database which you can interrogate by telnet. Gopher will open the session for you, hand over control to telnet, and return when you've ended the telnet session. This ability to access the basic TCP/IP functions makes Gopher very useful. All you need to know is how to use Gopher. If you wish, you can avoid the intricacies of anonymous logins or accessing ftp and telnet directly.

Until the advent of World Wide Web browsers, Gopher was the only utility which allowed you this kind of flexibility. And it is still sometimes a useful means of finding information in cyberspace, although Web browsers are fast making it obsolete. Most Unix platforms have Gopher installed already, so to initiate Gopher on a Unix platform all you have to do is to type gopher and follow the menus which this command shows you.

2.4.3   WAIS

The last search utility which we'll discuss here is **WAIS**, which is an acronym for "Wide Area Information Service." Like Gopher, it relies on indexes. But it differs from Gopher in that these are indexes of the text inside files rather than an index categorizing files by content. For example, suppose you wish to find a file of Hungarian recipes for soup. WAIS will make an index of the words occurring in the file itself, e.g., *cabbage, paprika, sour cream,* whereas Gopher will index the file under larger category headings like Food > Hungarian > Recipes > Soup.

WAIS has one feature that is potentially very useful: it gives each word in the document a relevancy score. This means that if you institute a search using the word *cabbage*, WAIS will not only retrieve a list of documents which includes the Hungarian recipe file but it will also tell you how important a word *cabbage* is within that document. It is able to tell you this because WAIS databases are indexed by a special program called *waisindex* which gives each word a score based on:

- the word's frequency per 1000 words. Words occurring more frequently in the document get higher scores.
- the position of the word in the document. Words in titles and headings, for example, get higher scores.
- the rarity of the word in all the documents WAIS knows about. Words which are generally rare in documents get higher scores. This may, at first, seem counter-intuitive, but consider a document that contains both the words *language* and *anaphora*. *Anaphora* is certainly the rarer word, and if it occurs in this document, there must be a reason – probably that the document is about anaphora.

To institute a WAIS search on a Unix platform, you can type

```
waissearch <searchterm>
```

e.g.,

```
waissearch anaphora
```

at the root prompt. If your machine has a WAIS client, this will connect you to the default host machine and search the default database. If you want to search another database, you must specify the host machine and database, following the flags -h (host) and -d (database), respectively. So if you want to search for the word "syntax" in the Welsh database maintained on the sunsite.unc.edu host, you would type:

```
waissearch -h sunsite.unc.edu -d Welsh syntax
```

One of the problems with WAIS is that for *waissearch* to query a WAIS index, someone must already have gone to the trouble of producing such an index. To date, we have not found many WAIS-indexed databases relevant to linguistics. Another problem with using WAIS is that only Mosaic among the graphics Web browsers can handle WAIS addresses. Using other Web browsers, you have to contact WAIS servers indirectly, by going through a Web-to-WAIS search facility or using a Web-to-WAIS gateway. For these reasons, we find WAIS to be a less useful search facility than Gopher or Archie.

2.4.4 News

News is not so much a search facility as a place where computer users can interact, and thus find information by asking questions, or by downloading files individuals have posted to News. News works somewhat differently from the other Internet utilities, in that it uses multiple servers, as well as a user-oriented client. The major News facilities are USENET and ClariNet. Each is a distributed network, which means that news items sent to one USENET or ClariNet server are "propagated," or distributed by the server to all the other servers which act as clearinghouses for USENET or ClariNet news items. To read News, you must have access to a news client and a news server which is part of the News network. The news server may also serve as a central site for news items sent to purely local newsgroups (e.g., groups advertising rental property or jobs in the area). Because all news servers organize newsgroups in the same way, news items originating at ClariNet, at USENET, or a local server can be treated the same way by the client; that is, they can be displayed on your screen as part of the same hierarchical list.

ClariNet is a News system which takes its news items from wire services such as The Associated Press or Reuters and organizes them into newspaper-like categories, e.g., World News, Entertainment, Syndicated Columns. A subject listing of ClariNet newsgroups can be ftp'd from:

```
ftp.clarinet.com/clarinet_info/quickref
```

USENET is the very large set of newsgroups which take their news items from individual posters. When an individual posts a message to a

USENET newsgroup, a client at the local site sends these messages to the server which distributes ("propagates") the message to other servers which handle this newsgroup. Each server acts as a distributor, or *newsfeed*, for a chosen set of newsgroups. The systems administrator at each site decides which groups to make available to its clients. Your local news server may get newsfeeds from one server or from many different servers, depending on the diskspace available and the predilections of your systems administrator. (Some local sites – e.g., universities with timid administrators – filter out the more risqué USENET newsgroups.)

If you wish to read News, you start up your local client, which is called a *newsreader*. This newsreader goes to the local server and asks for a listing of the newsgroups which are available. Because there are many newsgroups (USENET alone has thousands), many newsreaders only list the groups to which you have previously subscribed. If you are a first-time user, however, the newsreader will ask if you want a listing of all the newsgroups available to your local server. Retrieving this list can take a considerable time, but it may be the only way for you to find groups you want to subscribe to. When the client displays the list of available newsgroups, you select one to read, and the client goes back to the news server for a list of headers of all relevant news items. When you select a news item to read, the newsreader goes back to the news server once again to get the item you requested.

There are many different kinds of newsreaders. If you read News from a Unix account on a mainframe, you may activate your newsreader by typing rn ("read news"), trn ("threaded rn") or even nn ("no news" – a name spawned by the saying "No news is good news"). Figure 2.5 below is part of the screen we got when we typed trn at a Unix prompt.

Note that in Figure 2.5 the bottom of the screen tells us how to subscribe to groups using the syntax "g" followed by the newsgroup name. Then it tells us there are 48 unread news items in the newsgroup news.announce.newusers and asks us if we want to read these. We don't. So it tells us that we are at the end of our subscribed newsgroups and asks "What next?" At that point we subscribe to the newsgroup sci.lang.

In addition to Unix news clients like *trn*, there are clients which can be run on your personal machine. These are often much easier to use than a mainframe newsreader, since they often provide menus of permissible operations (reply to the newsgroup, save the news item as a file, etc.), present newsgroup choices as an organized list, allow you to *thread* (i.e., to group together) news items having the same topic or subject line, and allow you to use a mouse.

Furthermore, later versions of most Web browsers, e.g., Netscape 2.0 or later, can function as newsreaders, giving you all the advantages listed above, plus the ability to view pictures contained in news items, and even to play sound files. However, a newsreader must have access to a local

```
hdry-ut{12}%>trn
Trying to set up a .newsrc file — running newsetup...
Welcome to trn. Here's some important things to remember:
o Trn is an extension of rn and has a similar command
  syntax.
o Typing a space to any prompt means to do the normal
  thing. You could spend all day reading news and never
  hit anything but the space bar.
o If you have never used the news system before, you may
  find the articles in news.announce.newusers to be
  helpful.
o Please consult the man page for complete information.

Creating /home/uts/li/ligt/hdry/.newsrc to be used by
news programs.
Done.
To add new group use "a pattern" or "g newsgroup.name".
To get rid of newsgroups you aren't interested in, use
the 'u' command.
Unread news in news.announce.newusers    48 articles
****** 48 unread articles in news.announce.newusers —
read now? [ynq]
****** End of newsgroups — what next? [npq] g sci.lang
Newsgroup sci.lang not in .newsrc — subscribe? [ynYN]
Put newsgroup where? [$^Lq]
****** 472 unread articles in sci.lang — read now? [ynq]
****** End of newsgroups — what next? [npq]
```

Figure 2.5   The initial screen of the *trn* newsreader

news server; if your Web browser can not read News, it may be because it lacks such access.

Newsgroups are usually presented as hierarchical lists, because News is organized into categories and sub-categories, ostensibly by subject. For linguists the best metaphor for this arrangement is the tree. Every newsgroup is dominated by a node that includes all groups whose topics are, in the opinion of the organizers of News, sub-categories of the node topic. In the name of the newsgroup, each node is separated from its dominating node by a dot. So, for example, a newsgroup called *rec.art.folk* would be a group on the recreational activity of art which deals specifically with folk-art.

The hierarchical organization of News, it may be observed, follows its own rules. The dominating node *alt* for "alternative" (e.g. *alt.abortion.*

recovery, alt.arts.ballet), for example, indicates not so much similarity of content, as an implication of similarity of attitude on the part of those who post messages there. Groups dominated by *alt* tend to be groups where anything goes. The content of these groups is hard to predict, and ranges from the quirky to the frankly obscene. Groups dominated by *soc* (for "social"), on the other hand, tend to be more serious. Groups dominated by *sci* discuss scientific issues. This is where the major linguistic newsgroup, *sci.lang*, resides.

To some degree News fills the same role as e-mail discussion lists, but it has important differences. For example, the reason why so many people like News is that reading News is a maintenance-free occupation. Subscribing to an e-mail discussion group is not. When you receive e-mail you have to do something with it, even if only delete it. With News, if you fail to read anything for weeks, all that will happen is that you will get behind in the discussion. Items you failed to read will eventually disappear all by themselves. You can, what is more, move freely between groups, reading a little here, dropping the group for a while, and going back later if you wish. It's easy to stumble across a newsgroup on an interesting topic (your newsreader, after all, will provide a list), post a few messages to it, and move on.

The easy availability of newsgroups has, however, some bad effects. It's as easy for the uninformed as for the expert to post a message on a topic, and thus newsgroups tend to contain a very mixed set of items. *Sci.lang*, for example, supposedly treats the scientific study of language. In practice, however, it mixes news items reflecting "scientific study" with news items of awe-inspiring linguistic naiveté. (This can also be true of mailing lists, of course; but mailing lists on specific topics do require some knowledge and initiative to find, qualities presumably lacking in the "drive-by" poster.) Newsgroups are also hard to keep focused and are often subject to flame-wars, since personal connections between posters are tenuous and, if a dispute arises, no one has the authority to intervene.

2.5 WORLD WIDE WEB

Each of the Internet functionalities discussed so far does only a few, specific things: mailers send and receive mail, ftp servers transfer files, Gopher servers find information, and so on. The World Wide Web, however, is different. It is an Internet functionality which can do something none of the other utilities can: it can do everything.

2.5.1 What is the Web?

The Web does not exist as a concrete entity. "Web" is a metaphor for the multiplicity of links effected by the new technologies called web browsers and web servers. Unlike a Gopher client, which requires a

Gopher server on the other end, a browser can interact with (almost) any kind of server, as long as it knows the server type. Thus the information it exchanges can also be of virtually any kind: a text, a photograph, a sound, a movie, a program, or a mail-message.

However, the facility which has made the Web what it is is the use of **hypertext** as a way of accessing Internet facilities. And the HTTP server, i.e., a server running HyperText Transfer Protocol, is the facility that has come to be known as a "Web server." As most users know by now, hypertext is text which has links to other texts embedded in it, so that the user can select a link with a mouse or a keystroke and "go to" the linked text. On the World Wide Web, the links are called ***URL***'s (Universal Resource Locators); and they have a three-part syntax:

a) The kind of resource being accessed. Is it an HTTP server, a Gopher server, a WAIS service, an ftp site, telnet site or a News group? Each of these has a different prefix: HTTP, GOPHER, WAIS, ftp, TELNET and NEWS.
b) The address of the service, in domain name form, preceded by a colon and two slashes. If a port has to be designated, it follows this, preceded by a colon. The address ends with a slash.
c) The path to the right file. This will include the name of each subdirectory in the path, followed by a slash, and the filename if you know it.

Thus, if a file called `default.html` exists inside the directory `files` and is present on a machine called `engserve.tamu.edu` which has an HTTP server and uses Port 8000, the correct URL would be

`http://engserve.tamu.edu:8000/files/default.html`

A telnet connection would appear as follows:

`TELNET://engserve.tamu.edu/`

2.5.2   Hypertext

Even though you can use a browser to access a Gopher server and retrieve plain text or an ftp server and retrieve files, it is most likely that you will want to access an HTTP server and retrieve documents in hypertext, because it is hypertext documents which contain links to other documents. If, for example, your browser displays a hypertext document that lists the datasources collected by The LINGUIST List, e.g., the homepage at:

`http://www.linguistlist.org/`

and you decide you want to see the list of sites dedicated to specific linguistic topics, you select that link and retrieve another hypertext document, this one containing links to these sites (Figure 2.6).

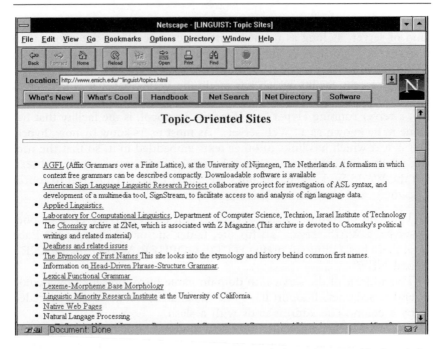

Figure 2.6 Hypertext page listing WWW sites dedicated to specific linguistics topics (From the LINGUIST List website)

Selecting a link to a specific site, e.g., Lexical Functional Grammar, will retrieve yet another hypertext document, this one listing (and potentially linking you to) information about LFG (Figure 2.7). It is this ability to link one text to another which has caused the set of protocols we are talking about to be called a "web."

2.5.3   Web browsers

Web browsers, which run on the user's own machine, are the key Web technology. There are a number of browsers available for different platforms. There are text browsers, such as Lynx, which cannot handle graphics but which have the advantage of not requiring that the machine run TCP/IP. Text browsers will work over a serial line, i.e., one which transmits series of characters, not data in Internet Protocol. This means that you can use a text browser with your ordinary modem and phone line and very basic software. However, you won't be able to take advantage of the full capacity of the Web. For that, you need a graphics browser. The earliest graphics browser was NCSA Mosaic, but it has been largely superseded by browsers such as Netscape and Explorer. Both Netscape and Explorer are available by anonymous ftp.

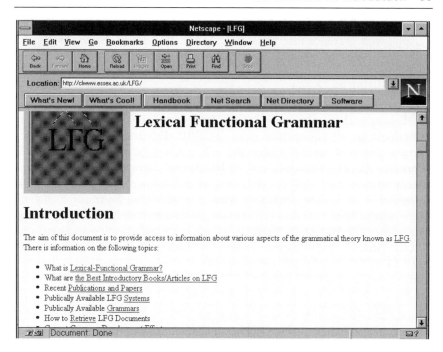

Figure 2.7   Homepage of the website dedicated to Lexical Functional Grammar

The addresses are:

```
ftp.netscape.com
```

and:

```
ftp.microsoft.com
```

Ftp to one of these sites as described in section 2.3.2 above, log in using "anonymous" and download the browser version which is appropriate to your machine. Netscape is free to educators, though others must pay a small fee. Explorer is free to everyone.

Browsers not only know how to ask different kinds of servers for information, they know what to do with the different types of information they retrieve. If the file is a graphics file, the browser will display it on screen as a picture. If the data is text, the browser will display it in a text window. If the connection is to an ftp port, the browser will save the data as a file. This means that users can do highly sophisticated things without ever needing to learn the specific technologies operating behind the scenes.

Browsers themselves are very easy to learn. To use a browser, all you need to know is how to run the browser software, how to distinguish a hypertext link from other text (by color, underlining, or shading), and how to open links (by selecting them with a mouse or the keyboard). For persons with graphics interfaces (e.g. MAC, Windows), browsers are the epitome of "point-and-click" technology: you open a browser by clicking on its icon and you access its functions and links by clicking on menu items or highlighted text.

However, in order to use a graphics browser like Netscape, Explorer or Mosaic, and thereby enjoy all the features of the Web, your machine must have an IP connection (e.g., TCP/IP, Ethernet), or run software using a protocol which makes the other machine think it does. *PPP* (*Point to Point Protocol*) and *SLIP* (*Serial Line Internet Protocol*) are protocols that fool the Internet into thinking that your personal computer is an Internet machine. However, they can be tricky to install. Many universities are now giving out an Internet connectivity package which includes MacTCP, TCP/IP, or Winsock and which – theoretically, at least – installs itself using an easily-run setup program. If such a package is available to you, by all means use it.

However, you should know that you will need a good deal of memory (at least 8 MB) and a fairly fast connection. Otherwise Web access can be painfully slow. The Web makes no distinction between different kinds of text; and some of these "texts" – like movies, pictures, and sounds – are very bulky. A single short computer movie is the size of all of Jane Austen's combined works. To move this kind of information around at all requires at the minimum a high speed modem. An ethernet connection is even better.

2.5.4   Writing a Web page

One of the reasons that the Web has been so successful is that it's very easy to set up a Web site. You have to have a certain amount of know-how to make information available on the Internet via Gopher or WAIS or Archie, but setting up a Web page with all the hypertext links you want is so easy that individuals who have absolutely no computational expertise can do it. All you need is an account on a machine where a Web server is running and some introduction to a simple *markup* language called *HTML*.

If you're a student or employee of a university, it's very likely that you have access to an HTTP server through the same account as you use for e-mail. Even if such a server is not running on your own machine, it's probably running on other university machines, and you can request an account on one of these for your Web page files. In that case, all you have to do is create a hypertext document and store it as a file in a directory which is accessible to the server.

To create a Web page, the first thing you should do is download a Web browser like Netscape or Explorer, since the browser will help you download all the additional software you need. See Section 2.5.3 for instructions.

Next you will need to learn how to write HTML (HyperText Markup Language), so you may wish to download the hypertext primer available at the URL:

```
general/internet/www/HTMLPrimer.html
```

Just access this URL through your browser and save it as a file on your own machine. (Your browser will probably have a "Save as" option in the File menu.) Then you can print it out and refer to it as you mark up your Web page. The grammar of HTML is very easy to learn, but – if you're like us – you may have trouble remembering the vocabulary items and be grateful for a glossary.

2.5.4.1 HTML basics

In HTML, the analogue of a vocabulary item is the *tag*. A tag consists of a left angle bracket (<) followed by the name of the tag, e.g. B for *bold*, or I for *italic*. A right angle bracket preceded by a slash (/>) closes almost all of the tags. The two exceptions are the <P> tag, which marks the end of a paragraph, and the <BR> tag, which marks a line break.

Tags are instructions to the Web browser. Most of these instructions tell the browser how to format the page it is displaying. So, for example, in the markup below

```
<B> This is boldface. </7>
```

the tag <B> tells the Web browser to bold the text until it finds the </B>, when it will stop bolding the text. (Case never matters inside a formatting tag.[4] So <b> and </b> would work just as well.)

Titles are marked by the <TITLE> tag, and end with the </TITLE> tag. Every Web page should have a title, as this is what is displayed at the top of the window when the page is read with a browser. Headings are indicated by tags beginning with H, e.g. <H1> </H1>, <H2> </H2>. The larger the number to the right of the H, the smaller the heading. Lists of various kinds (bulleted, indented, numbered, etc.) can also be formatted by using appropriate tags.

Consider the following HTML text:

```
<TITLE>This is an Example of HTML</TITLE><H1>Now we have
a heading</H1>Now we have some text, followed by a
paragraph break<P>And then another<P>And then <B>some
bold text</B>
```

This will display in Netscape as in Figure 2.8.

In addition to formatting commands, you will almost certainly wish to add *link*s to your document, so that the user can move from your page

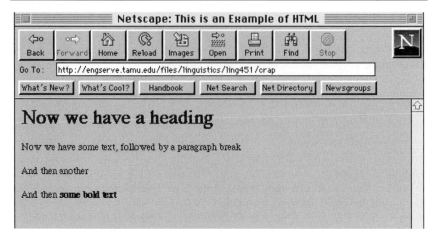

Figure 2.8   The sample HTML text as displayed by Netscape

to related files or documents. Links are added by surrounding the address of the resource and the words you wish to use as a link with anchor tags. The browser will indicate that the selected words are a link by changing their color and/or underlining them.

The hyperlink anchor tag always starts with <A. It is followed by HREF, which tells the browser that this is a Hypertext REFerence. Then comes an equals sign, then the quoted address of the file you wish to link. If the file is local, and in the same directory, the filename will serve as the address, e.g.

```
<A HREF="subgrouping.html">
```

If the file is on a remote system, however, you must use the URL scheme (see Section 2.5.1) to specify the file.

After specifying the address, you type the words you wish to be high-lighted in your text to indicate the link, i.e., the words you want the user to "click" on. Then you close the link with </A>, as in:

```
<A HREF="subgrouping.html">This is a link</A>.
```

2.5.4.2   *Mounting your Web page*

Once your page is furnished with links and formatted to your liking, you simply save it as a file in the proper subdirectory. If it is your main page, you should give the file a name that the Web server recognizes – usually *index.html* or *default.html* – so that it will display this page first when someone visits your site with a browser.

The directory to which you save the file can be a subdirectory within your own account, but it too must be a directory that the HTTP server can read, so you may have to ask your local help desk administrator what the directory should be called, and how to set protections so that outsiders can read it. Most HTTP servers are programmed to read directories called either *www* or *public_html*.

For example, if you have a university account with the address

```
foobar@sloppy.emich.edu
```

and the machine called "sloppy" is running a Web browser, you can place your Web page in a subdirectory of this account, perhaps one called */usr/local/foobar/www/*. Anyone wishing to read the page with a Web browser would access it at the URL:

```
http://sloppy.emich.edu/~foobar/
```

By convention, the main Web server at each site has the alias *www*. So, if "sloppy" houses the main Web server, your page can also be accessed as

```
http://www.emich.edu/~foobar/
```

This URL tells the browser to contact the machine at Eastern Michigan University which is running the primary WWW server and to go to the WWW-accessible directory in the account of "foobar." The server will find the file called *index.html* in this account and – if the HTML markup was done correctly – display it with proper formatting and live links.

2.5.5   Setting up a Web server

If you do not already have an account on a machine running an HTTP server, you may be required to set up a Web server in order to make your Web pages available to the public. If you have a certain amount of computational experience, you will find setting up a Web-server only about as complicated as installing a word-processor. However, this chapter is intended for beginners, so we will not go into this process in detail.

Many Web servers are free; and you can find a list of available servers at a number of different sites on the Web, e.g.:

```
http://www.uiuc.edu/help/servers.html
```

Note, however, that running an HTTP server on your own machine requires that:

- your machine be directly connected to the Internet. If you have an Ethernet connection, you automatically have an Internet connection too.
- your machine be running all the time. Once you set up an HTTP server, you'll receive connections from all over the world at all hours of the day.

If you decide to set up a Web server, we recommend that you consult a book on the subject; the most helpful book we know is an O'Reilly and Associates Nutshell book called *Managing Internet Information Services* (Liu *et al.*, 1994).

2.6 CONCLUSION

In this chapter we have tried to outline the nature of the Internet, and how you, as a linguist or linguistics student, can take advantage of it. In this space, it has been impossible to do more than introduce the eight Internet technologies we have discussed; but we have tried to provide enough information to allow you to decide which of these are likely to be most useful to you. The Appendix to this chapter lists resources which will allow you to learn more about the ones you choose to investigate further.

Many of the resources are themselves on the Internet, so we urge you to sit down at the computer and try to find them. Simply surfing the net is probably the best way to learn – certainly, a lot of the information in this chapter was acquired that way; and it was (dare we say it) a lot more fun than going to a library. This is fortunate, since we all need to continue exploring the Internet: so much valuable linguistic information now appears there that we cannot ignore it for long without losing contact with important research.

NOTES

1 One of the authors of this chapter had a paper accepted in 1991. It did not appear in print until 1995. And this is probably not at all unusual.
2 For a more extensive overview of the Internet and how it works, we refer readers to Liu *et al.* (1994), from which much of the following information is drawn.
3 IP numbers, then, are ordered the opposite way to domain names. The left-most octet of an IP number indicates the widest network, whereas the widest domain is indicated by the rightmost portion of a dotted domain name.
4 It does matter in addresses, e.g., filenames, when talking to a Unix machine. So, when enclosing material within anchor tags, make sure that upper and lower case are quoted exactly.

Appendix

PART I BOOKS

Krol, Ed. 1994. *The Whole Internet.* Sebastopol, CA: O'Reilly & Associates. There is an Academic Edition adapted into a textbook by Bruce Klopfenstein. One of the best books for those who want a good introduction to how the Internet works. There is considerable detail here, and it's very clearly written.

Liu, Cricket, Jerry Peek, Russ Jones, Bryan Buus, and Adrian Nye. 1994. *Managing Internet Information Services.* Sebastopol, CA: O'Reilly & Associates. A more advanced book for those who want set up their own site. It will teach you how to set up Web servers, e-mail lists and ftp sites.

Miller, D., S. Fowell, N. Ford. Forthcoming. *Information Skills in an Electronic Age: The Student's Handbook.* London: Routledge. A book aimed at the particular needs of students who use the Internet as part of their education and research.

Quarterman, John S. 1995. *The Matrix: Computer Networks and Conferencing Systems Worldwide.* Bedford, MA: Digital Press. This is the standard handbook on the Internet. It is bulky, and can be very complex, but it is well worth reading nevertheless.

Unicode Consortium. 1996. *The Unicode Standard: Version 2.0.* Reading, MA: Addison-Wesley. (See also http://www.unicode.org.) The standard reference work on Unicode, the character encoding system which will allow linguists (and a whole lot of other people) to use any script they wish on the Internet.

PART II SOFTWARE

Web browsers

Internet Explorer: Produced by Microsoft, this is one of the fuller featured browsers available. The latest version of Explorer is Unicode-compatible. http://www.microsoft.com/msdownload/default.asp

Netscape: Another full-featured browser, and, at the moment, probably the most common. The latest version of Netscape is Unicode-compatible.
http://www.netscape.com/

Tango: The first of the new wave of browsers whose native character encoding is Unicode. This makes it particularly interesting to linguists, since it makes the display of unusual characters possible.
http://www.alis.com/index.en.html

HTML editors

Netscape: Some versions of the Netscape browser have editing software added on. Netscape Gold is one such version, as is the browser package called Netscape Communication. The Windows version is better than the Mac versions, but this is changing fast and both are good ways to begin writing HTML. You don't need to know a lot of HTML with these editors. They will do much of the work for you.
http://www.netscape.com/

Word: Later versions of Microsoft Word also function as HTML editors and are integrated with the Explorer browser.

PART III   NETWORK RESOURCES

A Beginner's Guide to HTML: One of the better guides to writing HTML on the Web.
http://www.ncsa.uiuc.edu/General/Internet/WWW/HTMLPrimer.html

Deja News: A quick and easy way to read News without having access to a news server. It will also allow you to search all news postings and retrieve those you're interested in.
http://www.dejanews.com/

E-mail addresses of linguists: A service of the LINGUIST list. This lists most of the ways you can find a linguist's address, and includes search facilities for some of these.
http://linguistlist.org/addresses.html

Killersites: Creating good websites is not as easy as it seems. This site attempts to explain what good pages should look like.
http://www.killersites.com/core.html

Library Catalogs on the Internet: A list of libraries available by telnet.
http://library.usask.ca/hywebcat/

The LINGUIST List: A good place to start in tracking down linguistic information on the Web.
http://www.linguistlist.org/

Searchable List of Mailing Lists: If you want to find a mailing list in some particular area, this is a good place to begin.
http://tile.net/lists/

SIL: Another good site from which to find good linguistic information. Includes the famous Ethnologue, a description of all the World's known languages.
http://www.sil.org/linguistics/linguistics.html

Virtual Library in Applied Linguistics: An excellent, well-maintained site for information on this topic.
http://alt.venus.co.uk/VL/AppLingBBK/

The World Wide Web Consortium: If you want to find out more about how the World Wide Web works, this is the place to go to.
http://www.w3.org/pub/WWW/TheProject.html

Chapter 3

Education

Henry Rogers

3.1 INTRODUCTION

Linguistics is a discipline of great intricacy: students have to learn to manipulate and interrelate small bits of data. At the same time, linguistic theory tends to be quite abstract; to neophytes the theory they read about seems quite unconnected to the phonemes and morphemes they see strewn across a homework assignment. Bloomfield's sentence "Phonemes contrast" is straightforward to the initiated – indeed, elegant in its simplicity; to the uninitiated, however, it is opaque and unhelpful. Linguistics instructors are challenged to make visible both the forest and the trees.

Computers add to the techniques in a linguist's pedagogical repertoire. Computers can be used to help instructors in presenting new information, and to help students in practicing new techniques. They can allow us to combine and examine more information in a greater variety of ways and in less time than was previously feasible.

For teachers, using computers in teaching offers several advantages. Visual and sound presentations in lectures can be improved. More class time can be spent on difficult or interesting issues, and less on repetitive drill. Complex data, large corpora, and sophisticated analytical techniques can be introduced earlier or more easily than with traditional methods.

From the students' point of view, computers allow them to work at their own pace receiving immediate feedback without academic penalty – in short, they can "play" with the data. For some students, using a computer means that they can master the basics, rather than merely survive the course. In other cases, students are able to make a better analysis of a problem than they could have done using traditional methods. Most students find educational programs on the computer enjoyable, even if they are not previously familiar with computers.

All computer programs require learning how to use them. In general, there is a trade-off between ease of learning and power. Programs which are easy to learn generally have fewer features and are less flexible and can do fewer things. The programs with powerful features usually have high learn-ing curves. In this chapter we survey some of both types. See the appendix to this chapter (and the online appendices at http://www.routledge. com/routledge.html) for details of the programs mentioned in the text.

3.2 SOFTWARE FOR TEACHING LINGUISTICS

This section explores ways of using computers as a teaching assistant. Here the computer imitates some of the activities of an instructor. Information is presented to the student, questions are asked, and the student's answers are evaluated. Occasionally someone suggests that in future all teaching will be done by computers and that teachers will become redundant. These suggestions are more commonly advanced by those with little experience in teaching or computing. In my view, teachers are a basic requirement of a complex civilization; computers are tools. Good teachers have a responsibility to use the most advantageous tools available; for many tasks, a computer is a useful tool.

Teaching linguistics is a complex endeavor. In elementary courses, students have to comprehend a number of difficult concepts, and they have to acquire certain skills requiring considerable practice. Fortunately, some students will learn linguistics no matter how it is taught. These we can forget about in this chapter: there is no need to devise better ways of teaching mathematics to young Newtons. However, instructors in intro-ductory linguistics courses typically find that there are some students who, although they are motivated and clearly capable in other fields, never come to control basic notions in linguistics – they are not easily able to "see" relationships in data in the way linguists do. Many of the ideas developed in this section relate particularly to lessening the difficulties these students experience in elementary courses.

In more advanced undergraduate courses and in graduate courses, students have to develop research skills in finding order in large sets of data, in formulating hypotheses in terms of a theory, and in testing those hypotheses. Certain areas of linguistic education involve specialized training. In phonetics, for example, students need ear training and prac-tice in transcription; they need to learn to acquire and interpret acoustic and physiological data. In some fields, students need to learn statistical techniques. As students progress in their education, the difference between their study and the work of an experienced scholar lessens, and the computer shifts from an instructional to a research tool. The use of the computer in research is more fully discussed in other chapters of this book.

We are still at the beginning of using computers as teaching tools. Linguistics, so far, has rather little in the way of such software. Although I have mentioned existing programs where I am aware of them, much of the material that follows is hypothetical in that it discusses the types of programs that might be developed rather than ones which are currently available.

3.3   COMPUTER ASSISTED INSTRUCTION

Computer assisted instruction (CAI) is a term applied to situations in which the student works alone at a computer to study material presented as structured lessons. (For recent general discussion, see Hockey (1992b) and Irizarry (1992); also Bantz *et al.* (1989), Burns *et al.* (1991), and Psotka *et al.* (1985). For discussion specifically aimed at linguistics, see Ansel and Jucker (1992)). The software containing these lessons is known as courseware. Typically, students go to an instructional computer laboratory where computers containing the programs are found; they select the appropriate program and follow the instructions provided. Increasingly, CAI programs are made available through the electronic network.

Courseware may present new material; more often, however, it extends the activity of the lecture or tutorial. CAI is particularly suited for introductory courses and for teaching specific skills.

The simplest format of CAI is an explanation of the point at hand, followed by a question to which the student responds. A correct answer allows the student to proceed to the next lesson. With incorrect answers, the student tries again. The computer might, for example, present a set of Arabic data as in Figure 3.1.

After examining these data, the student can be asked a question such as: "What consonants do all these forms have in common?" The student then enters the answer. If the answer is the correct one – /k t b/, the computer shows a message such as "CORRECT," and the student goes on to the next question. If the student gives an incorrect answer such as /ʔ k t b/, the computer shows a message that the answer is incorrect, possibly providing some help such as "You have too many consonants; not all of these occur in every form." At this point the student tries again.

kataba	'he wrote'	jaktubu	'he writes'
kitba	'writing'	kattaba	'to make write'
kātaba	'correspond'	takātaba	'to keep up a correspondence'
ʔiktataba	'copy'	kitāb	'book'
maktaba	'library'	miktāb	'typewriter'
kātib	'writer'	maktūb	'letter, note'

Figure 3.1   Arabic data for a morphology problem

We can easily image how this lesson might be expanded with further questions: "What meaning do all these forms have in common?" "If /ð k r/ is the root meaning 'remember,' what would be the Arabic for 'he remembered'?"

Essentially, problems of the sort traditionally found in workbooks have been moved to the computer. The difference lies in the ability of the computer to give immediate feedback to the student. Some materials are better suited to CAI than others. In general, questions which have clear-cut, finite answers work well; for example:

What is the underlying form of X?

Which phonemes belong in the class defined by the features shown?

'What you need most is a good rest.' This sentence is a cleft sentence, pseudo-cleft sentence, neither?

The passive of 'Mary bit the snail' is _____.

Familiar pedagogical techniques such as problem solving, matching, filling in the blanks, multiple choice, and true or false can be used. Questions requiring discussion or explanation do not work so well.

Courseware may cover an entire course, or it may deal with only certain aspects. The program LX Problems by Labov (Figure 3.2) presents a wide range of material appropriate to an introductory course. Programs of a larger scope have the advantage of providing a unified approach over a longer period of study. The smaller programs are more easily modified and thus more easily used by other instructors and in other situations. Computer programs are more rigidly structured than books. Where the instructor's own method of teaching follows the same structure as that of the program, there is of course no problem. However, two teachers rarely follow the same syllabus. In my own department, some instructors prefer to introduce phonology before morphology in Introductory Linguistics; others reverse this order. Designing a single computer program that allows this kind of flexibility is difficult.

An alternative approach to the large, all-inclusive program is a modular approach with a series of smaller programs each focusing on a specific area. An example of the smaller program is Phthong (described more fully below) which teaches a specific skill, the phonemic transcription of English.

One particular type of program which should be mentioned here is **hypertext** (specific versions are produced under several names, such as HyperCard, SuperCard) which has been used extensively for courseware (Figures 3.3a and b). The basic conception of hypertext is a stack of cards through which the user navigates. The user sees one card at a time. The card typically presents text along with various buttons; by clicking

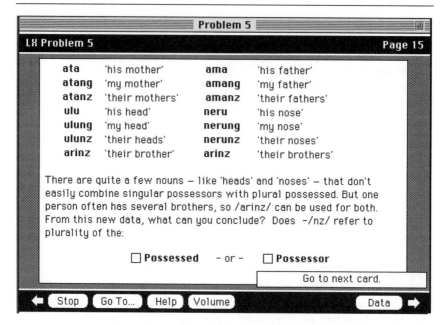

LX Problem 5			Page 15
ata	'his mother'	ama	'his father'
atang	'my mother'	amang	'my father'
atanz	'their mothers'	amanz	'their fathers'
ulu	'his head'	neru	'his nose'
ulung	'my head'	nerung	'my nose'
ulunz	'their heads'	nerunz	'their noses'
arinz	'their brother'	arinz	'their brothers'

There are quite a few nouns — like 'heads' and 'noses' — that don't easily combine singular possessors with plural possessed. But one person often has several brothers, so /arinz/ can be used for both. From this new data, what can you conclude? Does -/nz/ refer to plurality of the:

☐ **Possessed**   - or -   ☐ **Possessor**

Go to next card.

Stop   Go To...   Help   Volume   Data

Figure 3.2   A lesson on inalienable possession from William Labov's *LX Problems*. The student has already divided the words into morphemes. When this card is introduced, the student hears the voice of a native speaker pronouncing the forms. After checking "Possessed" or "Possessor," the student's answer is evaluated. The boxes at the bottom allow the student to perform various actions, such as quit, go elsewhere in the program, get help, change the speaker volume, or go to the next card.

on the appropriate button, the user can go to the next card or return to the previous card. Other buttons can take the user to a related card. For example, if one card mentions "isogloss," the program could be set up so that by clicking on "isogloss," the user is taken to a card explaining isoglosses. Any number of such connections is possible. A different situation might allow the user to see how different theoreticians have analyzed the same point. Cross-references, footnotes, bibliographic references, and explanations can be made available as necessary. A collection of cards is known as a "stack," hence the term "stackware" which refers to a set of material that can be run using a hypertext program.

The advantage of hypertext is that students are encouraged to interrelate information and to examine it from different perspectives rather than just to process ideas in a linear fashion (the ordinary way of reading a book). Ansel and Jucker (1992) discuss specific uses of hypertext; see also the description of Phthong below. Hypertext systems generally allow someone without programming skills to produce simple educational stacks

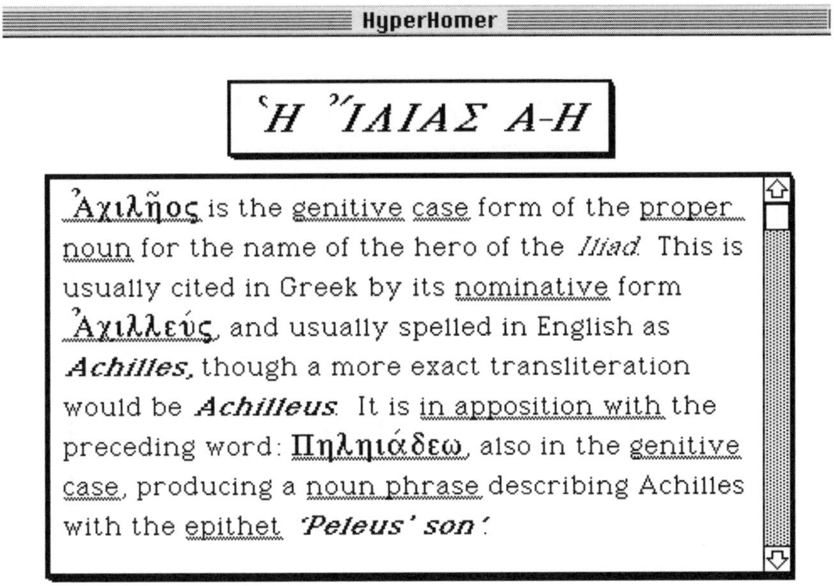

῾Η ᾽ΙΛΙΑΣ Α-Η

᾽Αχιλῆος is the genitive case form of the proper noun for the name of the hero of the *Iliad.* This is usually cited in Greek by its nominative form ᾽Αχιλλεύς, and usually spelled in English as *Achilles,* though a more exact transliteration would be *Achilleus.* It is in apposition with the preceding word: Πηληιάδεω, also in the genitive case, producing a noun phrase describing Achilles with the epithet *'Peleus' son'.*

Figure 3.3a In *A World of Words,* John Lawler presents a hypertext version of a short passage in the Iliad. In this card, we see that the genitive form of "Achilles" occurs. Note that certain words in this card are underlined. If the user clicks on one of these words, another card explaining that term appears. For example, a student who does not understand the meaning of "genitive case" can click on "genitive case" and the card shown in Figure 3.3b will appear.

without a great deal of difficulty. Professional programmers can use an associated programming language for much more sophisticated results.

3.4 THEORY MODELING

In research, computers are often used to model theories: that is, the computer program produces the same results as those which the theory predicts, given the same input. In linguistics, a model might simulate the way government and binding works, or feature geometry. For a specific situation, such as for a particular language, we propose hypotheses framed in terms of our theory. The computer model could then test our hypothesis.

Much research in linguistics involves applying a theory to a set of data. By being able to test hypotheses using a theoretical modeling program, we can formulate better hypotheses and identify points where the theory has difficulty in accounting for data.

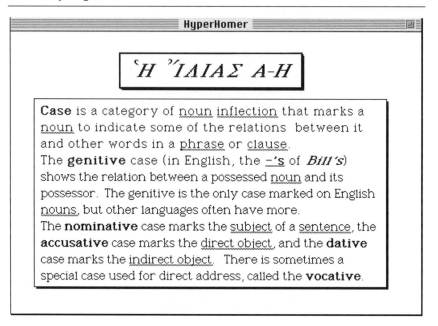

Figure 3.3b This card from *A World of Words* explains "case," including the "genitive case." The bold face print makes it easy to identify the technical terms. If students are uncertain about other terms such as "noun," clicking on "noun" will take them to another card which explains that term. Students can retrace their steps or return to the original card when they wish. Moving through a text in this nonlinear fashion is known in hypertext as "navigating."

In introductory classes, students need to learn about the basic relationship of theory and data. For example, they have to learn how a phrase structure grammar can be used to generate sentences. Computer programs which model theories can be useful in this type of teaching. A possible syntactic program could provide students with practice in a variety of tasks. Students could be given a grammar and some sentences and asked to determine whether the sentences are grammatical or not. In a different problem, students could be given a simple grammar with appropriate lexical items and asked to generate grammatical sentences. A more complex task would be to ask students to modify an existing grammar to account for additional sentences, or to create a grammar to account for certain data.

Many students not specializing in linguistics experience difficulty in learning linguistic theory. Part of this difficulty for some students is clearly the formal nature of theory; for many students, linguistics is their first encounter with this type of thinking. Rather than avoiding theory at the elementary level, Sobin (1991) suggests that we meet this fear of formalism head-on. He describes the use of the programming language Prolog in teaching basic syntactic skills in an elementary course. Sobin argues that by allowing students to construct grammars and to manipulate them, the process "turns an otherwise very abstract subject into a much more concrete one, which makes non-majors much more comfortable dealing with the subject matter. Prolog materials are frequently aimed at audiences with background in logic, linguistics, or computer science. However, I have found that it is quite possible to use the Prolog generative rule facility successfully with an audience untrained in any of these."

Another area where modeling could be of use in teaching is phonology. Here, for example, feature trees could be introduced. Students could practice construction of these trees to match segments against feature trees. They could be given a phonemic inventory of a language and asked to construct appropriate trees for the segments.

From such exercises in modeling, students become familiar with a theory; they learn its internal rules, how it accounts for data, the difference between grammatical and ungrammatical data, how rules and constraints are used to account for data and to exclude non-occurring possibilities.

At a more advanced level, computer simulations of models could be used to test descriptions of languages. A model could be used to point out any rules in the description which are inconsistent with the theory or with each other.

A practical difficulty is that computer models of theories require considerable programming effort and theories change rapidly, possibly rendering a model useless. Further, the computer requires specificity whereas the theorist may prefer to leave various points vague. The field of computational linguistics has done quite sophisticated work in this area, particularly with English syntax and morphology. See the chapters in this book on natural language processing (Chapters 7 and 8), and also Ide (1991), Dresher and Kaye (1990); and GTU, SysPro, YOUPIE in the appendix.

3.5   COMPUTERS IN SPECIFIC AREAS OF LINGUISTICS

Butler (1985), Ide (1991), and Roach (1992) are general sources of information on the use of the computer in linguistics.

3.5.1   Core areas of linguistics

3.5.1.1   Phonetics

Computers have enormously changed our ability to do phonetic work, and they have great potential to improve the way we teach phonetics (Knowles, 1986).

To be used by a computer, sounds must be digitized. This is easily accomplished with a tape recorder (or microphone) and a digitizer. Computers are now available with a digitizer built-in; traditionally, however, the digitizer has been separate: either a card placed inside the computer, or a separate device attached between the tape recorder and the computer. One difficulty is that digitized sounds take up a great deal of memory, requiring a large hard disk or other storage device.

Ear training and transcription are areas in which the computer can help the instructor. The Phonetic Symbol Guide – Electronic Edition by Allen, Pullum, and Ladusaw allows the user to hear the sounds of the International Phonetic Alphabet. The Electronic Edition is a talking accompaniment to the *Phonetic Symbol Guide* (Pullum and Ladusaw, 1996). Similarly, the sounds accompanying Ladefoged's *A Course in Phonetics* (1992) are available in a digitized form. Jonesphones allows the user to hear Daniel Jones pronounce the cardinal vowels, as well as providing a limited drill in identifying the cardinal vowels. Courseware for ear training can be further useful in that students can work on their weak spots, those with poor preparation can upgrade their skills, and anyone planning field research could brush up on the sounds likely to be encountered.

Phonemic transcription can be taught using a computer (see discussion of Phthong below). Essentially items are presented to the student who enters a transcription, and the transcription is evaluated by the computer for accuracy. The phonetic symbols are entered by clicking on an area of the screen where the symbols are shown. The open-ended nature of narrow transcription presents a problem for the computer. If the number of possibilities is limited, however, then the same type of format used for phonemic transcription can be used to teach narrow transcription. Access to the larger number of symbols required for this type of transcription can be provided by a palette of symbols lurking in the background of the screen.

Most students find practical work with vowels particularly difficult, needing a great deal of practice to be able to perceive, produce, and place them on a vowel chart accurately. Courseware could be used to teach them, starting with a limited number of vowels and gradually increasing the number that the student must discriminate. A related type of exercise would require students to put a dot on a cardinal vowel chart corresponding to the vowel they hear, with the computer evaluating the answer. A more complex program would make an acoustic analysis of the students' vowels and chart the formants.

The Sounds of the World's Languages (see Figure 3.4) provides examples of a large number of contrasts found in languages around the world. For example, one can hear preaspirated consonants in Icelandic or clicks in Nama. This program is a valuable source of material useful for

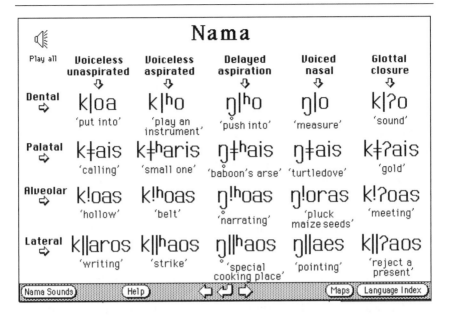

Figure 3.4 Words containing clicks in Nama from *Sounds of the World's Languages.* Individual words are played by clicking on the word. Columns or rows can be played by clicking on the titles at the top or at the left. The loudspeaker plays all words. "Nama Sounds" provides further information. "Maps" and "Language Index" takes the user to cards with further information; there is also an index of sound types. The sound files can be opened by other programs, such as an acoustic analysis program for making spectrograms. This large database showing contrastive sounds makes an excellent source for laboratory projects in acoustic phonetics.

classroom presentations and for student research projects. These sounds can be analyzed acoustically.

Computers offer excellent opportunities for teaching the anatomy needed in phonetics. Interesting exercises could be devised where the student has to assemble a larynx on the screen by dragging the cartilages into their correct positions. Three-dimensional models could be made which would allow the student to rotate a model of the larynx and view it from different angles. Some of the work that our medical colleagues are doing might well be useful to us in this area.

The UCLA phonetics laboratory has developed a program which models the vowel sounds that would be made with a vocal tract of a particular shape. A similar program might model the sounds produced by varying the position and tension of the vocal folds.

Waveforms and spectrograms can easily be used for classroom demonstrations and discussions (Signalyze). Laboratory exercises using prepared materials can be used for more advanced assignments. UCLA's *Sounds of the World's Languages* provides excellent material for student projects in acoustic phonetics. In future years, we should see much more in the way of databases of digitized sounds which can be used for teaching purposes. The acoustic program by Randolph Valentine (Figure 3.5) allows the user to measure and compare the fundamental frequency of speech from a child and from an adult.

One example of this is the Oxford Acoustic Phonetic Database which has appeared as a CD-ROM. The disk contains spoken words from several languages or dialects: English (US, RP), French, German, Hungarian, Italian, Japanese, and Spanish. The **corpus** was constructed to illustrate the consonants and monophthongal vowels of each language. This sort of material seems ideal for individual projects in acoustic phonetics. Students could be assigned topics such as "Geminate length in Italian," "A comparison of glides in XYZ," "Moraic duration in Japanese," "Taps and trills in Spanish."

We can easily foresee the appearance of similar collections of data in other areas of linguistics. Databases can be of various forms in linguistics (Knowles, 1990). They can be corpora of raw materials, or structured in some fashion; they can be in ordinary orthography or in a phonemic

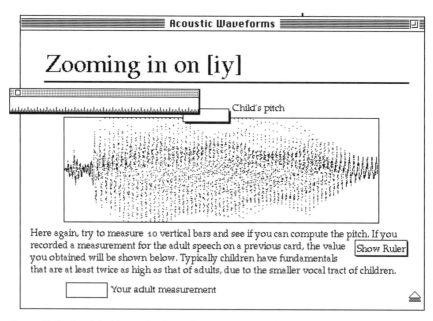

Figure 3.5 In this HyperCard stack on acoustics from Valentine's *Introduction to Linguistics*, students use the ruler to measure fundamental frequency of a sound. A subsequent card allows the student to compare the measurements made for the fundamental frequency used by the two speakers.

transcription. They can be digitized sound for phonetic research, as in the Oxford collection, and they can be coded to identify morphological and syntactic units.

The computer provides not only the access to the data, but also the tools for the analysis. CD-ROMs (very similar to compact disks for music) are particularly suitable for this as they are capable of storing large amounts of data and they can be produced quite inexpensively.

3.5.1.2 Phonology

Phonemic transcription needs a great deal of drill, and thus it is an area especially well suited to CAI. Programs for this are CAPTEX, Phonetics, Phonetics Tutor, and Phthong (discussed in some detail below).

Elementary phonology problems could easily be used on a computer. Structured lessons could be effectively used to supplement the lecture and tutorial material to give students a large number of problems exhibiting a variety of phenomena. Structured lessons could also drill students in recognizing typical phonological processes such as palatalization. Valentine's *Introduction to Linguistics* (Figure 3.6) teaches phonological feature specification.

One difficulty in learning phonology is to learn to distinguish probable solutions from far-fetched ones. We have all had students who are frustrated because their answer was marked wrong although it "worked": e.g., "voicing of the initial consonant is determined by the height of the second vowel in the following word." Multiple choice questions could address this problem directly by asking students to choose the best answer among various ones that technically "work."

At a more advanced level, computers are a useful way to present students with more complex sets of data. Even basic tools such as a spreadsheet could be used to reorder the data in various ways or to search for all occurrences of an item.

Phonological theories can be implemented as a computer program. Dresher and Kaye (1990) developed a program YOUPIE to model the cognitive ability a child uses to learn the stress system of a language.

The UPSID database of phoneme inventories which Maddieson has constructed provides an excellent source for projects in phonological universals.

3.5.1.3 Morphology

At the elementary level, students can use appropriate courseware to learn basic notions by practicing basic tasks such as dividing a word into morphemes, listing other allomorphs, identifying cranberry and portmanteau morphs (See the example from LX Problems in Figure 3.2). A

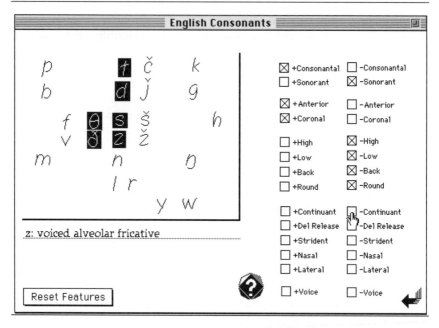

Figure 3.6 From a HyperCard stack: English Consonants from Valentine's *Introduction to Linguistics*. Here the student is asked to describe the set of features for /z/. At the beginning of the exercise, all the sounds in the panel at the upper left are highlighted. As the student selects plus or minus values for each of the features, highlighting is removed from those sounds which no longer fit the features selected. At the moment of the picture, the student is about to select a wrong answer [–continuant] (note the position of the hand) which will remove the highlighting from all the sounds indicating that the student has made a wrong choice.

more demanding program could ask the student to show the constituent structure of a word, labelling each portion.

Klavans and Chodorow (1991) used an instructional morphological parser to teach morphological theory at the graduate level allowing students to test analyzes that morphological theory predicts. See also PC-Kimmo (Figure 3.7).

3.5.1.4 *Syntax*

Instructors in elementary linguistics courses are reporting that many students arrive at university nowadays unfamiliar with simple grammatical notions such as subject, preposition, and prefix – never mind gerund, relative clause, or subjunctive. Exercises can be developed to bring students up to speed who have deficiencies is this area. The individual

```
PC-KIMMO TWO-LEVEL PROCESSOR
Version 1.0.5 (26 February 1991), Copyright 1991 SIL
Type ? for help
PC-KIMMO>take demo
PC-KIMMO>cd :English
PC-KIMMO>load rules english
Rules being loaded from english.rul
PC-KIMMO>load lexicon english
Lexicon being loaded from english.lex
PC-KIMMO>generate `fox+s
   foxes

PC-KIMMO>recognize foxes
   `fox+s        [ N(fox)+PL ]

PC-KIMMO>generate `spy+s
   spies

PC-KIMMO>recognize spies
   `spy+s        [ N(spy)+PL ]
   `spy+s        [ V(spy)+3sg.PRES ]

PC-KIMMO>quit
|
```

Figure 3.7 A short demonstration from *PC-KIMMO* which relates lexical representations with their surface forms. Here we see two examples: *foxes* and *spies*.

use of the computer allows students to work on those areas which are a problem for them without requiring the time of the entire class.

Certain notions in syntax are quite challenging for some students: e.g. the relationship of an underlying string to a surface string. At Toronto, Arbourite is being developed to provide students with help in mastering this concept. Arbourite will, as well, have a tree-drawing facility. Students will be required to draw an accurate tree for a particular sentence. Ultimately, we would like to have a program that could parse strings for us; to avoid dealing with the complexity of a parser immediately, however, we are going to use exercises with prepared answers, stored in the computer as labeled bracketed strings which the computer will convert to trees. Several people in our department teach introductory linguistics at various times. No two of these use exactly the same theory; therefore, we want to make our program adaptable to all of them, and to even greater variation at other universities. Different instructors will be able to modify the analysis used by other instructors to suit their own needs.

For advanced work in syntax, there is a great deal of work in natural language processing (see Chapters 7 and 8 in this book); see also Bakker *et al.* (1988). LFG-PC, ProfGlot, Stuf, SYNTACTICA, and PC-PATR.

3.5.1.5 Semantics

Some students find semantics difficult, particularly in making fine distinctions of meaning. Computers offer a good opportunity for extensive practice in this area. Probably some ideas could be borrowed from programs used for teaching logic such as Tarski's World.

Advanced students in semantics will find much of the work in natural language processing of use (see Chapter 7); see also FrameBuilder, Semantic Tutorial, and SEMANTICA.

3.5.2 Other linguistic courses

3.5.2.1 Structure and history of English

Many universities offer courses titled something like "The structure and history of English," where English could be any language. Here the opportunities for computers are not in set exercises, although they could be used, but in the wealth of material that could be made available to students. For structure, sizeable corpora of various sorts could be used; any of the topics mentioned above – phonology, morphology, syntax, etc. – could be available. For history, a wealth of interesting material could be made available, such as digitized reconstructions of historic pronunciations, maps, dialect information, pictures of manuscripts, etc.

3.5.2.2 Languages of the world

Here the need is for a breadth of material covering linguistic, anthropological, and sociolinguistic data. Multimedia presentations of text, sound, and video could give students a concentrated look at important and interesting aspects of a language and its culture; maps (Figure 3.8), samples of texts, speech, and writing could be used. These presentations could be used both for individual work and classroom presentation. The large storage capacity of CD-ROMs could provide a large variety of materials from which instructors could select the ones most useful to their purposes. A basic source of information about most of the world's languages is the Ethnologue.

3.5.2.3 Dialectology and historical linguistics

Courses in these areas share a good deal: they often present data in a geographical and temporal dimension. The geographic dimension can

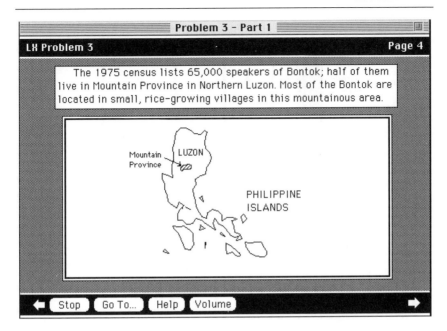

Figure 3.8 This example from *LX Problems*, showing where Bontok is spoken, is an example of the kind of information that could be provided in a course on Languages of the World. The map is accompanied by a short recording in Bontok.

easily be shown by maps; computers, however, can add the temporal dimensions showing changes over time (*World of Words*, Figure 3.9). These features can be accompanied by sound illustrating these and other dimensions of dialect such as social class, age, sex, etc. Theoretical models could be used to test hypotheses of language change. Programs available now can convert data to charts and maps, providing excellent ways of illustrating dialectal information. Computers also can ease the introduction of statistical methods. See also Smith (1987) and IVARB/ MacVARB.

3.5.2.4 *Sociolinguistics*

In sociolinguistics, multimedia presentations could show language in action in different social situations. Kinship studies (Findler, 1992) might especially find computers useful. Classroom presentations could be quite effective in demonstrating different kinship systems. Theories of kinship could be simulated and tested. Projects on color terminology could be set up with a computer, replacing the need for color chips.

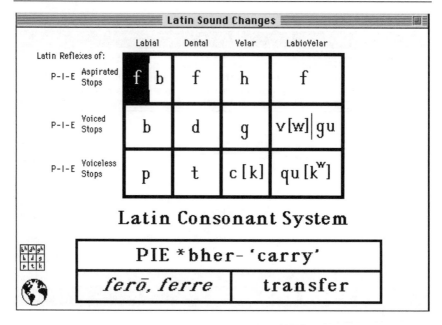

Figure 3.9 One part of *A World of Words* shows the relationship of Indo-European and Latin consonants. Here the user has selected Latin /f/. The program shows a reconstructed root in Indo-European, as well as a Latin example, together with an English word containing the Latin form.

3.5.2.5   Psycholinguistics

Student projects in psycholinguistics often involve experiments in areas such as the response time in various situations. The questions can be posed on the computer screen and the response time can be calculated by having the computer determine and record how long the subject takes to press a key. Graphic programs offer easy ways of turning numerical data into more readily understood charts. Many psycholinguistic experiments require the use of statistical programs. See EDW in the appendix.

3.5.2.6   Writing systems

The ease with which different fonts for alphabets and scripts can be used on a computer is an asset in teaching writing systems both in presentations and in structured lessons. Exercises could be used for learning about a writing system as students often do in a general course, or they could be used for more intensive practice aimed at mastering a particular writing system. A large number of computer fonts are available through the

```
senatus popvlvsqve romanvs
imp caesari divi nervae f nervae
traiano avg germ dacico pontif
maximo trib pot xvii imp vi cos vi p p
addeclarandvm qvantae altitvdinis
mons et locvs tantis operibvs sit egestvs
senatus popvlvsqve romanvs
imp caesari divi nervae f nervae
traiano avg germ dacico pontif
maximo trib pot xvii imp vi cos vi p p
addeclarandvm qvantae altitvdinis
mons et locvs tantis operibvs sit egestvs
```

SⲤⲚⲢTVꟅ ⲚOⲢVⳐVꟅⲨⲦV((ⲨⲞⲘⲢⲚVꟅ
Ⅰ(((Ⲣ ⟨Ⲣ((ꟅⲢⲨⳐ Ⲏ|Ⅵ Ⲛ((ⲨⲨⲢ((⅄‹ Ⲛ((ⲨⲨⲢ((
TⳐⲢ|ⲢⲚO ⲢVⳐ Ⅼ(((ⲨⲘ δⲢ‹|‹O ⲚOⲚTⅠ⅄‹
(((ⲢⲬⅠ(((O TⲨ|δ ⲚOT ⅩⅥⅠ Ⅰ(((Ⲣ Ⅵ ‹OꟅ Ⅵ Ⲣ Ⲣ
Ⲣδδ((‹ⳐⲢⳐⲢⲚδⲨ(((ⲨⲨⲢⲚTⲢ((ⲢⳐTⅠTVδⅠⲨ|Ʂ
(((OⲚꟅ ((T ⳐO‹VꟅ TⲢⲚTⅠꟅ OⲚ((ⲨⅠδⲨꟅ ꟅⅠT ((Ⅼ((ꟅTVꟅ

Figure 3.10   Trajan's Inscription from the Roman Forum. The upper form uses a typeface closely resembling the original inscription; the lower form shows how it might have looked in Roman handwriting of the time.

Internet from computer archives. Figure 3.10 illustrates how two fonts can be used to demonstrate different ways of writing Latin in ancient times.

3.5.2.7   *Speech pathology*

Many of the techniques of phonetics are easily adaptable to teaching speech pathology simply by varying the content somewhat. In phonetics, for example, sounds of disordered speech, such as denti-labial stops or cleft palate speech, could be added to those of the normal speaker. Programs could be organized so as to give students practice in particular interview schedules, guiding them in entering, sorting, and interpreting data from interviews (PEPPER). Exercises aimed at learning to recognize disorders could be devised; for example, sound recordings could be available along with acoustic and physiological data. Computer simulations could be used to introduce students to various laboratory instruments.

2.5.2.8 Lexicography

Lexicography is rather seldom taught as a course on its own, but problems could well be presented using a computer with collections of relevant citations. Many dictionaries are now available in electronic form and could be used for student projects. See Conc, FrameBuilder, and MacLex in the appendix to this chapter.

3.6 DEVELOPING TEACHING SOFTWARE

I have been involved in developing two projects: Phthong and Arbourite. My remarks in this section are clearly personal, stemming from my own experience in these two programs. I use Phthong as an example, not as any sort of ideal, but because I know the history of its development best.

3.6.1 Design

Developing linguistic software requires two types of expertise: linguistic and programming. These may be found in the same person or in two. Many programs have been developed by linguists cum amateur programmers. The efficiency and sophistication, however, that a professional programmer can bring to a project should not be underestimated. Phthong was developed by a linguist and a programmer.

At the outset, the scope of the project needs to be considered. In developing Phthong, we wanted a rather small, self-contained program to teach the phonemic transcription of English. It is also important not to reinvent the wheel; so we checked available sources as much as possible to make sure that no one had developed or was developing a similar program. Other programs existed but were different in some way from what we hoped to achieve.

We also knew that we wanted two kinds of flexibility. First, instructors have rather strong preferences as to the symbol inventory and transcription systems that they use. Since we wanted the program to be used at other universities, we saw the need for a flexibility that would allow instructors to choose various transcription systems. Second, we wanted to be able to change the examples; this ability would also allow instructors to modify the answers to suit their own preferences or dialect areas. Ultimately, we achieved this flexibility by having a separate set-up module which allows the instructor to choose the transcription system and to modify the entries.

The linguist was responsible for the basic design and the linguistic content and accuracy. For Phthong, we decided to use a simple linear design in which the sounds would be presented one by one. The effect is like being shown a series of cards with questions on each. For each sound we have a short introduction showing the use of the sound, then a set of about five or six cards is presented in sequence with each card giving a word illustrating the sound in phonemic transcription and asking the student to supply the ordinary English orthography. Then, the process is reversed: the student is presented with a similar number of cards giving the English orthography and asked to provide the phonemic transcription; then, on to the next sound.

The programmer was responsible for preparing the program, a set of instructions in a computer language which directs the computer to perform the desired task. It is not always easy to remember or to figure out what the computer code is trying to accomplish at each point in the program. For this reason, it is important that the programmer document the code fully, by inserting explanatory notes.

At the outset, basic programming decisions have to be made. For Phthong, we chose the Macintosh computer because that was the ordinary machine used in our department and the university had a Macintosh teaching site in place, and we chose to use HyperCard (see the general discussion on hypertext above), which is not a language in the usual sense, but a program itself which allows programs, called stacks (sets of interactive cards), to be constructed. We knew that HyperCard stacks had been quite successful in other educational programs. The basic conception of HyperCard as a stack of cards through which the user navigates fit our own design well.

To start the actual development on its way, we made an initial mock-up of what each type of card should look like, and we picked a couple of examples for each type of card. The programmer then was able to make a small prototype of Phthong.

Fairly early on, the design of the interface (Schneiderman, 1987) was a joint concern for the linguist and the programmer. Two considerations were important: function and appearance. Ideally one wants the operation of the program to be immediately apparent and natural to the student. Small items are extremely important: size and placement of each item on the screen, the number of items on the screen at once, and the method of signaling correct or incorrect answers to the student.

Figure 3.11 illustrates a phonemics-to-English card in Phthong. Here, students are given the phonemic transcription and asked to produce the ordinary English spelling – *seat*. The right and left arrows are buttons, which, when clicked on, take the student to the next or to the preceding card. LISTEN plays the sound of the word. TEST lets students test their answer. ANSWER shows the correct answer for as long as the mouse button is depressed. The HELP button in the upper left corner gives assistance with this type of card. The TOC button in the upper right corner takes students to the Table of Contents, a point from which they can go to other lessons or exit the program.

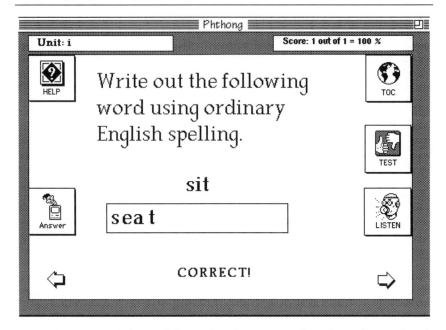

Figure 3.11   A card from *Phthong* showing an exercise where the student is given the phonemic transcription and asked to produce the ordinary English orthography. Here the student is testing the answer by pressing on the "TEST" button, and receives a message "CORRECT."

Figure 3.12 shows the other type of card where students are given *teak* and asked to enter the phonemic transcription – /tik/. Each of the phonetic symbols at the top of the card is a button. When the student clicks on a symbol, that symbol is entered in the answer box.

If the student's answer is correct, the word "CORRECT" appears at the bottom of the card. For incorrect answers, a hand appears below the answer with a finger pointing to the leftmost error with a short message such as "you have too many symbols," "you don't have enough symbols," or "you have the wrong symbol here." We had hoped to have more detailed messages such as "you have forgotten that mid tense vowels in English are diphthongs," but incorporating such messages proved quite difficult.

When students are completely stymied, they can click on ANSWER, and the answer will appear for as long as the mouse button is depressed. We felt that providing this device would help prevent students from giving up in complete frustration.

Programs inevitably have problems. Once a basic model is running, it is important to test it as much as possible. Programs need to be tested on different machines and with different users. With Phthong, the early

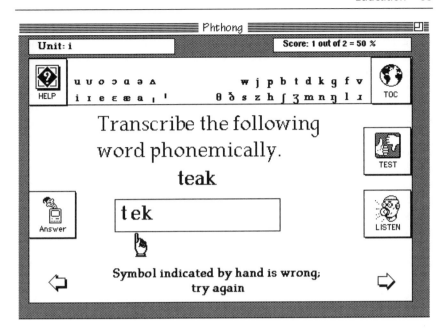

Figure 3.12 A card from *Phthong* showing an exercise where the student is given the ordinary English orthography and asked to produce the phonemic transcription. Note the buttons at the top allowing phonemic symbols to be entered. Here the student has entered a wrong answer, and Phthong has provided some help in identifying the error.

testing was done by the linguist, with the program shuttled back and forth between the linguist and the programmer for revisions. We tried to use only one version at a time so as to avoid any confusion.

Once we had a working model, Phthong was tested with three volunteers. Using inexperienced people is important in finding out whether the interface works properly. Fortunately, the university computer services staff were willing to run these tests. We also felt that it would be useful for the developers not to be present for the testing. Various suggestions for improvement emerged. For example, we realized that we needed some basic instructions on using the computer when one student was observed waving the mouse in mid-air at the screen as if to say "Beam me up, Scotty."

Further testing involved trying it out as a part of regular courses. The next step was to send it to instructors at different universities; this phase is known as beta-testing.

For the full scale model, we needed a full list of words to be used. The linguist was responsible for providing these with the appropriate transcriptions in order that each example included only sounds already introduced. When the longer list of words was introduced, we found that using HyperCard directly was unpleasantly slow in moving to the next item. The programmer was able to solve this problem by storing the data in text *file*s which HyperCard could use more efficiently. A structural change such as this required a major programming change.

An important part of any program is the documentation for the user, the printed materials that accompany the software disks. In commercial enterprises, the writing of documentation is a specialty of its own, experience having shown that developers are not always the best people to explain a program to new users. Linguistic programs are unlikely to have that kind of luxury, and documentation will probably be prepared by the developer. Fortunately, our basic trade skill is explaining complexities.

As the program matures, developers think about improvements which make the program more interesting – bells and whistles. In Phthong, we have done little yet in this direction, but some possibilities include an animated vocal tract showing the production of each new sound as it is introduced, accompanied by a playing of the sound itself. We could use a more imaginative "CORRECT" message: perhaps a random choice of flares of rockets, polite golf applause, trumpet fanfares, or a genteel "Good show!" These adornments are clearly optional, but they use the computer to merge work and play, an old-fashioned teaching technique.

After Phthong had been used for some time, the electronic network increased significantly in importance. The university wanted to shift teaching programs to the Web and to restrict computer laboratories to Internet use only. We are currently developing a Web version of Phthong which students can access from a computer, either in the lab or by modem from home. The advantage is that anyone can use any platform and no longer has to go to a specified laboratory during certain hours.

At some point, ownership and copyright of the program have to be dealt with. Universities typically have policies which regulate such matters, at least in part. Clarifying such issues at an early point will help prevent unpleasantries from emerging later.

Distributing software successfully is difficult. Software can be distributed commercially, whereby unlicensed copies are illegal. Unfortunately, the distributional infrastructure for educational software is not as well developed as it is for books. Software can be distributed free, with unlimited copying allowed. A third method is called shareware, in which anyone can make a copy to try out the program; users are expected to remit a fee (usually small) to the developer if they keep the program, otherwise to destroy it. Sometimes, programs start out as freeware or shareware and become commercial after their value and reliability are proven.

Linguists developing teaching software will obviously use it in their own classes if the institution has appropriate facilities. Like-minded colleagues in other universities are often interested in trying out a program. Many of our colleagues use computers mainly for wordprocessing and have little special interest in trying new methods of teaching. In helping such linguists to see the possibilities of teaching with computers, it is important to be clear about meeting their needs. A program has to help them do their job better, otherwise it is just a toy.

Arbourite is a program for drawing syntactic trees and teaching the relationship of underlying and surface structure. My colleagues in syntax were clear that this was an area of difficulty for beginning students. Although I do not teach syntax, I felt that this was an appropriate area for a CAI program. We formed a steering committee for general supervision, and we have gone through course outlines and homework assignments to see what teaching strategies used in traditional teaching might be implemented on a computer. We have tried to make Arbourite a departmental project to ensure that it meets the needs of those who will use it.

3.6.2   Problems

3.6.2.1 *"There is a really neat program for doing just what you want that will be out real soon now."*

The computing world has developed a bound morpheme *-ware* as in *software, hardware, shareware*. An unfortunately common species is *vaporware*, software which lives in the heart and soul of the developer, but not on the machine quite yet. In developing software, there is many a slip twixt conception and fruition.

An instructor wanting to use CAI is likely to have trouble finding a suitable program. Little is available. Linguistics is a small discipline. Few people have the combination of knowledge, time, and incentive to develop materials for such a small audience. At present, there is no well-developed distribution scheme for getting what does exist to the instructor. Book publishers, on the whole, have not been enthusiastic about publishing software, and traditional software publishers have not been terribly keen on the academic market. Occasionally, a potentially useful program is available on a platform (e.g., IBM v. Macintosh) which is unsupported at the local institution.

The appendix lists programs which might be of use in teaching. Some of these are quite general in their purpose, and their use is obvious. Others emerged from quite specific needs; adapting them to someone else's course might be quite difficult. A program might, for example, be an excellent tool for teaching morphology using an item-and-arrangement approach with Greek examples, but of little use to someone using a different theoretical framework or who was teaching the structure of English.

3.6.2.2   *"This program is fantastic, and I just don't understand why it isn't working right this afternoon."*

Medieval scribes had a patron demon Titivillus who caused them to make errors in their writing. With the increasing cutbacks in manuscript production, Titivillus has shifted his operations recently to the equally fertile field of computer programming. Bugs can and do happen in every aspect of program development. Trained programmers are an asset here: first, they have experience in locating problems and fixing them, and second, they have a reassuring professional perspective that views bugs as an ordinary part of programming life.

Robustness describes a program's ability to operate well in different environments. Large software developers have the resources to test their products in a wide variety of settings (and even then they cannot completely eradicate Titivillus' work); linguistic programs are usually developed under much more constrained circumstances with inevitable problems as they are moved to different machines and to different sites. Realistically, users of linguistic teaching software have to be prepared to deal with a lower level of robustness and reliability than they would tolerate in commercial, general-purpose products.

Even when a program is available and works properly, its usefulness can be undermined by its design. We can imagine a wonderful syntax program capable of analyzing complex sentences. It is less easy to imagine two syntax instructors using exactly the same theory. This is a particularly difficult problem at the elementary level. An instructor may feel that an AUX node is a troublesome nuisance for beginners, but our wonderful syntax program may stick them in faithfully. Students at more advanced levels can deal with this kind of diversity; beginners have more trouble. In doing exercises in a traditional manner, the instructor can tell students just to omit the AUX. The computer program, however, tells students they are "wrong" every time they omit the AUX. Teaching programs need to allow flexibility for instructors to modify them to suit their own needs and teaching styles.

3.6.2.3   *"Our present budget projections do not envision further expenditures on what many of my decanal colleagues frankly consider frills."*

Computing costs money. Administrators have to carefully dispense the little money they have. Given the experimental nature of computers in teaching, finding money for computer sites may be an uphill struggle. Sites also require security and maintenance, items with costs attached. The software itself is usually a more manageable expense.

Some of our older colleagues immediately think of steel pen-nibs at the mention of "high-tech"; they tend not to be well disposed to spending money on "frills" such as computers. Others see computers as limited to the "hard" sciences, with strong doubts about their usefulness in linguistics.

Any academic contemplating software development should be aware that it can be very time-consuming. Further, administrators tend to view such work with little enthusiasm in making decisions about tenure, promotion, and merit increases.

Ideally, to develop teaching programs, we need projects combining linguistic and programming expertise; unfortunately, educational development grants for producing instructional software are rare.

3.7 PROSPECTS

A colleague has often told the story that manufacturers thoughtfully equipped the earliest automobiles with buggy-whip holders because of their proven use on vehicles to that date. Our normal pattern is to use new technology very conservatively to make old methods better and easier. Gutenberg tried to make his bible look like a manuscript, and laser printers still come with fonts to look like a typewriter.

Predictions about how computers will change our lives are unreliable. We are still waiting for the paperless office. Predicting how computers will affect teaching is no easier. The presentation of information will remain as much of a skilled craft – or art form, if you prefer – as it is today with books. Textbooks will likely continue as a major component for instruction. They offer a convenience and ease of reading that is hard to replace.

For providing access to data, computers will likely prove superior to printed alternatives. The ease with which data can be manipulated, analyzed, and presented in various formats is very persuasive. In many cases we are likely to see linguistic workbooks replaced with computer programs. Larger problem collections will become available.

Teaching aids, which have been rare in linguistics, are likely to become much more common allowing instructors to make livelier and more sophisticated presentation of certain material in their lectures.

Software can help teaching in three areas: providing interesting exercises where basic skills must be learned, allowing data to be manipulated in various ways to reveal the underlying structure; testing hypotheses with various models.

Given the opportunity of studying philosophy with Aristotle or with a computer, most students would choose Aristotle. Nevertheless, computers do offer many opportunities in teaching; most of those opportunities are still not clear to us.

Appendix

PART I   SOFTWARE

See the online appendices (http://www.lsa.umich.edu/ling/jlawler/routledge) for price and current status information.

Acoustic phonetics

Explains the basic concepts of acoustic phonetics. There are demonstrations of the movements of the air particles in a sound wave, and interactive displays allowing the user to superimpose two waves and see and hear the result. Later sections allow the manipulation of damped wave trains similar to formants and show the user how the air in the vocal tract vibrates. Basic notions of formant speech synthesis are demonstrated, using recordings showing the building up of a synthesized sentence, one parameter at a time. Fourier analysis is explained graphically. HyperCard.

Systems supported: Macintosh

Developer/Distributor: Phonetics Laboratory, Dept. of Linguistics, UCLA, 405 Highland Ave., Los Angeles, CA, 90024–1543, USA.

Barlow HyperCard STACKS

Simple interactive exercises for introductory course: Indo-European roots, exploring the relationship of PIE, Latin, Greek, and English; Grimm's Law; three morphology problems, comparative reconstruction of Polynesian; American English phonemic transcription; recognition of vowel of American and British English.

Systems supported: Macintosh

Developer/Distributor: Michael Barlow, Dept of Linguistics, Rice University, Houston, TX, 77005, USA.

barlow@ruf.rice.edu

http://www.ruf.rice.edu/~barlow/#soft/

Calling

HyperCard stack for introductory linguistics.
Systems supported: Macintosh
Developer/Distributor: Marmo Soemarmo, Ohio University.
soemarmo@oak.cats.ohiou.edu

CAPTEX

Teaches phonemic transcription by setting, correcting, and scoring exercises. It also gives help and error feedback and logs student activity. Teachers may use the program to create new phonetic symbols and exercises, and to treat different accents of English or other languages.
Systems supported: MS–DOS
Developer/Distributor: Oxford University Phonetics Laboratory, 41 Wellington Square, Oxford, OX1 2JF, UK.

CG laboratory [categorial grammar]
DCG laboratory [definite clause grammar]
PATR laboratory
PSG laboratory [phrase structure grammar]

A group of programs for writing grammars in a form which can be manipulated by students to explore formal grammars. It helps the student understand the relationship between strings, rules, and trees, and to grasp parsing, generation, ambiguity, and recursion.
Systems supported: Macintosh
Developer/Distributor: Linguistic Instruments, Department of Linguistics, University of Göteborg, S-412 98 Göteborg, Sweden.
li@ling.gu.se

Conc

A concordance program for the Macintosh specially designed for linguistic analysis. Conc produces keyword-in-context concordances of texts. The sorting order is defined by the user. The user can restrict which words will be included in or excluded from a concordance on the basis of frequency, length of word, inclusion in a list, or pattern matching. Conc can concord both flat text files and multiple-*line* inter-linear texts produced by the IT program. Can also produce letter (*character*) concordances to facilitate phonological analysis.
Systems supported: Macintosh
Developer/Distributor: John V. Thomson. International Academic Bookstore, 7500 W. Camp Wisdom Road, Dallas, TX, USA.
academic.books@sil.org

http://www.sil.org/computing/conc/conc.html
Review: Bauer, Christian. 1992. "Review of Conc," Literary and
Linguistic Computing 7(2):154–156.

Ear tour

Illustrates anatomy of the ear. HyperCard.
Systems supported: Macintosh
Developer/Distributor: David B. Williams. Office of Research in
Technology, Illinois State University, Normal, IL, 61761, USA.

EDW

A speech display and editing program for preparing stimuli in speech
perception experiments and as an aid in the acoustic analysis of digitized utterances. A spectrogram based on the waveform can be
displayed along with the waveform itself. EDW has no built-in capability to digitize speech and relies on other programs to create the
waveform files it is used to edit. Several auxiliary programs are included
for basic acoustic analysis and measurement and for manipulating
X-Ray Microbeam data.
Systems supported: MS-DOS; Sun
Developer/Distributor: H. Timothy Bunell, Applied Science and
Engineering Labs., Alfred I. duPont Institute, 1600 Rockland Rd.,
Wilmington, DE, 19899, USA.
bunnell@asel.udel.edu
ftp://asel.udel.edu/pub/spl

Ethnologue

An online database of basic information about most languages in the
world. It can be searched by language name, country or linguistic affil-
iation.
http://www.sil.org/ethnologue/ethnologue.html

FrameBuilder

Allows creation of lexical database with semantic definitions. As an
aid to lexical database acquisition, FrameBuilder makes possible the
efficient creation of theoretically sound and internally consistent
lexical/semantic definition to a lexical database by a linguistically inexperienced student. HyperCard.
Systems supported: Macintosh
Developer/Distributor: Donalee H. Attardo, Purdue University, West
Lafayette, IN, 47907, USA.

GOLDVARB See IVARB

Grammar and trees

A HyperCard stack containing a context free phrase structure parser and a tree drawing routine for students to explore context free phrase structure grammars, and particularly to see the relationship between rules and trees. Some sample exercises are included.
Systems supported: Macintosh
Developer/Distributor: Christopher Culy, Linguistics Department, The University of Iowa, Iowa City, IA, 52242, USA.
chris-culy@uiowa.edu

GTU [Grammatik-Text-Umgebung]

Tutorial software in computational linguistics. The program takes a given sentence, parses it, and displays its PS-tree.
Systems supported: MS-DOS
Developer/Distributor: Martin Volk, Institute of Computational Linguistics, Universität Koblenz-Landau, Rheinau 3–4, 5400 Koblenz, Germany.
martin.volk@informatik.uni-koblenz.de

Introduction to Linguistics

Several stacks for use in an introductory class in linguistics, including phonetic transcription, phonological features, and acoustics. Hyper-Card.
Systems supported: Macintosh
Developer/Distributor: J. Randolph Valentine: jvalent@facstaff.wisc.edu

IT [Interlinear Text]

A tool for building a *corpus* of analyzed texts. The analysis is embodied in user-defined annotations which are displayed in a form that is unsurpassed for clarity of presentation – the form of interlinear, aligned text. IT also manages the database of lexical information derived during the analysis of texts.
Systems supported: MS-DOS, Macintosh
Developer/Distributor: Gary F. Simons and Larry Versaw. International Academic Bookstore, 7500 W. Camp Wisdom Road, Dallas, TX, USA.
academic.books@sil.org
(MS-DOS) gopher://gopher.sil.org/11/gopher_root/
computing/software/linguistics/text_analysis/it/
(Mac) ftp://ftp.sil.org/software/mac/

IVARB (MacVARB for Macintosh; also known as GOLDVARB)

Performs variable rule (VARBRUL) analysis on naturally occurring data in all areas of linguistics. A VARBRUL study analyzes the choice made by speakers between discrete alternatives during language performance: different pronunciations, lexical items, word orders, syntactic structures, etc. This choice may be influenced by many factors, such as syntactic or phonological environment, discourse function and style, age, socioeconomic class, and sex of the speaker. VARBRUL is suited to corpus-based research where the number of occurrences of different contexts varies.

Systems supported: MS-DOS, Macintosh

Developer/Distributor: IVARB – Sharon Ash, Dept. of Linguistics, Univ. of Pennsylvania, Philadelphia, PA, 19104–6305, USA; MacVARB – David Sankoff, Centre de recherches mathématiques, Univ. de Montréal, CP 6128, succ. A, Montréal, P.Q., H3C 3J7, Canada; also UMich.

JonesPhones

A digitized version of Daniel Jones pronouncing the cardinal vowels. Some exercises are included. HyperCard.

Systems supported: Macintosh

Developer/Distributor: Tom Veatch, 619 Williams Hall, Univ. of Pennsylvania, Philadelphia, PA, 19104, USA.

K-TEXT

KTEXT is a text processing program that uses PC-KIMMO to do morphological parsing. KTEXT reads a text from a disk file, parses each word, and writes the results to a new disk file. This new file is in the form of a structured text file where each word of the original text is represented as a database record composed of several fields. Each word record contains a field for the original word, a field for the underlying or lexical form of the word, and a field for the gloss string.

Systems supported: MS-DOS, Macintosh, UNIX

Developer/Distributor: Evan Antworth, Academic Computing Department, Summer Institute of Linguistics, 7500 W. Camp Wisdom Road, Dallas, TX, 75236, USA.

evan@sil.org

LX Problems

A series of programs for introductory linguistics, covering phonetics, phonology, morphology, dialectology, and sociolinguistics. The

problems combine sound and graphics to bring the user into close contact with the phonetics and culture of a particular dialect of a language. Analytical problems use a variety of computational techniques to lead the student to the correct solution. The program stores each action taken by the student in a separate file so that teaching assistants can review students' progress and problems. HyperCard.
Systems supported: Macintosh
Developer/Distributor: William Labov, Linguistics Laboratory, Univ. of Pennsylvania, 1106 Blockley Hall, Philadelphia, PA, 19104, USA. labov@central.cis.upenn.edu.

MacLex

Creates and maintains a lexicon.
Systems supported: Macintosh
Developer/Distributor: Bruce Waters
ftp://ftp.sil.org/software/mac/

MACVARB See IVARB

PC-Kimmo

Program for computational phonology and morphology. Typically used for testing morphological descriptions by relating lexical and surface forms. Takes two files – a rules file specifying the phonologic rules of language, and a lexicon file with glosses and morphotactic constraints – and takes the lexical form and produces the surface form, or takes the surface form and produces the lexical form with its gloss.
Systems supported: MS-DOS, Macintosh, UNIX
Developer/Distributor: David Smith, Gary Simons, and Stephen McConnel
International Academic Bookstore, 7500 W. Camp Wisdom Road, Dallas, TX, USA, tel. (214)709–24045, fax (214) 709–2433.
http://www.sil.org/pckimmo/

PEPPER

Programs to Examine Phonetic and Phonologic Evaluation Records. Ten programs for phonetic analysis in normal and disordered speech.
Systems supported: MS–DOS
Developer/Distributor: Lawrence D. Shriberg. Dept. of Communicative Disorders. Univ. of Wisconsin-Madison, Room 439, Waisman Center, 1500 Highland Ave., Madison, WI, 53705, USA.

Phonetic Symbol Guide – Electronic Edition

A talking encyclopedia of phonetic symbols; accompanies Pullum and Ladusaw (1986). Organized by the shapes of symbols, each entry gives a name for the symbol, its usage – by the IPA, by American phoneticians, and by others – variations on its shape, its source, and additional useful comments. There are 311 entries, plus an explanatory introduction, a glossary a list of references, and a dozen pages of symbol charts. HyperCard.

Systems supported: Macintosh

Developer/Distributor: George D. Allen, Michigan State University, College of Nursing, East Lansing, MI, 48824, USA.

Phonetics Tutor

A tutorial program that assists in phonetic transcription of English, employing American symbols, with IPA symbols in sample lessons as an option. The lessons can be edited. The program also teaches phonetic terminology and distinctive features.

Systems supported: MS-DOS.

Developer/Distributor: Center for Applied Linguistics, Language and Linguistics Software, 1118 22d St. NW, Washington, DC, 20037, USA.

Phonetics

Teaches phonemic transcription of RP.

Systems supported: MS-DOS

Developer/Distributor: Martin Sawers, 71a Westbury Hill, Westbury-on-Trym, Bristol, BS9 3AD, UK.

Phono

Phono is a software tool for developing and testing models of regular historical sound change. An ordered set of sound-change rules is tested either on a data file or interactively. It is accompanied by a model for Spanish.

Systems supported: MS-DOS

Developer/Distributor: Lee Hartman, Dept. of Foreign Languages, Southern Illinois University, Carbondale, IL, 62901–4521, USA.
lhartman@siu.edu
http://www.siu.edu/~nmc/phono.html

PHTHONG

HyperCard stack for teaching phonemic transcription, using a graded set of cards introducing material in a cumulative fashion. First the transcription is from a phonemic transcription to ordinary English orthography, then from English orthography to phonemic transcription. Reviews and other exercises are also used. A setup module allows instructors to customize the transcription to fit their preferences or dialect area.

Systems supported: Macintosh

Developer/Distributor: Henry Rogers, Dept. of Linguistics, Univ. of Toronto, Toronto, Ont., M5S 3H1, Canada.

rogers@chass.utoronto.ca

http://www.chass.utoronto.ca/~rogers/

http://www.chass.utoronto.ca/~rogers/phthong.html

ProfGlot

Implementation of the theory of Functional Grammar as described in Dik (1989). The program is an integrated system in that it can deal with different languages in terms of very similar structures and procedures, and it has the capacity not only of producing linguistic expressions in those languages, but also of parsing them, of translating between these languages and of drawing certain inferences.

Systems supported: MS-DOS

Developer/Distributor: Amsterdam Linguistic Software, P. O. Box 3602, 1001 AK Amsterdam, The Netherlands.

Semantic Tutorial

Tutorial in semantic/pragmatic portion of introductory linguistics course; part of a proposed larger series of courseware in linguistics. Part of a larger "Linguistics Online" project. HyperCard.

Systems supported: Macintosh

Developer/Distributor: Victor Raskin, Purdue University, West Lafayette, IN, 47907, USA.

SEMANTICA

Produces semantic interpretation of sentence from phrasal and lexical rules provided by user. The program also presents a World Window, which depicts a three-dimensional graphical landscape and various kinds of geometric *object*s in it. In this window, the student can explore the relation between the first-order interpretation and a depicted world.

Systems supported: NeXT

Developer/Distributor: Richard Larson.

rlarson@semlab1.sbs.sunysb.edu

Signalyze

An acoustic analysis program. It allows digital speech signal editing, analysis, and manipulation. It includes multiple window display and zoom. It includes three types of pitch analysis; a variety of spectral analyses including Fourier analysis with several bandwidths, linear predictive coding, and cone kernel analysis; and cepstral analysis. Further functions include exportable data scoring, arithmetic and transcendental transformations, power and RMS envelopes, down- and up-sampling, derivative differences, and zero-crossings. Several sound formats are supported.

Systems supported: Macintosh

Developer/Distributor: InfoSignal Inc. Distributed by Network Technology Corp. 91 Baldwin St., Charlestown, MA, 02129, USA, and by InfoSignal Inc., C.P. 73, CH-1015, Lausanne, Switzerland. gopher://uldns1.unil.ch:70/11/unilgophers/gopher_lett/ LAIP/speech/Signalyze/

Sounds of the World's Languages

Illustrates phonological contrasts in about 100 languages. A phonetic transcription and a gloss of each word is given. The pronunciation of each word can be heard. For each language there is a general information card, and in a few cases, additional data such as reproductions of aerodynamic data or tracings of X-rays. The location of each language is shown on a map which also serves as an ***index*** to the languages. Other indexes include the list of languages, a list of sound types, and IPA charts. HyperCard.

Systems supported: Macintosh

Developer/Distributor: Phonetics Laboratory, Dept. of Linguistics, UCLA, 405 Highland Ave., Los Angeles, CA, 90024–1543, USA.

Speechlab

An introductory course on phonetics, explaining acoustics, physiology and spectrography interactively, with a complete lexicon of German/ American speech sounds, with videos, anatomical illustrations, acoustic analysis and detailed description of each sound, and a bibliography of 4,000 items.

Systems supported: Windows (3.2, 95, NT). Sound card recommended.

Developer/Distributor: office@media-enterprise.de

http://www.media-enterprise.de

Stamp

Tool for adapting text from one dialect to another.
Systems supported: MS-DOS, Macintosh, UNIX
Developer/Distributor: SIL.
gopher://gopher.sil.org/11/gopher_root/computing/
software/linguistics/cada/stamp/

SYNTACTICA

A program for exploring grammars (phrase structure and lexicons) and
the structures they generate. It generates syntactic trees using phrase-
structure rules and lexicon.
Systems supported: NeXT
Developer/Distributor: Richard Larson.
rlarson@semlab1.sbs.sunysb.edu

SysPro

Simulates network models of language using systemic theory. SysPro
simulates system network models of language, permitting the user to
enter, store, recall, and display networks graphically in standard notation and derive from them linguistic expressions that represent each
of the logical states implied by the networks.
Systems supported: MS-DOS
Developer/Distributor: M. Cummings, English Dept., Glendon College,
York Univ., Toronto, Ontario, M4N 3M6, Canada.
GL250004@yuvenus

Tarski's World

A program teaching modern logic. Allows students to build three-
dimensional worlds and to describe them in first-order logic.
Systems supported: Macintosh, Windows, NeXT
Developer/Distributor: Jon Barwise and John Etchemendy, Cambridge
University Press
http://kanpai.stanford.edu:80/hp/Logic-software.html#Tarski

UCLA phonetics lab programs

Group of instructional programs that treat articulatory–acoustic relations: drawing parameter controlled diagrams of vocal tract configurations, calculating formant structure of vowel articulations, data plotting,
and displaying vocal tract shapes required for given formant frequencies.
Systems supported: Macintosh

Developer/Distributor: Phonetics Laboratory, Dept. of Linguistics, UCLA, 405 Highland Ave., Los Angeles, CA, 90024–1543, USA.

UMICH phonetics training tools

An ensemble of HyperCard stacks to assist beginning students of phonetics in associating symbols, sounds, and production. Includes sound files, animated vocal tracts, and X-ray movies for each speech sound. Can be accessed through an IPA-table interface or by manipulating a vocal tract on screen. Also, an IPA training game and a testing module, in which students are tested on their ability to associate IPA symbols, static vocal tract shapes, and physiological descriptions.
Systems supported: Macintosh
Developer/Distributor: UM-PTT@umich.edu
demo version at http://www.tmo.umich.edu/ling.html

UPSID (UCLA Phonological Segment Inventory Database)

Contains inventories of segments found in 450 languages. The inventories are designed to enable matters such as the relative frequency of occurrence of segments, the structure of segment inventories, and segment cooccurrence patterns to be studied using an unbiased language sample. The sounds are coded using an extensive set of phonetic features and can be accessed and sorted by use of these features. A version named PHONEME is available without an editing facility for use in the classroom.
Systems supported: MS-DOS
Developer/Distributor: Phonetics Laboratory, Dept. of Linguistics, UCLA, 405 Highland Ave., Los Angeles, CA, 90024–1543, USA.

WinSAL-V

A speech analysis program allowing recording, segmenting and playing of audio and video files in multiple windows. Includes FFT, LPC, cepstrum, and pitch analysis.
Systems supported: Windows (95, NT)
Developer/Distributor: office@media-enterprise.de
http://www.media-enterprise.de

WORDSURV

Analyzes word lists using lexicostatistics, phonostatistics, and comparative reconstruction. The program can be used in helping students to identify tentative comparative series for further testing.

Systems supported: MS-DOS
Developer/Distributor: SIL

A World of Words

Eight stacks about how Indo-European languages have changed over time. Topics include Grimm's law, Greek and Latin sounds, Maps and trees, Root and branch, a close transcription of a Frost poem, a hypertext version of the Proöemium of Homer's *Iliad*. HyperCard.
Systems supported: Macintosh (requires MacInTalk; System 6 recommended)
Developer/Distributor: John Lawler, University of Michigan. john.lawler@umich.edu

YOUPIE

Attempts to learn stress system of any language using parametric approach. Sample words with stress indicated are input; they are first parsed into syllable and then sent to a stress-learner. The learner attempts to set the value of stress parameters. If successful, YOUPIE produces a prose description of the stress pattern of the language.
Systems supported: MS–DOS
Developer/Distributor: Elan Dresher, Dept. of Linguistics, Univ. of Toronto, Toronto, Ont. M6J 2X8, Canada.
dresher@epas.utoronto.ca

PART II   NETWORK RESOURCES

http://www.umich.edu/~archive/linguistics/
The best general source for educational software in linguistics.

http://www.sil.org/computing/
SIL has produced a large number of programs over the years useful in teaching linguistics.

http://babel.uoregon.edu/yamada/guides.html
The best source for information on the net about language.

http://babel.uoregon.edu/Yamada/fonts.html
An excellent source for finding fonts useful in linguistics.

http://www.umich.edu/~archive/linguistics/jml.795.htm
A large collection of useful links, with a special section on Teaching Resources.

http://www.arts.gla.ac.uk/IPA/ipa.html
    The homepage of the International Phonetic Alphabet.

http://fonsg3.let.uva.nl/Other_pages.html
    Links to many sites on phonetics and speech.

There is an unmoderated discussion group TEACH-LING devoted to
    teaching linguistics. To subscribe, send a one-line message to
    listproc@lists.nyu.edu
    saying:

```
subscribe teach-ling YOURADDRESS YOURFIRSTNAME
YOURLASTNAME
```

e.g.

```
subscribe teach-ling smith@uplonk.ca Jean Smith
```

Chapter 4

Textual databases

Susan Hockey

Textual databases are becoming major resources for research in language and linguistics. By "textual database" we mean continuous text, either written or transcribed from speech. It may be a complete text or texts, in the literary sense, or samples of text. This chapter discusses important issues in the acquisition and use of these databases. An overview of existing resources is given, followed by an examination of *markup* schemes and software tools. The emphasis is on tools for the ordinary working linguist and the chapter concludes with a brief assessment of what he or she can expect to achieve using these techniques.

4.1 ACQUIRING AND CREATING ELECTRONIC TEXTS

Acquiring or creating an electronic text is of course the first stage of a project. Unfortunately there is as yet no single source which identifies all or even most existing texts. Until very recently almost all electronic texts were created either by individuals for their own specific research projects (for example, study of style of an author or comparison of vocabulary in specific genres) or by research institutes such as the Istituto Linguistica Computazionale Pisa or the Institut National de la Langue Française, which were established for large scale studies of their own language. At the time of writing it is estimated that about 25 per cent of texts are in the hands of individuals and about 70 per cent in research institutes. It is not known how many of these texts are available for other scholars to use, but very few of them were created originally for multi-purpose use by different scholars. The remaining 5 per cent form the growing number of texts which libraries are beginning to acquire and make available for general use.

4.1.1 Sources of texts

Here we can only note some long-standing sources of electronic text which can claim some reliability. The Web sites listed in the Appendix provide an obvious starting point for further exploration.

The **Oxford Text Archive** (OTA) at Oxford University Computing Services has a collection of more than 1000 texts in some 30 different languages, which it makes available to researchers at low cost. The OTA was established in 1976 to provide long-term storage for electronic texts which are of interest in literary and linguistic scholarship. It accepts any text which is offered and undertakes to ensure that the electronic copy is not lost. The texts are in many different formats, and the level of accuracy and *encoding* varies greatly. The OTA includes several corpora and collections of text which are of interest to linguists as well as electronic dictionaries and thesauri. Some OTA texts are available for widespread distribution; others need the permission of the original compiler before copies can be made. The OTA catalog also includes a number of texts which have been purchased for use by Oxford University and cannot be distributed further. It also gives a note of the source or depositor of the text and an indication of its size.

The Humanities Computing Yearbook, published by Oxford University Press, is a compendium of information about humanities computing, containing extensive bibliography and information about software and text resources. Volume 1, edited by Ian Lancashire and Willard McCarty, appeared in late 1989. Volume 2 edited by Lancashire alone, appeared in mid-1991 and contains much new material as well as updating significant Volume 1 entries. The editors have done their best to verify that the information is comprehensive and reliable, certainly at the time of publication. The major focus is on the humanities, and some areas of linguistics are not covered.

The **Georgetown Catalog of Projects in Electronic Text** is a database of information on electronic text projects throughout the world. It compiled well over 300 entries during 1989–92 concentrating on machine-readable versions of primary text. It is a useful compilation of organizations and institutions that are working on electronic text *file*s, but it does not give much information about the availability of the texts and does not list very many individual texts.

More recent information can be obtained from various electronic discussion lists and newsletters. This information may or may not have been verified. In particular, it has become common practice to announce new projects on discussion lists before those projects have achieved very much, and in some instances before they have begun. It is therefore advisable to check whether a project which has been announced electronically is in fact more than what has come to be called "vaporware."

Besides The LINGUIST List <linguist@linguistlist.org>, useful discussion lists are

```
humanist@lists.princeton.edu
```

and

```
corpora@hd.uib.no
```

The Humanist list began in 1987 as a forum for humanities computing specialists. Under the editorship of Willard McCarty it has become a major international forum for discussion of intellectual, scholarly, pedagogical, and social issues, as well as for exchange of information, including the availability of electronic texts. The Corpora list is moderated by the Norwegian Computing Centre for the Humanities and also has many queries about the availability of corpora.

Institutions which hold electronic text are too numerous to mention here, but a few are worthy of note. Many have substantial collections of text in one natural language which, although not initially created for this purpose, can be used as a basis for linguistic research. The **International Computer Archive of Modern and Medieval English**, administered at the Norwegian Computing Centre for the Humanities, collects and distributes information on English language material available for computer processing and on linguistic research completed or in progress on the material. The whole of Ancient Greek literature up to 600AD is available on CD-ROM from the **Thesaurus Linguae Graecae** and a companion CD-ROM of Classical Latin is distributed by the Packard Humanities Institute. Also available for individual use are the complete *corpus* of Old English, which forms the basis of the material for the **Old English Dictionary** being compiled in Toronto, several versions of the Bible in Hebrew, Greek and other languages, and a miscellaneous collection of mostly modern American newspapers and technical documents assembled by the **Association for Computational Linguistics** (ACL). In summer 1994 the **European Corpus Initiative** (ECI) released its first CD-ROM, which has a collection of corpora (texts, word lists, and dictionaries) in twenty-five languages including some multilingual parallel texts. The **Linguistic Data Consortium** (LDC) at the University of Pennsylvania has been funded by ARPA to collect and disseminate large amounts of language data for research in natural language analysis, speech processing and other language technology applications. There is a subscription fee for membership but some texts can also be purchased by non-members.

The **Brown** and **LOB** (Lancaster–Oslo–Bergen) **Corpora** are the two most widely known and used language corpora, and various other corpus-building projects have been modeled on them. Each contains one million words first published in 1961. The Brown Corpus is American English and the LOB Corpus is British English. Each consists of 500 samples of approximately 2000 words taken from a variety of genre. Samples from the newspaper and humor sections of the Brown Corpus have been used for the concordance examples in this chapter (see Section 4.3). The **British National Corpus** (BNC), a much larger enterprise consisting of 100 million words of British English, was completed in 1994. About ten per cent of the material is transcriptions of conversations.

The compilation and usage of these corpora and others have led to discussions and some empirical research on what constitutes a representative corpus.

In general, compiling information about electronic texts is not an easy task. Apart from a few well-known collections and corpora, information is scarce and is in many different formats. Compilers who created electronic texts for their own specific projects often embedded information about the texts in their own purpose-built software. Others developed their own *ad hoc* procedures for documenting the texts, resulting in different methodologies which are not easy to merge. Recent experiments using the rigor of bibliographic records to catalogue electronic texts have shown that these provide very well for some details that users of electronic texts need to know, but not well for markup and other information needed by processing programs. The TEI header (see Section 4.2.1) was developed as a solution to these problems.

4.1.2   Raw text or package?

A very large majority of existing electronic texts, and all those created newly by scholars, are what is called here *plain ASCII text*; that is, they are sequential files which can be displayed or printed by, for example, the DOS *command* type, or the Unix command cat. Software to use these texts must be acquired from another party or written by the user. Most of the texts which are becoming available on CD-ROM are accompanied by searching software and are not accessible in any other way. The user is constrained to the facilities which the developer of the software has chosen to include.

Nevertheless some of these resources provide a simple introduction to what computers can do for the linguist. The **ICAME CD-ROM** contains the texts of some of the ICAME corpora together with two retrieval programs, TACT and WordCruncher, both of which are widely used in the humanities. The **CETEDOC CD-ROM**, which contains major works of the early Christian Fathers, must be used via its own software interface, and other software interfaces come with the CD-ROMs of **the New Oxford English Dictionary** and the **Global Jewish Database** (Responsa material). The TLG, PHI, ACL, and ECI CD-ROMS do not come with any software and the texts are not *index*ed in any way. The user thus has complete flexibility in potential application functions on these CD-ROMs, but also needs to write or acquire software to use them.

At the time of writing there are only two large well-known collections of humanities-related material generally accessible by on-line searches over the Internet. **ARTFL** (American Research on the Treasury of the French Language) is based at the University of Chicago. It contains over 2000 texts of French language and literary material mostly from the eighteenth, nineteenth and twentieth centuries, with a smaller group of seventeenth-century texts as well as some medieval and Renaissance texts. Genres include novels, verse, journalism, essays, correspondence, and treatises. **The Dartmouth Dante Project** contains the Divine Comedy and over sixty commentaries in Latin, Italian, and English and is accessible free of charge over the Internet from Dartmouth College Library. In late 1996 Chadwyck-Healey began an on-line subscription service **Lion** (Literature Online) for their full-text English literature databases, where the focus appears to be on looking up words for reference.

4.1.3   Copyright issues

Finding out about electronic texts is not easy for other reasons. Copyright issues are a cause for concern in many quarters. When electronic versions of printed texts first began to be created over forty years ago, the full implications were not known. Many scholars created electronic versions of texts without getting appropriate copyright permissions, either because they did not know how or where to ask, or because publishers did not know how to answer. The copyright permission of many existing texts is unclear and, with the advent of networking, is further compounded by different laws in different countries. Neither do we have a clear defini-tion of what constitutes a new edition of an electronic text, since it is so easy to make changes on a continuing basis. Whether or not the present copyright laws are adequate to deal with all possible situations that may arise in the use of this new medium is not clear, but those who have most to gain by protecting copyrights tend to be those who distribute text in a fixed form, only accessible via software provided with the text. While this makes a medium which is easier for publishers and librarians to handle, it does not provide as well for the innovative ideas and uses which electronic texts can stimulate. Other researchers have sought to avoid getting embroiled in copyright issues and deliberately chosen to work with texts which are out of copyright, but which may not neces-sarily be the best data from a scholarly perspective. Given the rate of technological change, it seems unlikely that a general-purpose solution to the copyright issue will be found in the near future.

4.1.4   Optical character recognition and scanning

If no suitable text is available from any of these sources, the prospective user must then create his or her own electronic version. By the begin-ning of the 1980s *optical character recognition* (*OCR*) was possible for some texts. This permits a conversion of a text to electronic form without the need for keyboarding. The most usual OCR configuration now consists of a flatbed scanner attached to a PC or Macintosh, which has software to convert the scanner's *bit*-mapped image into ASCII text. Some have output options to convert the text into a format used by common wordprocessing programs.

Texts which are of interest to the linguist are likely to be suitable only for the more sophisticated scanners, most notably those which can be trained to read a specific ***character set***. Handwriting and old printed books, where the baseline is uneven, are not usually suitable; neither are texts which contain a lot of italic or bold face material. These latter include dictionaries, which have many type face changes. The poor quality of the paper and uneven inking makes newspapers difficult, but magazines can be much better. Some scanners are able to read non-standard characters, but any script where the letters are joined together is almost certainly not possible. There may also be difficulties with accented characters, particularly those which are not very common.

The best way to determine whether a text is suitable for scanning is to try it out, being aware first that a scanner will rarely produce an entirely accurate text. Variations in the ink or paper can lead to misreads such as the confusion of **c** and **e**, or **h** and **b**, even in what appears to be a clearly printed original. Some scanning software includes a dictionary to confirm doubtful readings, but this will not be of any use if the text is in an uncommon language. An advertised accuracy rate of 99.9 per cent means approximately one character error every ten lines, so it is necessary to proofread scanned text carefully for errors. Often a pattern can be detected in errors and some special software or macros can be written to correct a good percentage of them.

Optical character recognition sees only the typographic features on the page, and additional information is needed to create a usable text. Encoding needs to be added to identify such features as author, title, page number, and speaker, or whatever are the appropriate units of division within the document. It may be possible to provide automatic conversion of some of these from a scanned document, but some manual editing is very often necessary, since these structural divisions do not always map automatically on to typographic features, which are all the scanner can see. (For a detailed discussion of text encoding and markup see Section 4.2.)

The choice between scanning and keyboarding depends very much on the nature of the text, on the circumstances of the scholar, and the resources available. However, it is essential to remember that the scanning on its own is not sufficient to produce an accurate text and may take only perhaps a quarter of the time that is needed to create a usable text. Proofreading and adding markup to make the text useful for computer processing are much more time-consuming. In general, scanning rarely turns out to be as successful as many people expect, and it is worth knowing that most large text database entry projects such as the

Thesaurus Linguae Graecae and the New Oxford English Dictionary have found it more convenient to have data keyboarded professionally. A much better accuracy rate can be achieved and structural encoding can be inserted at the same time.

The term "scanning" is often used now for the creation of digitized images, where a picture of the page, not a transcription of the text itself, is stored in the computer. While this provides an effective means of delivering text for reading, the text itself in such an image cannot be processed in any way by the computer. The potential of image delivery of texts is strongest in the library environment, particularly for providing wider access to fragile manuscripts, but also to reduce duplicate purchases of the same material. In the longer term both image and text representation together will begin to show the real potential of the electronic library. In the meantime, linguists will find texts rather than digitized images to be more useful for their research.

4.1.5   Typesetting tapes

Typesetting tapes have sometimes been used as a source of electronic text. These are more appropriate when a substantial amount of text will be received from the same source, possibly on a continuing basis. Typesetting tapes often contain an idiosyncratic markup scheme which is typographic and needs substantial effort to decode. Corrections at proof stage are often typeset separately and not inserted into the main text so that the original tape is not a completely faithful rendering of the printed version. Publishers also find it cheaper in many instances to throw away their typesetting tapes and disks rather than incur costs in keeping them. As more publishers move to more standard markup formats these problems will diminish, but it is as well to be aware of them at this point. Using a typesetting tape seems most feasible if a standard encoding scheme is employed.

4.2   MARKUP SCHEMES

Electronic texts become much more useful when additional information called *markup* or *encoding* is inserted into the text. Markup makes explicit for computer processing those features which are implicit for the human reader of a text. In the case of wordprocessing and text formatting, markup serves to identify words to be printed in italic or bold, or to make a new page and center a heading. For text analysis applications, markup can serve two major purposes. One is to identify specific areas of text to be analyzed. The other is to locate words which have been retrieved from the text. For example, if a corpus is divided into subsections denoting different genres, words which are retrieved can be identified by their genres, thus showing their pattern of usage among genres. The types of analyses that can be performed on a text without markup are somewhat limited. Markup can be used to encode many different features within a text. In general the more markup there is in a text, the more useful that text can be, and the more expensive it is to create.

Markup can be used to encode both structural and analytic features. Structural features may include paragraphs, lists, headings, lines (of verse), stage directions (in drama), quotations, parts, sections, chapters, and bibliographic citations. Almost anything can be included as analytic information, but most effort so far has been directed to finding ways of representing linguistic analyses of various kinds. Very many markup schemes have evolved over the last forty or so years, most of which are incompatible with one another. Some have been created for use with specific programs or as part of larger ongoing research projects. Others have been *ad hoc* in nature and created by individual scholars for their own purposes, and reflect only the needs of one project. Electronic texts which were created some time ago often have fairly limited markup and some have only upper case letters.

Figure 4.1, the beginning of Section A of the Brown Corpus, shows one method of inserting locators. Each *line* begins with a fixed field identifier. A01 indicates that this is Section A1 of the Corpus; Section A2 begins with A02, and so on. The number in character positions 5 to 8 on each record is a line number. The numbers go up in tens so that additional lines can be inserted, as for example 0011, 0012 without having to renumber all the lines. Thus the first eight character positions are an identifier for each line of text and can be used to give a reference locator for each word within the line. In this example note also *Jr* written *Jr&* in line 10. Throughout the corpus the ampersand is used to mark an abbreviation in order to distinguish the full stop in an abbreviation from that at the end of a sentence. In line 21, *#MERGER PROPOSED#* is obviously a headline or subheading within the article.

Placing locators at the beginning of every line as in Figure 4.1 is repetitive and wasteful of space. It might only be necessary to insert a section number at the beginning of each new section. This can be done using the so-called *COCOA* method of encoding text. COCOA was first used widely by a concordance program of that name, developed at the Atlas Computer Laboratory in England in the 1960s. Figure 4.2 shows the beginning of Shakespeare's *The Merchant of Venice* encoded according to this scheme. The items within < and > serve as locators within the text. <T Merchant of Venice> indicates that the title is *Merchant of Venice*. <A 1> means Act 1 and <S 1> means Scene 1. Within the COCOA scheme a different letter category is used to denote each type of reference. Here C is used for speaker within the play, as S has already been used for *scene*. A C locator has been inserted in the text every time the speaker

```
A01 0010    The Fulton County Grand Jury said Friday an investigation
A01 0020    of Atlanta's recent primary election produced "no evidence" that
A01 0030    any irregularities took place. The jury further said in term-end
A01 0040    presentments that the City Executive Committee, which had over-all
A01 0050    charge of the election, "deserves the praise and thanks of the
A01 0060    City of Atlanta" for the manner in which the election was conducted.
A01 0070        The September-October term jury had been charged by Fulton
A01 0080    Superior Court Judge Durwood Pye to investigate reports of possible
A01 0090    "irregularities" in the hard-fought primary which was won by
A01 0100    Mayor-nominate Ivan Allen Jr&. "Only a relative handful
A01 0110    of such reports was received", the jury said, "considering the
A01 0120    widespread interest in the election, the number of voters and the size
A01 0130    of this city". The jury said it did find that many of Georgia's
A01 0140    registration and election laws "are outmoded or inadequate
A01 0150    and often ambiguous". It recommended that Fulton legislators
A01 0160    act "to have these laws studied and revised to the end of modernizing
A01 0170    and improving them". The grand jury commented on a number
A01 0180    of other topics, among them the Atlanta and Fulton County purchasing
A01 0190    departments which it said "are well operated and follow generally
A01 0200    accepted practices which inure to the best interest of both governments".
A01 0210    #MERGER PROPOSED# However, the jury said it believes "these
A01 0220    two offices should be combined to achieve greater efficiency and reduce
A01 0230    the cost of administration". The City Purchasing Department,
A01 0240    the jury said, "is lacking in experienced clerical personnel
A01 0250    as a result of city personnel policies". It urged that the city "take
A01 0260    steps to remedy" this problem. Implementation of Georgia's
A01 0270    automobile title law was also recommended by the outgoing jury.
```

Figure 4.1   The beginning of Section A of the Brown Corpus showing the fixed format locators

changes. The scope or value of a locator thus holds true until the next instance of the same locator. If the word *caught* in the third line of Antonio's speech here was retrieved it would have the locators T Merchant of Venice, A 1, S 1 and C Antonio. The actual letters used for each category are chosen by the encoder of the text and they are case sensitive, thus allowing up to 52 different categories.

The COCOA scheme assumes that whatever program is processing the text can keep track of line numbers automatically. Non-sequential numbers can be handled by inserting an explicit line number reference within the text. In Figure 4.2, stage directions are enclosed within double round brackets. This allows a program to ignore these if desired, so that occurrences of *enter, exit* etc. within the stage directions are not included within counts of these words throughout the text. A linguist may want to use this mechanism for notes about the source of the text, or for comments on speakers if the text is a transcription of a conversation.

```
<T Merchant of Venice>
<A 1>
<S 1>
((Enter Antonio, Salerio, and Solanio))
<C Antonio>
In sooth, it know not why I am so sad.
It wearies me, you say it wearies you,
But how I caught it, found it, or came by it,
What stuff 'tis made of, whereof it is born,
I am to learn;
And such a want-wit sadness makes of me
That I have much ado to know myself.
<C Salerio>
Your mind is tossing on the ocean,
There where your agosies with portly sail,
Like signiors and rich burghers on the flood,
Or as it were the pageants of the sea,
Do overpeer the petty traffickers
That curtsey to them, do them reverence,
As they fly by them with their woven wings.
<C Solanio> ((to Antonio))
Believe me, sir, had I such venture forth
The better part of my affections would
Be with my hopes abroad.
I should be still
Plucking the grass to know where sits the wind,
Peering in maps for ports and piers and roads,
And every object that might make me fear
Misfortune to my ventures out of doubt
Would make me sad.
```

Figure 4.2   The beginning of *The Merchant of Venice* showing COCOA-format markup

Many existing texts use either the COCOA encoding scheme or the method of locators shown in the Brown Corpus examples, but experience has highlighted problems. One syntax is used for encoding locators. Another is used for other kinds of information. It is sometimes not clear which is best for information such as foreign language words. The locator method can be used for substantial amounts of text in a different language. For example, using F for foreign language,

```
<F French>
```
lines of text in French
```
<F English>
```
lines of text in English

but single words or very short sections of text might better be treated in the same way as the stage directions as follows:

John exhibited a certain ((joie de vivre)).

or by adding specific markers at the beginning of each word, for example:

John exhibited a certain $joie $de $vivre.

where a search for all words beginning with $ retrieves the French words, a method which has been widely used. The same text may often contain different markers with different functions. Regrettably, documentation explaining what the markers indicate is less often provided.

4.2.1 SGML and the Text Encoding Initiative (TEI)

Two encoding schemes (with variants of them) have been illustrated above but many others exist. By 1987, as scholars interchanged texts more and more, it became clear that this plethora of encoding schemes was hampering progress. It was also recognized that most existing schemes were deficient in one way or another. Some were designed for one software program and were thus machine-specific. Others reflected only the views of their originators and could not readily be applied to other projects. Almost all were very poorly documented and none was rich enough to cope with the variety of applications and purposes for which an electronic text might be created. At the end of 1987, a major international project, called the *Text Encoding Initiative* (*TEI*), began under the sponsorship of the Association for Computers and the Humanities, the Association for Computational Linguistics, and the Association for Literary and Linguistic Computing. It produced its *Guidelines for Electronic Text Encoding and Interchange* in May 1994. The TEI Guidelines, as they are usually called, are the result of six years of work by volunteers in over twenty countries, coordinated and written up by two editors. The *Guidelines* consist of almost 1300 pages of specifications of encoding tags for many different discipline areas and provide a much sounder basis for encoding electronic texts.

The Guidelines use the *Standard Generalized Markup Language* (*SGML*) which became an international standard in 1986. SGML is a metalanguage for defining markup schemes. It is built on the assumption that a text can be broken down into components (paragraphs, lists, names, chapters, titles, etc.) which can nest within each other. The principle of SGML is "descriptive," rather than "prescriptive." The encoder indicates what a textual object is, rather than what the computer is supposed to do with that object. This means that different application programs can operate on the same text. For example, if titles embedded in the text are encoded as such, a retrieval program can search all the titles, an indexing program can *index* them, and a printing program can print them in italic, all without making any changes to the text.

The creator of an SGML application, as it is called, defines those features of a text which may need to be encoded as objects and gives specific *element* names to them. All the elements which may occur in a text are defined in an SGML ***Document Type Declaration*** (***DTD***) which also specifies the relationship between them. This means that a computer program can use the DTD to validate the encoding in a text. For example, an error is detected if the DTD specifies that the text must have at least one title element, but no title element is given. Non-standard characters are denoted by *entity* references in SGML, for example, "—" for an emdash or "é" for *é* as in *état* for *état*. This mechanism can also be used for boilerplate text, but is hardly feasible for large sections of text where other methods of defining writing systems are needed.

The SGML element names are embedded in the text in the form of encoding tags. Each element has a start and an end tag, although in many cases it is possible to omit the end tag. Elements can also have attributes which modify them in some way. Figure 4.3 shows the beginning of Walter Pater, *The Child in the House,* encoded in TEI-conformant SGML. This example was prepared by Wendell Piez as one of the TEI pilot projects produced at the Center for Electronic Texts in the Humanities in 1995–6. It begins with the front matter consisting of the title and a publication note. Only the first paragraph of the body of the text is shown. The paragraph tag <p> has an identifier *attribute* giving the chapter and paragraph number. In the <date> element an attribute gives a date value more suitable for computer processing than "Aug. 1878" which would be treated as two words "Aug." and "1878."

The TEI has attempted to define a comprehensive list of over 400 features which linguists and humanities scholars might want to use. The Guidelines describe each of these features and give examples of their use. However, since no list can be truly comprehensive, the Guidelines provide for extension and modification when needed. Very few tags are absolutely required. It is up to the encoder of a text to determine what he or she wishes to tag. The encoding process is seen as incremental, so another researcher may take that text and add encoding for a different set of features. SGML provides for different and possibly conflicting views to

```
<text id="ch">
<pb id="MS.172" ed="MS" n="172">
<front><head><title rend="Capitals">The Child in the
House</title>
<note>Published in <title rend="Italic" level="J">Macmillan's
Magazine</title>,
<date value="18780900">Aug. 1878</date>.</note></head></front>
<body><p id="ch1.01">
As Florian Deleal walked, one hot afternoon, he overtook by
the wayside a poor aged man, and, as he seemed weary with the
road, helped him on with the burden which he carried, a
certain distance. And as the man told his story, it chanced
that he named the place, a little place in the neighbourhood
of a great city, where Florian had passed his earliest years,
but which he had never since seen, and, like a reward for his
pity, a dream of that place came to Florian, a dream which did
for him the office of the finer sort of memory, bringing its
object to mind with a great clearness, yet, as sometimes
happens in dreams, raised a little above itself, and above
ordinary retrospect. The true aspect of the place, especially
of the house there in which he had lived as a child, the
fashion of its doors, its hearths, its windows, the very scent
upon the air of it, was with him in sleep for a season; only,
with tints more musically blent on wall <pb id="MS.173"
ed="MS" n="173">and floor, and some finer light and shadow
running and out along its curves and angles, and with all its
little carvings daintier. He awoke with a sigh at the thought
of almost thirty years which lay between him and that place,
yet with a flutter of pleasure still within him as the fair
light, as if it were a smile, upon it. And it happened that
this accident of his dream was just the thing needed for the
beginning of a certain design he then had in view, the noting,
namely, of some things in the story of his spirit&mdash; in
that process of brain&dash; building by which we are, each one
of us, what we are. With the image of the place so clear and
favourable upon him, he fell to thinking of himself therein,
and how his thoughts had grown up to him. In that
half&dash;spiritualised house he could watch the better, over
again, the gradual expansion of the soul which had come to be
there&mdash;of which indeed, through the law which makes the
material objects about them so large an element in children's
lives, it had actually become a part; inward and outward being
woven through and through each other into one inextricable
texture&mdash;half, tint and trace and accident of homely
colour and form, from the wood; and the bricks; half, mere
soul&dash;stuff, floated thither from who knows how far. In the
house and garden of his dream he saw a child moving, and could
divide the main streams at least of the winds that had played
on <pb id="MS.174" ed="MS" n="174">him, and study so the first
stage in that mental journey.</p>
```

Figure 4.3   Part of Walter Pater, *The Child in the House,* encoded in TEI SGML by Wendell Piez

be embedded in the same text and a researcher who works on that text may choose to ignore some of the encoding.

HTML is also an SGML application, but it consists only of elements intended to be interpreted by Web **browser**s for display. They are not suitable as locators in a retrieval system.

The TEI Guidelines are built on the principle that all texts share some common core of features, to which may be added tags for specific disciplines or theoretical orientations. The common core consists of a header, which provides a bibliographic and encoding description of the text, and some sixty elements such as title, list, name, date, abbreviation, quotation, note, and the like. Because of the very wide variety of structural divisions possible in the texts which the TEI is addressing, a general purpose structural element <div> is used with an attribute for the type of division (chapter, part, volume, stanza, book, quatrain, etc.). Together, the header, core, and structural tags form a base tag set. Specialized base tag sets exist for verse, drama, transcriptions of speech, dictionaries, and terminological data. The base may be supplemented by any of the following additional tag sets: linking, segmentation and alignment, simple analytic mechanisms, feature structures, certainty and responsibility, transcription of primary sources, critical apparatus, names and dates, graphs, networks and trees, tables, formulae and graphics, and language corpora. The construction of a TEI DTD has thus been likened to the preparation of a pizza where the base and then the toppings (in the form of additional tag sets) are chosen.

SGML is used for many different applications and the market for SGML software is growing, although much is still expensive for the academic user. Putting the tags into the text can be aided by SGML-aware programs like Author/Editor or the latest versions of WordPerfect which ensure that the document is valid as it is being tagged. Of the SGML-aware retrieval programs or browsers, only SoftQuad's Panorama is within the financial reach of the individual researcher. The Opentext search engine is used by many libraries which provide network access to SGML-encoded electronic texts. Electronic Book Technologies' Dynatext and SoftQuad's Explorer provide more of a browsing capability with **hypertext** linking. For those who have access to it, the SARA program written to search the British National Corpus is a good example of what can be done with an SGML-aware retrieval program.

More tools exist for those who are comfortable with Unix. These include a public domain parser sgmls and some corpus handling routines. (See Chapter 5.)

It is expected that more SGML software will become available and that some will be specific to the TEI DTDs. Researchers who are beginning a project should not consider the current lack of cheap software as a reason for choosing not to use the TEI and SGML. Experience has shown that the TEI remedies almost all the defects in pre-TEI encoding schemes. It addresses the scholarly needs in much greater depth and can be treated as an archival *format* of the text from which other formats can be derived. However, since we do not yet have any general-purpose SGML-aware desktop text analysis software, the examples in the next section were created with the **Oxford Concordance Program** (**OCP**), which predates the TEI. In most cases it is easy to convert an SGML-encoded text to the format required by OCP and similar programs.

4.3   BASIC ANALYSES

The computer's basic functions of counting, searching, and sorting (alphabetizing) have been applied to textual data ever since 1949 when Father Busa began the first humanities computing project, his concordance to the works of St Thomas Aquinas and related authors. These functions are used to create concordances and word lists which serve as the underlying tools for many linguistic computing projects. Packaged concordance programs are especially suited for the ordinary working linguist who does not have large-scale computing facilities and assistance. When applied judiciously they can be used for many different purposes in both research and teaching.

4.3.1   Word lists and concordances

A word list is a list of words where each word is accompanied by a number indicating how many times that word occurs. In an index, each word is accompanied by a list of references indicating where that word occurs in the text. A word list in alphabetical order is shown in Figure 4.4. This example uses Section A of the Brown Corpus, a sample of newspapers. As in almost all other examples, only a portion of the results is illustrated. The words are given in alphabetical order, beginning with the word *a* which occurs 2122 times, out of a total of 88912 words in this text. In this version of the Brown Corpus "~" and "&" represent abbreviations. Because of the way that words were defined when this list was created, *~A, A&, A&A&U&* and *A&A&U&*'s appear at the top. Note that *a* occurs many more times than the other high frequency words shown here, e.g. *about*. The hyphen at the end of *abstaining-* has also appeared because in this case it represents an em-rule which appears without a space before it in the text. A word list like this shows up misspellings very quickly as can be seen with the entry *accomodations*. It also immediately shows that the words are individual forms. The verb *achieve* appears in three different forms and the noun *achievement* in two. Note also *Achaeans* and *Achaeans'* as two separate entries.

a	2122	absent	2	accommodated	1
~A	2	absolute	1	accommodations	2
a&	39	absolutely	1	accomodations	1
Aaron	1	absorb	1	accompanied	4
A&A&U&	1	absorbed	4	accompanying	1
A&A&U&'s	1	abstaining-	1	accomplish	2
abandoned	3	abstention	1	accomplished	4
abandonment	1	abuse	1	accomplishment	1
Abatuno	1	abuses	2	accord	2
Abbey	1	acacia	3	according	23
Abe	1	academic	10	accordion	1
Abel	1	academics	1	accosted	2
Abell	1	Academy	4	account	10
abide	1	Accardo	1	accounted	2
abilities	1	accelerated	1	Accounting	1
ability	9	accent	1	accounts	2
ablaze	1	accented	1	accredited	1
able	24	accept	8	accumulation	1
Abner	1	acceptable	3	accurate	1
aboard	3	acceptance	4	accuse	1
abolish	2	accepted	5	accused	8
Abolition	1	accepting	2	Ace	3
abortive	2	access	3	Achaeans	1
about	147	accessories	1	Achaeans'	1
above	16	accessors	1	achieve	6
Abra	1	accident	7	achieved	3
Abraham	1	accidentally	1	achievement	15
abroad	4	acclaim	1	achievements	1
abrupt	1	acclaimed	2	achieves	1
absence	1	acclimatized	1	aching	1

Figure 4.4   Word list in alphabetical order

The words in the same text can also be sorted into frequency order as in Figure 4.5 where the most frequent word appears first. The word *the* is easily the top with over twice as many occurrences as the next word *of*. There is also a big gap between the top six words *the, of, and, to, a* and *in* and the next word *for*. Figure 4.6 shows part of a concordance of the word *I* in the humor section (R) of the Brown Corpus. Here each occurrence is identified by a reference consisting of the sample number and line number within the sample.

the	6383	have	265	home	131
of	2859	not	256	also	129
and	2184	Mrs&	253	her	121
to	2143	were	252	no	119
a	2122	would	246	over	119
in	2020	which	245	into	115
for	968	new	241	some	113
that	826	their	231	only	111
is	733	been	212	made	107
was	716	one	212	we	107
on	690	There	189	if	103
He	642	more	184	time	102
at	636	all	180	years	102
with	567	its	178	three	100
be	526	I	177	House	96
as	517	last	177	them	96
by	503	or	175	any	95
It	477	two	174	what	95
his	428	Mr&	170	can	94
said	406	when	169	week	94
will	389	up	168	before	93
from	353	other	164	him	93
are	329	out	162	may	93
This	319	first	158	City	91
an	311	state	153	under	91
has	301	After	151	could	87
but	283	about	147	now	87
had	280	president	142	school	87
who	268	year	142	four	82
They	267	than	138	Most	81

Figure 4.5   Word list in frequency order

4.3.2 Defining words

As we look at some other examples, the first question to consider is what constitutes a word. Some software packages include a built-in definition of a word. This is usually something surrounded by spaces, which is also almost always inadequate. The "words" in the Brown Corpus are relatively straightforward, but, as we saw in Figure 4.4, they include hyphens and apostrophes as well as numerals, percent and dollar signs, as well as additional symbols like "&" for an abbreviation in *Mr&* and *A&*. The

```
R01   026   and dunes They're better off,  I  tell you I saved their souls". The de
R01   026   hey're better off, I tell you   I  saved their souls". The detective, co
R01   061   rs I've been murdering women.   I  can lead you to every one of the bodi
R01   093   ean more publicity for Welch.   I  knew that both these cynics were wait
R01   100   eputation of a helpless girl!   I  studied Welch closely as the trial pr
R01   102   warted. It wasn't long before   I  sensed that there was something deepe
R01   108   erseded by some luckier chap.   I  did not rest until I had tracked the
R01   108   er chap. I did not rest until   I  had tracked the mystery down. Well, h
R01   141   these first days of the trial   I  didn't have as much time to commisera
R01   142   to commiserate with Viola as    I  should have liked. In the first place
R01   146   girl, no matter how innocent.   I  couldn't invite Viola to our house, f
R01   154   lly famous trade in pickles).   I  hated being dragged into the salons o
R01   164   at long last came a time when   I  broke away from Mother and her societ
R01   168   alas, to my own mother. When    I  arrived at Viola's I was shown, to my
R01   169   er. When I arrived at Viola's   I  was shown, to my surprise, into the <
R01   172   herself was preparing dinner.   I  sat and watched proceedings. There wa
R02   001   and cooked by Viola herself.    I  realized that Hamlet was faced with a
R02   005   themselves, after a fashion.    I  was saved from making the decision as
R02   013   clutched the hand with which    I  was trying to hold the phone, claimin
R02   016   ou hold on a second, please",   I  covered up the mouthpiece, and with m
R02   019   e remoter reaches of Siberia.   I  promised to illustrate the lecture, i
R02   021   n and recognizing the caller,   I  resumed my everyday voice. Soon we we
```

Figure 4.6   Concordance of word *I* in Section R of the Brown Corpus

user needs to decide whether these are in fact parts of words, and if so how they will be treated in the alphabetization process.

Non-alphabetic characters which have more than one meaning include

1 period (full stop), indicating the end of a sentence, an abbreviation, or a decimal point
2 apostrophe surrounding a quotation or direct speech, indicating the genitive or appearing in forms like don't and can't
3 hyphen, indicating a compound word or a typographic feature when a word is broken at the end of a line, or used as an em-rule

If a text is being keyboarded some of these problematic characters can be encoded at this stage. For example typographic hyphens can be eliminated and the entire word reconstituted, or periods which are abbreviations can be encoded as a different character.

At the simplest level, the text or other linguistic data is seen as a sequence of characters, most often corresponding directly to those characters on the keyboard or screen. These characters are almost always stored as 8-*bit bytes* giving, for example, a possible total of 256 characters, of which only 96 are easily accessible directly from the keyboard. These characters form a specific order within the computer, often called the internal collating sequence. In it upper and lower case letters appear different so that for example upper case *A* is different from lower case *a*. This fixed order is used by some software packages for sorting words, but even if upper and lower case letters can be made equivalent, it is inadequate to handle all but the simplest of texts.

In most applications for humanities research and teaching, much more flexibility is needed in the definition of an orthographic *word*. The user needs to be able to define the make-up of a word and the alphabetical sequence used for sorting words. OCP permits up to eight keyboard characters to represent one letter. This means that *ch*, *ll*, and *rr* in Spanish can be sorted as separate letters. In fact OCP has four major types of letter which are described below.

4.3.2.1 Alphabet: primary sorting

"Alphabet" letters make up the primary sorting **key** for alphabetizing words. They are defined in the order in which they are to be sorted with the possibility of declaring letters to be equal for sorting purposes, as is normally needed for upper and lower case letters. Figure 4.7 shows a word list of a short Spanish poem, where *chapotean* comes after *cuatro*, and *llega* after *Los*. It would be just as possible to define an alphabet where *z* is first and *a* is last, causing all beginning with *z* to appear first, followed by all beginning with *y*, *x*, *w*, etc. The numerals 0 1 2 3 4 5 6 7 8 9 are best treated as part of the alphabet since they occur frequently

A	3	escaleras	1	números	1
abandonados	1	esperanza	1	palomas	1
aguas	1	fruto	1	paraíso	1
al	1	furiosos	1	podridas	1
allí	1	gime	1	por	1
amores	1	habrá	1	porque	1
angustia	1	hay	1	posible	1
aristas	1	huesos	1	primeros	1
arte	1	huracán	1	que	4
aurora	3	inmensas	1	recibe	1
boca	1	juegos	1	saben	1
buscando	1	la	4	salen	1
cieno	2	las	4	sin	2
columnas	1	leyes	1	su	1
comprenden	1	Los	2	sudores	1
con	1	llega	1	sus	1
cuatro	1	mañana	1	taladran	1
chapotean	1	monedas	1	tiene	1
de	6	nadie	1	un	1
deshojados	1	nardos	1	van	1
devoran	1	negras	1	veces	1
dibujada	1	ni	2	y	4
en	2	niños	1	York	2
enjambres	1	no	2		
entre	1	Nueva	2		

Figure 4.7   Word list showing alphabetization of Spanish

enough as numbers, dates, currency symbols and weights and measures, all of which look like "words."

This mechanism for sorting words is adequate for most languages which use the Roman alphabet, but it is unable to place, for example, Old English *thorn* in the alphabetical position of *th*, that is in the middle of the *ts*. Neither can it easily handle Welsh and other languages which exhibit mutation. It is possible to define the correct alphabetical order for Greek, Hebrew, Russian, or other languages which do not use the Roman alphabet. In this case the display of a character on the screen or the printing of it must be treated as separate operations, independent of the functions of another application program.

Various utilities exist for screen display or printing of non-standard characters. In choosing suitable software, it is all too easy to be seduced by the ability to display or print certain characters, rather than to examine the functionality of the software to determine whether it is capable of performing the desired analyses.

4.3.2.2 Diacritics: secondary sorting

Some letters are better treated as **diacritic**s, that is, as a secondary sorting key for alphabetizing words. Hyphen and apostrophe are good examples in English. If the words *can't* and *cant* and *I'll* and *ill* occur, one might expect all the instances of *can't* to come immediately after all those of *cant* and all those of *I'll* immediately after all those of *ill*. These results cannot be achieved by placing the apostrophe anywhere in the alphabet. Figure 4.8 shows an example of *ill* and *I'll* followed by other entries beginning *ill-*. Note also that "*&*" used for abbreviations is also treated this way as is shown in *Ill&* for Illinois.

Accented characters are usually best treated in this way. Many existing electronic texts were created when only the 96 or so characters accessible directly from the keyboard were available. A common way of representing an acute or grave accent was to use / or \ immediately after the letter to which it belongs. For example *élève* would appear as *e/le\ve*. Other characters might be chosen for circumflex, cedilla, etc. Defining / and \ to be diacritics causes words which include these accented letters to appear in the alphabetical order in which they are normally found in a dictionary. For example *élève* would appear as a separate entry from *élevé*. OCP also provides a means for correctly sorting the accented characters on the PC's character set.

4.3.2.3 Padding: non-sorting letters

"Padding" letters have no effect on the way a word is sorted. Words containing them are sorted together with the same sequence of letters without them. Figure 4.9 shows the effect of this on *ill* and *I'll* which is now only one headword. If "*&*" was also defined as a padding letter, *Ill&* would also appear as the same headword as *ill*. Note also the effect on *its* where *it's* appears in entry A03 031.

4.3.2.4 Punctuation: word separators

Punctuation or word separators normally include all the regular punctuation characters, plus any other additional symbols which separate words, including space. Although in most situations it is better to treat a hyphen in English as a diacritic, Figure 4.10 shows what happens when it is defined as a word separator. The entries for *long* include *long-term*, *long-time*, *long-life*, and *long-bodied*. These entries would also appear under *term*, *time*, *life*, and *bodied*.

```
              ill  2
A04  157  early concluded that Laos was ill suited to be an ally, unlike its mo
A19  079  "fair". Police said he became ill while parked in front of a barber  s

              I'll  9
A06  177  r the primary", he promised, "I'll be explicit on where I stand to br
A11  092  ", Hansen added, "but I think I'll move better carrying a little less
A12  165  aid Stram, quipping, "I think I'll put that play in the book". The  e
A14  164  , a man who knows the rules. "I'll do as you say, but I'll also play
A14  165  les. "I'll do as you say, but I'll also play a provisional ball and g
A19  061  hese are the board's minutes. I'll write what you tell me to". For  a
A21  109  people anywhere in the world. I'll need more than a single day to fin
A39  110  boy. "that's [Yogi] Berra's. I'll never forget one time I struck out
A39  125  a team of nine angry men and I'll give you a team of nine gentlemen

              Ill&  5
A03  170  te Republican Leader Dirksen [Ill&] and House Republican leader Charl
A08  011  at Scott Field in Belleville, Ill&.   Before entering the service, Pfa
A15  132  ave a doubleheader at Quincy, Ill&, Saturday. #HAPPY HITTING# if it's
A17  162  & Howard M& Dean of Hinsdale, Ill&, and Mrs& James A& Reeder of Shrev
A28  001  ir fellow builders"._ELBURN, ILL&_ - Farm machinery dealer Bob Houtz

              illegal  3
A03  040  "by unfair and fundamentally illegal means". Karns said that the cas
A36  155  tion strike and would make it illegal for any union to act in concert
A39  022  t the knock-down pitch is not illegal. Experts point to the thinning
```

Figure 4.8 Concordance showing apostrophe and & as diacritics

```
                           ill              11

A04  157   early concluded that Laos was ill suited to be an ally, unlike its mo
A06  177   r the primary", he promised, "I'll be explicit on where I stand to br
A11  092   ", Hansen added, "but I think I'll move better carrying a little less
A12  165   aid Stram, quipping, "I think I'll put that play in the book". The e
A14  164   , a man who knows the rules. "I'll do as you say, but I'll also play
A14  165   les. "I'll do as you say, but I'll also play a provisional ball and g
A19  061   hese are the board's minutes. I'll write what you tell me to". For a
A19  079   "fair". Police said he became ill while parked in front of a barber s
A21  109   people anywhere in the world. I'll need more than a single day to fin
A39  110   boy. "That's [Yogi] Berra's. I'll never forget one time I struck out
A39  125   a team of nine angry men and I'll give you a team of nine gentlemen

                          Ill&              5

A03  170   te Republican Leader Dirksen [Ill&] and House Republican Leader Charl
A08  011   at Scott Field in Belleville, Ill&.  Before entering the service, Pfa
A15  132   ave a doubleheader at Quincy, Ill&, Saturday. #HAPPY HITTING# if it's
A17  162   Howard and M& Dean of Hinsdale, Ill&, and Mrs& James A& Reeder of Shrev
A28  001   ir fellow builders". _ELBURN, ILL&_ - Farm machinery dealer Bob Houtz

                           its              203

A01  044   which has been under fire for its practices in the appointment of app
A01  047   court "has incorporated into its operating procedures the recommenda
A01  050   's wards from undue costs and its appointed and elected servants from
A01  106   em which the party opposes in its platform. Sam Caldwell, State High
A01  114   rgia Legislature will wind up its 1961 session Monday and head for ho
A02  004   tered down considerably since its rejection by two previous Legislatu
A02  069   NATE} quickly whipped through its meager fare of House bills approved
A02  077   ulf Coast district. Money for its construction will be sought later o
A02  129   that Dallas is paying for all its water program by local bonds, and t
A03  031   retary, replied, "I would say it's got to go thru several more drafts
A03  176   g", but made no prediction on its fate in the House. _WASHINGTON, FEB
```

Figure 4.9 Concordance showing apostrophe as padding letter

4.3.2.5   Using the letter definitions

A "word" can then be defined as something which consists of a combination of letters of alphabet, diacritic and, possibly, padding status. Punctuation letters separate words. The word is most often the basic search unit, and, with a little ingenuity, the letter definitions can be manipulated to search for words when they occur only under certain conditions. For example, if the normal end-of-sentence punctuation is given alphabet status, it is possible to look for words only when they occur at the ends of sentences by including the punctuation as part of the word.

4.3.3   Sorting words

Words can be sorted by their endings, a process normally called **reverse alphabetical**. This is illustrated in Figure 4.11, part of an index of words ending in *ed*. Note that *glanced* comes before *financed* since, working backwards from the end of the word, the first letter that is different is *l* in *glanced* and *n* in *financed*. *Denounced, announced,* and *pronounced* are all close together. See Chapter 5 for more on reverse alphabetization.

As we have already seen, words can also be sorted by their frequency, starting with the most frequent word, or least frequent, or even by their length where the longest or the shortest word comes first.

4.3.4   Selecting words

The concordance may include every word or only selected words. Words can be selected in several ways. Wild card characters denoting any number of letters including none, or any single letter can be specified. It is also possible to look for words occurring a certain number of times, or for sequences of words (phrases) possibly also containing wild card characters. Here are some simple examples:

*ing   all words ending in *ing*
*as *as   all places where there are two consecutive words which end in *as*
in * of   all places where the word *in* is followed by *of* with one word intervening

Figure 4.12 shows the result of a search for all words ending in *ing*. As can be seen, it can be used in a fairly crude way to find all present participles. Although some unwanted words such as *anything* also appear, they can be deleted or ignored when the results are being studied. In many cases for the ordinary working linguist, this simple approach can be much more productive than attempting to use morphological or syntactic analysis programs, which are never completely accurate.

```
                                              long

A01   167   y raises. _COLQUITT_ - After a    long    , hot controversy, Miller County ha
A02   178   he report, culminating a year      long    study of the ~ADC program in Cook
A02   180   re consulting firm, listed 10      long    range recommendations designed to
A04   011   who have never, or not for a       long    time, had such problems. The night
A04   070   have to carry out obligations      long    since laid down, but never complet
A07   099    1958. This would provide for      long    -term Federal loans for constructio
A07   159   made by a panel of eight in a      long    and detailed report. The report wa
A08   032   deral buildings, some a block      long    and all about seven-stories high.
A08   065   serving the political scene a      long    time, no script from the past is w
A08   173   ne that most try to avoid, as      long    as they can see an alternative app
A10   024   the people in, and added, "so      long    as people rebel, we must not give
A10   189   The U&S& mails to defraud as       long    as there is evidence of a conspira
A11   060   ror. Then Robinson slammed a       long    double to left center to score bot
A12   063   ng, he said: "that won't last      long    ". It didn't; Monday, he had four L
A12   090   the game's, final play, was a      long    pass by quarterback Bob McNaughton
A13   177   ird Frank Robinson hammered a      long    home run deep into the corner of t
A14   079   , Shea owned and operated the      long    Island Indians, a minor league pro
A14   135   n gully. Willie's partner was      long    Jim Barnes, who tried to keep coun
A14   138   on project. "Thirteen", said       long    Jim. "Nae, man", said Willie, "ye
A15   036   ing back in the groove before      long    . Our pitching is much better than
A15   153   how they're handled, just as       long    as their names are spelled correct
A19   052   iams, Jr&, a board member and      long    -time critic of the superintendent,
A19   184   g market today. Trouble-free,      long    -life, quality components will play
A21   133   ern High School in June. The       long    crisis in Laos appeared nearing a
A22   014   h are available to it only so      long    as it conforms to the aforemention
A23   040   d, he said, and added Field's      long    service in state government and we
A24   197   o that he was associated with      long    Island University in Brooklyn. _AS
A26   020   he Morton Foods issue was hot      long    before it was on the market. Indee
A26   055   ic mind of late. Foods, which      long    had been considered "recession res
A29   034   use they are designed for her      long    -bodies silhouette. She also likes
A29   077   s must have ogled him all day      long    - but he dutifully kept his eye on
A29   145   hed panels decorate a 60-inch      long    chest. An interesting approach to
```

Figure 4.10   Concordance showing hyphen treated as a word separator

```
glanced     2   A40 116, A42 058        A17 007, A17 039, A19 001, A19 144,
                                        A20 055, A21 034, A21 096, A21 134,
financed    2   A03 086, A44 034        A21 139, A21 166, A22 001, A24 189,
                                        A25 084, A25 197, A27 097, A28 108,
advanced    6   A20 077, A27 065,       A32 004, A32 011, A32 080, A33 032,
A27 066, A34 163, A36 003, A44 022      A34 013, A37 192, A38 125, A40 046,
                                        A40 065, A41 122, A41 146
experienced 4   A01 024, A10 169,
A40 167, A44 121                        pronounced  3   A09 108, A19 037,
                                        A37 087
silenced    1   A42 125
                                        forced      8   A02 187, A06 031,
commenced   1   A41 114                 A14 023, A14 068, A19 194, A28 015,
                                        A36 056, A36 144
sentenced   3   A20 041, A20 166,
A23 069                                 enforced    3   A02 020, A03 187,
                                        A19 103
convinced   6   A31 128, A34 007,
A34 022, A34 051, A34 102, A42 020      divorced    1   A20 015

ensconced   1   A40 012                 reduced     6   A02 041, A11 119,
                                        A20 089, A28 069, A28 115, A35 183
bounced     5   A11 048, A11 056,
A11 123, A25, 193, A38 030              produced    6   A01 002, A33 070,
                                        A34 032, A34 036, A34 153, A39 025
denounced   1   A36 132
                                        reproduced  1  A20 058
announced   37  A01 085, A04 051,
A04 189, A06 085, A08 002, A10 002,     introduced  10 A02 036, A06 128,
A11 152, A12 121, A14 006, A15 011,     A06 166, A15 089, A20 145, A20 146,
```

Figure 4.11   Index showing words sorted by their endings

Figure 4.13 shows the results of a search for *in* * *of* where the three words together form a special kind of headword.

4.3.5 Sorting contexts

Normally all the occurrences of a specific headword in a concordance appear in the order in which they occur in the text, but it may also be interesting to look for patterns before or after these occurrences. In a right-sorted concordance the entries for each headword are given according to the alphabetical order of what comes after the headword. This has the effect of bringing together all the places where the head-word introduces or forms part of the same phrase. Figure 4.14 shows a right-sorted concordance of the occurrences of *that* in Section R of the

```
                               allotting    1
A26 006 the stock; it was more one of allotting a few shares to a number of c


                               allowing    5
A03 110 e care under a "unit formula" allowing more of such care for those wh
A20 090 size, and also in complexity, allowing a single propeller to be used,
A23 140 cal experience in business by allowing them actually to form small co
A30 157 e height of the light socket, allowing three to four inches above the
A36 029 Defense Department regulation allowing costs of a type generally reco


                               amazing    1
A39 033 d every challenger was Ruth's amazing September surge. In the final m


                               amending    1
A07 098 some quick progress on a bill amending the national Defense Education


                               announcing    2
A21 083 Association, followed that by announcing plans last night for a door-
A32 010 Cecilia Orchestra in Rome. In announcing Jorda's return, the orchestr


                               anything    10
A13 094 was a double-crosser and said anything he (Liston) got was through a
A13 155 ally they were helpless to do anything about the nationwide policy}.
A26 052 ket at, and everyone who knew anything about it expected the Morton s
A31 115 and business firms. It there  anything a frustrated individual can do
A31 125 ism, but never felt there was anything he, as an individual, could do
A35 126 cademic world there is seldom anything so dramatic as a strike or a b
A37 116 was the only man who could do anything effective. In a tense, closed-
A39 121 by Farrell: "I'm not learning anything on the bench. Play me". (Farre
A40 017 hing" just "in case he spills anything", Frankie got so made at the ch
A40 066 ste is gaudy. I'm useless for anything but racing cars. I'm ruddy laz


                               apartment-building    1
A19 176 uilders to concentrate in the apartment-building field. Although econ


                               appealing    2
A30 171 calloped edge is particularly appealing. TODAY'S trend toward furnit
A41 149 mumba was a Communist. Before appealing to the U&N& or to Russia, he
```

Figure 4.12   Concordance of words ending in *ing*

Brown Corpus. An examination of the references (R02 101, R06 151, R06 089, etc.) shows that these entries are not in the order in which they occur in the text. They begin with all the places where *that* is followed by *the*. We see three occurrences of *that the girls* and three of *that there was*. The entries can also be given according to what comes to the left of the headword. In Figure 4.15 we can see all the places where, for example *said that*, *say that*, *so that*, etc. occur. In either case the user can

```
A11  053  el's wild pitch into the dirt   in front of          8
A11  148  save place money only a head    in front of  the plate. The Flock added
A19  067  h a recording machine sitting   in front of  Glen T& Hallowell's Milties
A19  079  id he became ill while parked   in front of  him.   The Board of County C
A20  155  d his south bound express bus   in front of  a barber shop at 229 West P
A30  070  doesn't like to be driven up    in front of  Dunbar Vocational High scho
A30  085  of status when I am driven up   in front of  a school in a car driven by
A38  164  o he put the ball in a bunker   in front of  work in a car driven by my
                                                       the green. His bogey 4 on t

A16  151  ana Mason, also an ex-singer.   In honor of          2
A17  012  planning a luncheon next week   In honor of  the Wackers' new baby. Fur
                                          in honor of  {Mrs& J& Clinton Bowman}, w

A23  136  mpany set records with $2,170   in sales of          1
                                          in sales of  its products, a selection o

A25  178  ney for the loan association,   in satisfaction of   1
                                          in satisfaction of  mechanic's liens on

A22  126  ng into the home of relatives   in search of         1
                                          in search of  his wife, hitting his uncl

A23  076  ries of 15 Portland robberies   in spring of         1
                                          in spring of  1959 in which the holdup m

A30  021  pment industry to raise funds   in support of        1
                                          in support of  this cultural center for
```

Figure 4.13 Concordance of phrase in <anyword> of

```
R02 101  was wine in the pot roast or that the chicken had been marinated in
R06 151  ce fiction has always assumed that the creatures on the planets of a
R06 089  t you must have heard it said that the drawing-room disappeared forev
R06 153  ed fruit bats. It seems to me that the first human being to reach one
R02 004  on an ascending scale, seeing that the girls dressed themselves, afte
R02 168  e kitchen. Then, I remembered that the girls had had a banana for des
R02 029   and I be there. I discovered that the girls had shrewdly vacated the
R09 065  the widespread Western belief that the Lord Buddha is the most compas
R09 172  ovelist's carping phrase, was that the lower lip was a trifle too vol
R09 113  fter a while, we became aware that the money was disappearing as fast
R09 163  to continue your vocation, is that the next time you're attracted by
R09 130  rning, we discovered not only that the pennies were missing from the
R06 177   cardinal rules of writing is that the reader should be able to get s
R08 007  dead at his feet, informs him that the Saracens have invaded Silesia,
R08 162   Mailer), but no one can deny that the screen crackles with electrici
R07 011  ark and it's a city ordinance that the statues cannot be crawled on".
R03 018   two months, it was announced that the studio "owed" the government a
R04 094  sturdy legs to a heavy top so that the whole thing didn't wobble like
R08 035  probably very few people know that the word "visrhanik" that is bante
R02 076  ld be no dust anywhere and so that their children would color in the
R02 093  ite human. It seemed, indeed, that their house was not so much a home
R01 011  Avocado Avenue, they learned that their man, having paused to get oi
R02 045  mber, and sitter to call (not that there was much of a choice, since
R01 102  t wasn't long before I sensed that there was something deeper than ov
R02 100  ". She always let it be known that there was wine in the pot roast or
R04 020   became increasingly apparent that there were to be no dogs in the pi
R04 004  found it. It wasn't his fault that these things were so. The difficul
R08 111  vernment tutor. The innocence that they tried to conceal at the begin
R02 094  ther a perfect stage set, and that they were actors who had been hand
R02 057  she and Herb met and decided that they were in love. They were marri
R02 132  ia were distinguished only in that they were, to me at least, indisti
R04 025  they would become so confused that they would have nervous breakdowns
```

Figure 4.14   Concordance showing occurrences of *that* sorted by right context

choose whether punctuation should be examined as the concordance entries are sorted.

4.3.6 Word frequency distributions

Besides the simple word frequency lists, OCP and other programs can produce more sophisticated distributions. A frequency profile, as shown in Figure 4.16, shows the number of words which occur once, twice, three times, etc. up to the most frequent word. Cumulative and percentage totals are also given. The type/token ratio is a measure of the spread or richness of the vocabulary. Types are different words, and tokens are instances of each type. For example, if the word *and* occurs 100 times

```
R06 017  seem to remember", he said, "that in an interview ten years ago you
R06 089  t you must have heard it said that the drawing-room disappeared forev
R07 170  herself with curiosity. "say that again", she pleaded. She laughed a
R09 155  oks at it, therefore, I'd say that your horoscope for this autumn is
R06 110  I said. "Oh, I forgot to say that if one is taken to the funny house
R05 031  would you care to have us say that you were misquoted in regard to it
R06 101  disturbing, as when one says that a friend is acting funny; and frig
R08 174  gical culmination of a school that started with Monet, progressed thr
R07 172  ss. "You what"? She could see that Mr& Gorboduc was intrigued; the ho
R09 152  rly a man <in extremis>. "See that guy"? the operator asked pityingly
R05 055  standard device. ""Do you see that pretty girl standing next to the c
R02 004  on an ascending scale, seeing that the girls dressed themselves, afte
R02 031  in the living room. It seemed that I would be the gainer if I accepte
R01 002  ograph of Carco! For it seems that Barco, fancying himself a ladies'
R05 162  ", said the woman, "I've seen that picture already". Another brand o
R01 102  t wasn't long before I sensed that there was something deeper than ov
R02 147  that I mistrusted bake shops that called themselves "Sanitary Bake S
R03 007  round and Major Bowes shows) "That Man in the White House, like some
R02 175  received in a stunned silence that was evidence in itself of the dear
R04 130  n and it all seemed so simple that he didn't like to disclose his ign
R07 055  her feet, winking and smiling that enormous smile (she had lots of wo
R02 076  ld be no dust anywhere and so that their children would color in the
R03 138  Mother Cabrini, and timed so that its release data would coincide wi
R04 094  sturdy legs to a heavy top so that the whole thing didn't wobble like
R07 021  "Never mind. I know something that is much more fun that we can do on
```

Figure 4.15   Concordance showing occurrences of *that* sorted by left context

in a text, it is 1 type and 100 tokens. It will be seen that the type/token ratio yields a number between 0 and 1. The closer it is to 1, the richer the vocabulary. The type/token ratio can be used for comparisons between texts, but is dependent on the length of the texts and is therefore only effective when the texts are approximately the same length.

4.3.7 Concordances and interactive retrieval

Interactive retrieval programs provide some of the same facilities, but they work by querying an index which has previously been built by a special ancillary program. The retrieval of words is much faster, especially when the text is large. However, for this approach the word definitions must be made when the index is built, and cannot be redefined for each query. This can mean less flexibility overall. Some interactive retrieval programs do not allow a search on word endings, for example for **ing*. If they do allow it, they may take a long time because there is no reverse index to search and so they must do a sequential search on the word list. For the individual scholar, TACT is probably the most widely-used text retrieval program.

FREQUENCY	RELATIVE FREQUENCY	NUMBER SUCH	WORDS IN FREQUENCY	VOCAB TOTAL	WORD TOTAL	PERC. OF VOCAB	PERC. OF WORDS	PERC. OF WORDS IN FREQ
1	0.00112	6995	6995	6995	6995	52.82	7.87	7.87
2	0.00225	2053	4106	9048	11101	68.32	12.49	4.62
3	0.00337	1018	3054	10066	14155	76.00	15.92	3.43
4	0.00450	624	2496	10690	16651	80.72	18.73	2.81
5	0.00562	456	2280	11146	18931	84.16	21.29	2.56
6	0.00675	325	1950	11471	20881	86.61	23.49	2.19
7	0.00787	233	1631	11704	22512	88.37	25.32	1.83
8	0.00900	188	1504	11892	24016	89.79	27.01	1.69
9	0.01012	133	1197	12025	25213	90.80	28.36	1.35
10	0.01125	118	1180	12143	26393	91.69	29.68	1.33
11	0.01237	100	1100	12243	27493	92.44	30.92	1.24
12	0.01350	82	984	12325	28477	93.06	32.03	1.11
13	0.01462	77	1001	12402	29478	93.64	33.15	1.13
14	0.01575	61	854	12463	30332	94.10	34.11	0.96
15	0.01687	59	885	12522	31217	94.55	35.11	1.00
212	0.23844	2	424	132.6	57477	99.71	64.64	0.48
231	0.25981	1	231	13207	57708	99.72	64.90	0.26
241	0.27105	1	241	13208	57949	99.73	65.18	0.27
245	0.27555	1	245	13209	58194	99.74	65.45	0.28
246	0.27668	1	246	13210	58440	99.74	65.73	0.28
252	0.28343	1	252	13211	58692	99.75	66.01	0.28
253	0.28455	1	253	13212	58945	99.76	66.30	0.28
256	0.28793	1	256	13213	59201	99.77	66.58	0.29
265	0.29805	1	265	13214	59466	99.77	66.88	0.30
267	0.30030	1	267	13215	59733	99.78	67.18	0.30
268	0.30142	1	268	13216	60001	99.79	67.48	0.30
280	0.31492	1	280	13217	60281	99.80	67.80	0.31
283	0.31829	1	283	13218	60564	99.80	68.12	0.32
301	0.33854	1	301	13219	60865	99.81	68.46	0.34
311	0.34978	1	311	13220	61176	99.82	68.81	0.35
319	0.35878	1	319	13221	61495	99.83	69.16	0.36
329	0.37003	1	329	13222	61824	99.83	69.53	0.37
353	0.39702	1	353	13223	62177	99.84	69.93	0.40
389	0.43751	1	389	13224	62566	99.85	70.37	0.44
406	0.45663	1	406	13225	62972	99.86	70.83	0.46
428	0.48137	1	428	13226	63400	99.86	71.31	0.48
477	0.53649	1	477	13227	63877	99.87	71.84	0.54
503	0.56573	1	503	13228	64380	99.88	72.41	0.57
517	0.58147	1	517	13229	64897	99.89	72.99	0.58
526	0.59160	1	526	13230	65423	99.89	73.58	0.59
567	0.63771	1	567	13231	65990	99.90	74.22	0.64
636	0.71531	1	636	13232	66626	99.91	74.93	0.72
642	0.72206	1	642	13233	67268	99.92	75.66	0.72
690	0.77605	1	690	13234	67958	99.92	76.43	0.78
716	0.80529	1	716	13235	68674	99.93	77.24	0.81
733	0.82441	1	733	13236	69407	99.94	78.06	0.82
826	0.92901	1	826	13237	70233	99.95	78.99	0.93
968	1.08872	1	968	13238	71201	99.95	80.08	1.09
GT1000	1.12583	6	17711	13244	88912	100.00	100.00	19.92

TYPE/TOKEN RATIO:0.14896
TOTAL WORDS READ   = 88912
TOTAL WORDS SELECTED = 88912
TOTAL WORDS PICKED   = 88912
TOTAL WORDS SAMPLED   = 88912
TOTAL WORDS KEPT   = 88912
TOTAL VOCABULARY   = 13244

Figure 4.16   Part of a word frequency distribution

4.3.8   Limitation

It is important to understand these two limitations:

1 **Homograph**s (words which are spelled the same but have different meanings) are not separated. In a word list or index, only the head-word is given and there is no way to determine whether several meanings are present for a homographic word. It is only when the contexts given in a concordance are inspected that the different meanings of (for example) *lead* as a verb "to lead" and two meanings of the noun *lead* (as "leash" and "a metal") can be seen. These need to be separated manually if further analyses of word counts are to be performed. Some concordances omit common words, but this can also lead to problems with homographs; for example *will* as an auxiliary verb, as well as two meanings of the noun: "wish" and "testament".

2 **Lemmatization**, that is, bringing together different forms of the same lemma, is not normally carried out. Depending on the nature of the research, it may be necessary to lemmatize manually or at least not to be dependent on counts which have been performed on unlemmatized forms. In some languages most forms of the same lemma appear close together in an alphabetical list, e.g. *bring, brought, bringing, brings,* but for other lemmas, forms may need to be brought together from different parts of the list.

4.4   CONCLUSION

Much computer-aided text-based research in the humanities is carried out using the tools and techniques described in this chapter. Applications include lexical research, stylistic analysis, lexicography, and almost any other task based on finding specific instances or repeated patterns of words or "pseudo-words." It is important to be aware of the limitations outlined in Section 4.3.8, but it is also true that judicious use of wild card characters in specifying search terms can often yield useful results very quickly. Certain types of clauses or constructions can be identified by words which introduce them. Inflections can be studied by specifying words that end in certain sequences of characters. Punctuation or other special characters can also be used to find specific sequences of words. It is now generally accepted that common words or function words, those words which are not dependent on the content of a text, can be used in many circumstances to discriminate style and genre. Vocabulary frequencies can then be subjected to further statistical analyses. Numerical studies of style and vocabulary are not especially new, but with the advent of computers much larger quantities of texts can be analyzed, giving an overall picture that would be impractical to find by any other means.

If suitable electronic text is already available, progress in a text database project can be rapid. The linguist may find that he or she has too many results to digest easily. If the text needs to be created first, a project may not appear to produce visible results for a long time. A little experimentation with the chosen software on a small amount of text can be very encouraging to someone faced with a lot of proofreading and editing of data. Much time can be spent in reformatting data, from an OCR scanner, or for a particular program, and here it is sometimes worth investing time in learning a macro language or other tool which can speed this up rather than working through the text line by line with a word-processor or *editor*. The advice given in this chapter should help linguists determine how useful textual databases and the tools that work with them can be. Many examples now exist of successful projects and we can expect these tools to become part of the everyday working life of many linguists. With a clear understanding of the limitations, much can be accomplished with little investment of time.

Appendix

PART I PRINT RESOURCES

Biber, Douglas. 1998. *Variation Across Speech and Writing*. Cambridge: Cambridge University Press. Uses computational techniques to analyse the linguistic characteristics of different spoken and written genres. A useful place to start for topics more advanced than those discussed in this paper.

Johansson, Stig. 1994–5. Quo vadis? Reflections on the Use of Computer Corpora in Linguistics, *Computers and the Humanities*, 28:243–52. A survey up to 1994 with special attention given to the pitfalls. Also has a good bibliography.

Lancashire, Ian (ed.). 1991. *The Humanities Computing Yearbook 1989–90*. Oxford: Oxford University Press. Compendium of bibliography, software and electronic resources for humanities computing, all verified by the editor.

Lancashire, Ian, in collaboration with John Bradley, Willard McCarty, Michael Stairs, and T.R. Wooldridge. 1996. *Using TACT with Electronic Texts*. New York, Modern Language Association. Detailed description of the TACT programs, concentrating on their use for literature. Accompanying CD-ROM contains over 2500 texts.

Literary and Linguistic Computing. 1986– . Journal of the Association for Literary and Linguistic Computing. Published by Oxford University Press. See especially Volume 8, Number 4 (1993) and Volume 9, Number 1 (1994) for papers from the Pisa Workshop on Corpora, 1992.

Nijmegen Institute for Cognition and Information. 1993. *Optical Character Recognition in the Historical Discipline: Proceedings of an International Workgroup*. Netherlands Historical Data Archive, Nijmegen Institute for Cognition and Information. Papers assessing the value of OCR for the humanities. "Historical" is interpreted broadly.

Oxford University Computing Service. 1988. *Micro-OCP Manual*. Oxford: Oxford University Press.1993] rprt. Author: Susan Hockey. Contains description of COCOA markup format as well as functions of OCP program.

Sinclair, John M. 1991. *Corpus, Concordance, Collocation*. Oxford: Oxford University Press. Good introduction from the Editor-in-chief of Cobuild.

Sperberg-McQueen, C.M and Lou Burnard (eds). 1994. *Guidelines for the Encoding and Interchange of Electronic Texts*. 2 vols. Chicago and Oxford: Association for Computers and the Humanities, Association for Computational Linguistics, Association for Literary and Linguistic Computing. Also available in various electronic formats from the TEI Web site http://www.uic.edu/orgs/tei. Complete specification of the TEI Encoding Guidelines. Chapter 2, "A Gentle Introduction to SGML," is highly recommended.

PART II   SOFTWARE

MicroConcord: Concordance program for DOS developed by Mike Scott and Tim Johns. Produces various kinds of concordances and collocations. Designed specifically for intermediate and advanced students of English as a foreign language. Published by Oxford University Press. See MicroConcord and the MicroConcord Corpus Collections. Overview at http://www1.oup.co.uk/oup/elt/software/mc?

Monoconc for Windows: Concordance program for Windows developed by Michael Barlow. Designed for use by linguists, language teachers, and students. Published by Athelstan. See http://www.nol.net/~athel/mono.html

Oxford Concordance Program (OCP) and MicroOCP: Powerful concordance program developed at Oxford University Computing Service by Susan Hockey and Jeremy Martin. OCP runs on several mainframe platforms including Unix. MicroOCP is implemented for DOS and is available from Order Department, Oxford University Press, 2001 Evans Road, Cary, NC, 27513, USA. E-mail: orders@oup-usa.org; http://www.oup-usa.org

TACT: Text Analysis Computing Tools developed by a team at the University of Toronto. Suite of programs for interactive text analysis. Available via ftp from ftp.chass.utoronto.ca/pub/cch/tact/. See also Lancashire *et al.* (1996).

PART III   NETWORK RESOURCES

British National Corpus (BNC): A 100 million word collection of samples of written and spoken language from a wide range of sources, designed to represent a wide cross-section of current British English, both spoken and written. The corpus is encoded in SGML and searchable via the SARA retrieval program. Access is restricted to within Europe. http://info.ox.ac.uk/bnc

Catalog of Projects in Electronic Text (CPET): A catalog of projects that create and analyze electronic text in the humanities, compiled at Georgetown University. It includes more than 300 projects working on primary materials such as literary works, historical documents, and linguistic data available from commercial vendors and scholarly sources. Although it has not been updated since early 1993, CPET is a very useful source of information.
gopher://guvax.georgetown.edu

Cobuild: A department of HarperCollins Publishers, specializing in the preparation of reference works for language. Based within the School of English at the University of Birmingham, UK, Cobuild has developed a very large corpus of English known as the Bank of English. CobuildDirect, a 50-million word corpus, is available on-line as a subscription service. A free demo can be sampled.
http://titania.cobuild.collins.co.uk

Corpus Linguistics Web site: Maintained by Michael Barlow, Rice University. Contains pointers to corpora in many languages, software, courses and bibliography. A useful starting point.
http://www.ruf.rice.edu/~barlow/corpus.html

European Corpus Initiative (ECI/MCI): Founded to oversee the acquisition and preparation of a large multilingual corpus. It has produced Multilingual Corpus I (ECI/MCI), a CD-ROM containing over 98 million words, covering most of the major European languages, as well as Turkish, Japanese, Russian, Chinese, Malay, and more. It is available to researchers for a modest fee.
http://www.elsnet.org/resources/eciCorpus.html

International Computer Archive of Modern and Medieval English (ICAME): An international organization of linguists and information scientists working with English machine-readable texts. It has compiled an archive of English text corpora in machine-readable form, which resides at the Norwegian Computing Centre for the Humanities (NCCH) in Bergen, Norway. The ICAME CD-ROM contains several well-known corpora including Brown and its British English equivalent (LOB). The ICAME Web site also holds the archive of the corpora list.
http://www.hd.uib.no/icame.html

International Corpus of English (ICE): ICE began in 1990 with the primary aim of providing material for comparative studies of varieties of English throughout the world. A related aim is to provide resources for research into English as an international language. Each of the twenty participating countries is collecting, computerizing, and analyzing a corpus of one million words of their own national or regional variety of English, spoken or written between 1990 and 1996.
http://www.ucl.ac.uk/english-usage/ice.htm

Linguistic Data Consortium (LDC): An open consortium of universities, companies, and government research laboratories. Hosted at the University of Pennsylvania, it creates, collects, and distributes speech and text databases, lexicons, and other resources for research and development purposes. Includes ACL/DCI CD-ROM. Some of the LDC material can be purchased by non-members.
http://www.ldc.upenn.edu

Oxford Text Archive (OTA): Contains electronic versions of literary works by many major authors in Greek, Latin, English and a dozen or more other languages, including collections, and corpora of unpublished materials prepared by field workers in linguistics and electronic versions of some standard reference works. The total size exceeds a gigabyte and there are over 2000 titles in its catalogue.
http://info.ox.ac.uk/ota

SGML Web site: Maintained by Robin Cover of Academic Computing, Summer Institute for Linguistics, this Web site contains everything possible about SGML and its applications. There are many pointers to academic applications.
http://www.sil.org/sgml/sgml.html

Text Encoding Initiative (TEI): Contains information about the TEI, how to obtain copies of the TEI Guidelines in print or electronic form, archives of technical discussions and pointers to projects that are using the TEI.
http://www.uic.edu/orgs/tei

Tutorial: Concordances and Corpora: Catherine Ball's excellent tutorial derived from her Corpus Linguistics course at Georgetown University. Includes examples prepared on a Macintosh computer.
http://www.georgetown.edu/cball/corpora/tutorial.html

Chapter 5

The Unix™ language family

John M. Lawler

5.1 GENERAL

The Unix™[1] operating system is used on a wide variety of computers (including but not limited to most workstation-class machines made by Sun, Hewlett-Packard, MIPS, NeXT, DEC, IBM[2], and many others), in one or another version. If one is around computers almost anywhere, one is within reach of a computer running Unix. Indeed, more often than not Unix is the only choice available for many computing tasks like e-mail, number-crunching, or running file servers and Web sites. One of the reasons for the ubiquity of Unix is that it is the most influential operating system in history; it has strongly affected, and contributed features and development philosophy to, almost all other operating systems.

Understanding any kind of computing without knowing anything about Unix is not unlike trying to understand how English works without knowing anything about the Indo-European family: that is, it's not impossible, but it's far more difficult than it ought to be, because there appears to be too much unexplainable arbitrariness.

In this chapter I provide a linguistic sketch[3] of the Unix operating system and its family of "languages". I use the word *language* here in its usual sense in computing contexts; since computer languages are not at all the same kind of thing as natural human languages, clearly this is a metaphorical usage. However, modern linguistic theory, strongly influenced as it is by computer science, is capable of describing the Unix language family rather well, because these "languages" possess some of the ideal characteristics posited by linguistic theories: they are completely regular, they exist in a homogeneous community, they are unambiguous, they are context-free, they are modular in design and structure, they are acquired (by computers, if not by humans) instantaneously and identically, they are universally interpretable in an identical fashion (barring performance details), and there is in principle no difference between one user and any other. Consequently the metaphor has considerable utility here for anyone familiar with linguistics. This situation is not in fact coincidental, since Unix was designed in the first place by people familiar with modern syntactic theory and its computer science analogs, and it shows. As a result, linguists will find much here they can recognize, though perhaps in unfamiliar surroundings. To that extent this chapter is simply applied linguistics. But Unix is also useful for applying linguistics, as I attempt to demonstrate.

5.2   HISTORY AND ETHNOGRAPHY OF COMPUTING

Unix is an *operating system* (*OS*). This is a special type of computer program that is, in a very important sense, a syntactic theory that completely constrains (i.e., defines, enables, and limits) all the programs that can run on a particular computer. In effect, the computer *per se* runs only the OS, and the OS runs everything else. Up until the 1970s, and for some time thereafter, it was normal in the computer industry for an operating system to be *proprietary*; that is, it was typically developed and sold by the makers of a particular computer along with the computer, and was limited to running on that computer alone. Any program that was to be run on that computer would have to be compatible with its OS, which varied markedly from computer to computer, limiting the possibility of widespread use of any program. Apple's Macintosh-OS has been a proprietary operating system for most of its existence, for instance, and the same is true of DEC's VMS; thus a program that runs on a Macintosh will not run on any other machine[4]. MS-DOS, on the other hand (which has been influenced significantly by Unix), is an example of a non-proprietary (or *open*) OS. Unix was the first successful open operating system.

Unix began in 1969 at Bell Laboratories in New Jersey. Ken Thompson, a member of the technical staff, put together a small operating system, and over the next several years, modified and developed it in collaboration with his colleagues, notably Dennis Ritchie and Brian Kernighan. This group[5] was also instrumental in developing at the same time two programming phenomena that have become totally integrated into Unix, and vice versa: the Software Tools movement, often called a "philosophy"[6], and the *C* programming language.[7] They produced a number of enormously influential books[8] still to be found almost three decades later on the desks of most serious programmers and system designers. This is a signal accomplishment in a publishing era where one year's computer books are inevitably the next year's landfill.

The Software Tools "philosophy" gives an idea of why Unix is the way it is. The metaphoric image is that of a matched set of hand- or machine-tools that are capable of being snapped together *ad lib* into any number of super-tools for specialized work on individual problems. If you had to make table legs, for instance, you might, with this set of tools, in this virtual reality, hook up your saw to your plane, and then to your lathe, and finally to your sander, just so, feed in sticks of wood at one end of this *ad hoc* assemblage, and receive the finished table legs at the other end. Real tools don't work that way, alas, but software tools can, if they're designed right. The basic principle is to make available a number of small, well-crafted, bug-free programs (**tool**s) that:

- do only one well-defined task
- do it intelligently and well
- do it in a standard and well-documented way
- do it flexibly, with appropriate user-chosen options available
- take input from or send output to other program tools from the same toolbox
- do something safe, and if possible useful, when unanticipated events occur.

Linguists are familiar with at least the spirit of this concept as the principle of modularity in syntactic theory. Modular design is a watchword in computer science as well as syntax, however, since it allows easy construction of *ad hoc* assemblages of tools for individual tasks, just as English syntax allows easy construction of *ad hoc* assemblages of ideas for individual purposes, i.e., the proverbial infinite number of sentences.

For example, consider the task of preparing a lexical *speculum*. This is simply a wordlist in **reverse alphabetic order**, so that *bring* and *string* might be adjacent, for instance; in a suffixing language like English, such lists have obvious utility for linguists. (See Chapter 4 for more discussion of wordlists.) They are immensely difficult to prepare by hand, however, and they can be tedious to program even on a computer. Below I present the Unix solution to this problem in the form of a linguistic data analysis problem; the answer follows. First, some preliminary information: word.big is an old wordlist from the University of Michigan's *MTS* mainframe system, salvaged from its demise. It was used by faculty and students for 20 years to spellcheck their e-mail and papers, so it's full of unusual words, in all their paradigmatic forms. To be precise as to the quantity, if not the quality, wc reports that it contains 70,189 words on 70,189 lines, for a total of 681,980 bytes (including 70,188 newline characters):

```
% ls -l word.big ↵
-rw-r—r—    1 jlawler          681980 Mar 17 1995 word.big
% wc word.big ↵
    70189 70189 681980 word.big
```

And now the problem. The numbering is added for reference; the rest is verbatim. If you type A–D at the "%" Unix prompt, you get back 1–10. Describe the syntax and semantics of A–D. Are there any generalizations?

```
A. % head word.big ↵
    1. a
    2. A
    3. aardvark
    4. aardwolf
    5. aba
    6. abaca
    7. abaci
    8. aback
    9. abacterial
   10. abacus

B. % head word.big | rev ↵
    1. a
    2. A
    3. kravdraa
    4. flowdraa
    5. aba
    6. acaba
    7. icaba
    8. kcaba
    9. lairetcaba
   10. sucaba
```

Figure 5.1a   Data analysis problem (A–B)

Using software tools (specifically the Unix programs sort and rev, and the Unix conventions of **input-output (I/O) redirection**), and given a wordlist file (with one word to a **line**, easy enough to prepare from any text via other Unix tools[9]) named word.big, the following **command** will produce a file named speculum:

```
% rev word.big | sort | rev > speculum
```

A parse of this command line shows it to be very straightforward, and this is given in Figure 5.2. The command is executed by sending the line to csh, which interprets and executes it. This in turn is accomplished by pressing RETURN at the end of the line, which may be considered a performance detail.

The programs sort and rev are both *filters*[10]; i.e., they belong to a class of programs that read a file and do things sequentially to what they find, sending their output to a **standard output**.[11] This in turn can become the

```
C. % head word.big | rev | sort ↵
    1. A
    2. a
    3. aba
    4. acaba
    5. flowdraa
    6. icaba
    7. kcaba
    8. kravdraa
    9. lairetcaba
   10. sucaba
D. % head word.big | rev | sort | rev ↵
    1. A
    2. a
    3. aba
    4. abaca
    5. aardwolf
    6. abaci
    7. aback
    8. aardvark
    9. abacterial
   10. abacus
```

Figure 5.1b   Data analysis problem (C–D)

standard input to the next program in the pipeline. This is not unlike the kind of processing that linguistic theories posit for various components of a derivation, and is directly related to the modularity inherent in the Software Tools design philosophy. rev simply reverses the **characters** on each line it encounters, while sort sorts files alphabetically by line.

The first part of the command above tells the OS to use rev on the file word.big, producing a stream of individually reversed lines. In Figure 5.1, the stream was limited to ten lines by using the head program, which simply shows the first few lines of a text file, defaulting to ten; in this command, however, the full word.big file would be the stream.

This stream is piped as input to sort, and sort's output is repiped to another copy of rev, this time re-reversing the (now sorted) strings. Finally, the resultant stream is parked in a file called speculum; the original file word.big is not affected by this operation, since it is only read, not written. In a test on a Sun workstation, with a word.big of 79,189 words, production of a speculum file by this method took less than one second.

```
%......the Unix C-shell (csh) prompt; this is the context
for the command that follows
rev...... send to output a reversed copy of each line in
source file:
word.big.. name of source (unmarked ablative) file,
which is to be read only
    |..... a pipe marker, connecting the output of rev to
the input of:
sort..... sort input alphabetically by line
    |..... another pipe, linking the output of sort to the
input of:
rev...... (another copy of) the same program invoked in
the first clause
    >..... dative case marker, indicating where the output
stream should be stored
speculum . name of goal (dative) file containing final
output; to be written only.
```

Figure 5.2   Parse of command line: *rev word.big | sort | rev > speculum*

The success of this combination of Unix, Software Tools, and C is evident from the facts:

- that C is the programming language in which Unix, the most widely-used operating system in the world, is written;
- that all the Software Tools programs are available, in C, on Unix, which is designed for their use and fits them best (though they are also available elsewhere, and in other languages);
- that C is the most widely used professional programming language in the world; any popular microcomputer program, for example, was almost certainly written in C.

Many of the software tools on Unix had their origin in the Tools movement, all were written in C, and all shared a common interface language, differing only occasionally in details of semantics and grammar. In addition, many of these tool programs (e.g. awk, sed, perl; see Section 5.6 below) evolved sublanguages of their own with a common core of structure, and these in turn came to influence Unix. A well-thought-out set of tools, and ways of combining them into useful programs, has many similarities to a well-thought-out set of phrases, and ways of combining them into useful speech. And, while their complexity does not approach that of a real natural language, the structure can be apprehended in similar ways, and this fact was not lost on the developers: Unix has been oriented from the start toward the written word, with numbers only incidental. Indeed, its first user was Bell Labs' wordprocessing department.

Gradually, the fame of Unix spread outside the lab. AT&T, Bell Labs' parent company, was at that time enjoined as a regulated monopoly from engaging in the software business, and thus the unlooked-for advent of a popular software product with its attendant demand was something of an embarrassment to the company. Their solution to this problem was almost as remarkable as its origin: AT&T essentially gave away Unix. For educational institutions, AT&T granted inexpensive licenses to run Unix on appropriate machines (originally PDP, later Digital's VAX line, and eventually machines designed especially for Unix), with full source code (in C) included. This meant that not only were the universities (in the personae of the students and staff of computing centers and computer science departments, and interested others) able to run Unix, but they were also able to modify it by changing its source code. Development proceeded rapidly at a number of sites, most importantly at the University of California at Berkeley, resulting eventually in the various releases of the Berkeley Standard Distribution of Unix (BSD), which was also free, and rapidly became the standard operating system for many computers.

This was particularly significant for American academic computing, since the late 1970s and early 80s was the period in which most universities switched over from large mainframe centralized computing services to distributed departmental minicomputers, frequently running Unix. Many of the design decisions in BSD Unix and its successors were thus made by academics, not businessmen, and this strongly influenced subsequent developments. Perhaps more importantly, the on-line culture that grew up around Unix, and proliferated into Usenet and then the **World Wide Web**, was an academic culture, not a business culture, with significant differences that were to become far more evident and important.

By the time 4.2BSD was released in 1983, AT&T had become free under the law to do something commercial with the rights it still held to the Unix operating system. However, the commercial, business-oriented System V version of Unix (**SysV**) released by AT&T that year to take advantage of this opportunity had serious incompatibilities with the BSD Unix that had grown up in academe in the previous decade, and an anxious diglossia ensued. Decreolization of these and other Unix versions in the form of eventual standardization of the competing versions is now being pursued and in many cases has been effectively achieved; but to this day, every version of Unix has its idioms, its gaps, its own minor examples of *Traduttore, traditore*. In this survey I do not treat dialectal variations, but rather concentrate on the many mutually-intelligible characteristics found in every version of Unix.

There are many fuller accounts available of the diachronic and dialectal development of Unix. The best and most thorough is Salus (1994), which has the additional virtue (for the purposes of this chapter) of having been written by a historical linguist who was personally involved with the development of Unix. For synchronic analyses, the best source is Raymond (1996), the printed version of an ongoing electronic lexicography project of impressive linguistic sophistication.

5.3   BITS AND ASCII: PHONETICS AND PHONOLOGY

Unix, like all computing systems, makes use of the concept of the *bit*, or *binary* digit[12]. This is what linguists know as the concept of binary opposition, e.g, *voiced/voiceless*. Computing exploits binary oppositions in electronic data to form its infrastructure, just as language exploits binary oppositions in perceived phonation. Unix also exploits several important elaborations of the bit: the *byte*, the *line*, and the *byte stream*. These etic units, which are literally built into the hardware, are structured by an emic system of byte interpretation called *ASCII*.[13]

In computing, just as in distinctive-feature theories, all oppositions are binary: "plus" and "minus" are the only choices for any feature. In computing, these are represented by "1" and "0". Since these are also digits, and the only digits needed in the representation of *Binary* (base 2) integers, the possibility arises of combining these feature specifications in a fixed order to form sequences of digits, or numbers. The fixed order is set by the manufacturer and may vary considerably, but virtually all Unix machines assemble bits into convenient groups of eight, which are called bytes. These are convenient because they are sufficient to define a useful-sized set.

All linguists learn that in Turkish, eight phonologically distinct vowels are possible, because there are three significant binary features, and $2^3 = 8$; that is, there are eight different ways to combine all possible values of the three features. With bytes, the relevant equation is $2^8 = 256$; that is, there are 256 different ways to combine the eight binary digits in a byte. 256 is an order of magnitude larger than the size of the English alphabet, and indeed the English alphabet is quite useful, even at that size. In fact, of course, the English alphabet (upper- and lower-case, separately coded), punctuation marks, *diacritics*, and a number of other symbols are all commonly coded in bytes, and that is by far the most common use of the byte, so much so that it is useful mnemonically to think of one byte as one English letter.[14]

Here is a byte: 0 1 1 0 1 0 1 0. This is the binary number that corresponds to the decimal[15] number 106. It represents, in a textual context, the (lower-case) letter "j", which is number 106 in ASCII. In a different

	Ø 000	1 001	2 010	3 011	4 100	5 101	6 110	7 111
Ø 0000	00 NUL 0	10 DLE 16 P	20 Space 32	30 Ø 48	40 @ 64	50 P 80 DLE	60 ` 96	70 p 112
1 0001	01 SOH 1 A	11 DC1 17 Q	21 ! 33	31 1 49	41 A 65 SOH	51 Q 81 DC1	61 a 97	71 q 113
2 0010	02 STX 2 B	12 DC2 18 R	22 " 34	32 2 50	42 B 66 STX	52 R 82 DC2	62 b 98	72 r 114
3 0011	03 ETX 3 C	13 DC3 19 S	23 # 35	33 3 51	43 C 67 ETX	53 S 83 DC3	63 c 99	73 s 115
4 0100	04 EOT 4 D	14 DC4 20 T	24 $ 36	34 4 52	44 D 68 EOT	54 T 84 DC4	64 d 100	74 t 116
5 0101	05 ENQ 5 E	15 NAK 21 U	25 % 37	35 5 53	45 E 69 ENQ	55 U 85 NAK	65 e 101	75 u 117
6 0110	06 ACK 6 F	16 SYN 22 V	26 & 38	36 6 54	46 F 70 ACK	56 V 86 SYN	66 f 102	76 v 118
7 0111	07 BEL 7 G	17 ETB 23 W	27 ' 39	37 7 55	47 G 71 BEL	57 W 87 ETB	67 g 103	77 w 119
8 1000	08 BS 8 H	18 CAN 24 X	28 (40	38 8 56	48 H 72 BS	58 X 88 CAN	68 h 104	78 x 120
9 1001	09 HT 9 I	19 EM 25 Y	29) 41	39 9 57	49 I 73 HT	59 Y 89 EM	69 i 105	79 y 121
A 1010	0A LF 10 J	1A SUB 26 Z	2A * 42	3A : 58	4A J 74 LF	5A Z 90 SUB	6A j 106	7A z 122
B 1011	0B VT 11 K	1B ESC 27 [	2B + 43	3B ; 59	4B K 75 VT	5B [91 ESC	6B k 107	7B { 123
C 1100	0C FF 12 L	1C FS 28 \	2C , 44	3C < 60	4C L 76 FF	5C \ 92 FS	6C l 108	7C	124
D 1101	0D CR 13 M	1D GS 29]	2D - 45	3D = 61	4D M 77 CR	5D] 93 GS	6D m 109	7D } 125
E 1110	0E SO 14 N	1E RS 30 ^	2E . 46	3E > 62	4E N 78 SO	5E ^ 94 RS	6E n 110	7E ~ 126
F 1111	0F SI 15 O	1F US 31 _	2F / 47	3F ? 63	4F O 79 SI	5F _ 95 US	6F o 111	7F DEL 127

Figure 5.3   ASCII chart

context, this byte might represent the decimal integer 106 itself, or memory address 106, or instruction 106, or part of a more complex number, address, or instruction. Computers use binary notation; writing numbers graphically is for humans, and computers will write numbers any way they are told. This byte is therefore likely to exist, as such, not as one of a series of marks on paper, but rather as a series of magnetic charges in ferrite or silicon, or as a series of microdots on a compact disk (*CD*, or *CD-ROM*).

All Unix systems are built on ASCII, and all Unix *file*s (or streams) are byte files which can be interpreted in ASCII, whether they are intended to be or not. The history of ASCII will not be treated here, but it would not be unfair to stress the fact that the "A" in the acronym ASCII stands for *American*, with all that that entails from a linguistic viewpoint. That is, ASCII represents just about everything that an early twentieth-century American engineer might have thought would be useful in a character code. This includes the upper- and lower-case English alphabet (coded cleverly to facilitate alphabetization), the Arabic numerals, ordinary punctuation marks, a potpourri of non-printing *control character*s (like Line Feed), and virtually no "foreign" letters or symbols.

There is provision for representing some diacritics, as separate letters: thus Spanish, French, German, Italian, and other languages which use diacritics that have rough ASCII equivalents (circumflex [caret ^], umlaut [quote mark "], acute [apostrophe '], grave [backquote `], tilde [~]) can be represented, though with some difficulty, and not always completely (there is no ASCII character except comma that can function as a cedilla, for instance). Languages like Turkish, Hungarian, Polish, or Czech, which use letters or diacritics that have no ASCII equivalents, are very difficult to represent properly. Languages with completely different alphabets, like Russian, Arabic, or Hebrew, require heroic measures. And non-alphabetic writing systems like Chinese are out of the question; they require a completely different approach. Which is not to say that ASCII romanization is impossible, of course.

Within its limitations, however, ASCII is very well-designed; a number of structural characteristics are worth pointing out. There are, to begin with, two parts of ASCII: Low ASCII, represented in the chart in Figure 5.3, from Decimal, Hex, and Binary 0 through 127 (= 2^7–1: Hex 7F, Binary 01111111); and High ASCII, from Decimal 128 (= 2^7: Hex 80, Binary 10000000) through 255 (2^8–1: Hex FF, Binary 11111111). Only the Low ASCII characters are completely standard; High ASCII characters vary from machine to machine.

For instance, many of the same additional characters are included in both DOS/Windows and Macintosh text files, but not all; and they appear in different orders, with different numbers. This is one reason why DOS and Mac text files are different. Unix cuts this Gordian knot by not using High ASCII at all to represent characters; only Low ASCII, the first 128 characters, are meaningful in Unix, and we will restrict our attention henceforth to these.

The most recognizable characters in ASCII are the **alphanumeric**s, that is, the letters of the (English) Latin alphabet plus the (English) Arabic numerals. Since the upper-case letters and the lower-case letters are etically different, they are coded separately; since they are emically related, they are coded analogously. The upper-case letters begin with A at Hex 41 (Decimal 65, Binary 01000001) and proceed alphabetically through z at Hex 5A (Binary 01011010), while the lower-case letters go from a at Hex 61 (Decimal 97, Binary 01100001) through z at Hex 7A (Binary 01111010). It can easily be seen that the difference between any given upper- and lower-case letter is always exactly 32; in Binary terms, it's even simpler: an upper-case letter has "0" in the third-highest bit, while a lower-case letter has "1" there. Otherwise, they are identical; this fact makes it simple to design software to be case-sensitive, or case-insensitive, as desired.

One of the important facts about Unix, which often disconcerts novices, is that it is case-sensitive by default, since it uses Low ASCII fully. Individual programs may (and often do) ignore case, but unless told otherwise, Unix does not. This means that a directory named News is not the same as one named news, and will not be found or referenced by that name. And since sort order is determined by ASCII order, and uppercase letters precede lowercase, this also means that Zygote will appear in a sorted list before aardvark, unless the sorting software is told to ignore case. One convention that results from this fact is that the unmarked case for Unix commands, filenames, directories, and other special words is lower-case. Capitalized and ALL-CAP terms are normally reserved, by convention, for special situations and system software, though there is no absolute prohibition imposed. For instance, most Usenet newsreaders (like rn or trn) expect to use (and will create if they don't find one) a directory named News. (A further behavioral modification produced by this convention is the decided predilection of some Unix users to eschew upper case in ordinary written communication, even when not modulated by Unix.)

Another feature of ASCII worthy of note are the Control Characters, which are non-printing, and represent an action of some sort; these may be considered supra-segmental analogs. Control characters have their own official names, taken from their original purpose (usually on teletype machines), which are normally acronymic or mnemonic in English. For instance, character no. 7, BEL (^G or *Bell*), originally rang the bell on a teletype, and now it often produces a noise of some sort on a computer, while no. 8, BS (^H or *Back Space*), originally moved the print head on a teletype back one space; now it is the code produced by the "BackSpace" **key** on most[16] keyboards.

The control characters occupy the first two columns[17] of ASCII; thus their most significant bits are "0000" or "0001". Their least significant bits are the source of their more common names, however. Just as the last four bits of "J" and "j" are identical ("1010"), so are the last four bits of no. 10, LF (^J or *Line Feed*), which originally moved the teletype print head down one line, and is now found as the newline character in Unix, among other uses[18]. Since, like all Control characters, this can be produced on a keyboard by pressing the "Ctrl" or "Control" shift key simultaneously with another key – in this case the "J" key – LF is often called simply "Control-J", or "Ctrl-J", and frequently abbreviated, like all control characters, with a caret as "^J".

All computer media, like writing or speech, imply a serial order. In print, we are used to the convention of lines of serially-ordered characters arranged horizontally on the page. For readers, a line is a more or less natural phenomenon, governed by paper and type size. In a computer, however, there is no physical page, nor any type to have a physical size. So lines, if they are to be defined at all, must be defined, like everything else, by bytes. Text files are line files; they consist of strings of bytes with newline characters inserted wherever a text line should be displayed. An ASCII text file with 1000 lines of 60 characters each would thus have 61,000 bytes:[19] 60,000 letter bytes plus 1000 newline characters. Many of the tools in Unix, like rev, work at the line level; others, like sort, work on whole files (though with reference to lines).[20]

Files are often called **stream**s in Unix. Since a text file (and Unix is almost entirely composed of text files) is simply a string of bytes (some of which are probably newline characters), it is often convenient to view the file itself as a single string, and this is always the case whenever anything like reading, writing, or modification has to be done to a file. In a computer, since there is no question of moving the perceptor, conceptually it must be the bytes that are streaming past.

This metaphor is quite different from the static concept implied by **file**: a stream is in motion, can be used for power, provides a continuous supply of vital resources, is all of the same kind, and is one-dimensional. A file, on the other hand, just sits there and waits for you to do something with it, offers little help, is entirely passive, may consist of many parts of different kinds, and is at least two-dimensional. This distinction between the metaphors of stream and file is not unlike Whorf's presentation (1956:210) of the distinction between the two Hopi words for "water". It turns out that the stream concept lends itself to convenient programming.

The result is that many Unix resources are designed around the concept of manipulating, measuring, analyzing, abstracting, modifying, sampling, linking, comparing, and otherwise fooling around with streams of text data, and since they share a common structure of conventions, they can be used together in surprisingly powerful ways. This is inherent in the way the simple speculum example above works; further examples may be found in Section 5.6 below.

5.4   GRAMMAR

The Unix language family is inflected. This is not common (though not unknown,[21] either) in computing languages. There is, for instance, complex clausal syntax, including clitics, marked lexical classes, a case system, and a very powerful morphological system for paradigmatic matching called *regular expression*s.

Regular expressions permeate Unix. Originally developed by the logician Stephen Kleene (1956), they found their place as Type 3, the lowest, on the Chomsky Hierarchy (Chomsky, 1963), where they are equivalent to finite-state ("right-linear") grammars, or finite automata. The most common type of regular expression morphology is the use of "*" (the *Kleene closure*) to indicate "any string" in such contexts as *.doc, meaning (in context) all files with names ending in the string ".doc"; this is the *shell* regular expression dialect, the simplest but not the only one. The Unix program egrep, for instance, uses an elaborated version of regular expressions to search text files for lines containing strings matching an expression.

Suppose, for instance, one has a World Wide Web server, which stores a record of each "hit" (i.e., file request) on a separate line in a logfile with a long and unmnemonic name. Suppose further that one has decided to think of this file as weblog for convenience. Then one creates a *shell* variable, stores the name in it, and then uses weblog to refer to that file thereafter. This could be done by putting a line like the following in one's .cshrc file:

```
weblog=/usr/etc/bin/httpd/log
```

Once set, this variable is available, and may be referred to, in any command. Unix makes a philosophically nice use/mention distinction here between the variable itself and the *value* of the variable. That is, weblog is the variable, while $weblog is its content, namely the string

```
/usr/etc/bin/httpd/log
```

To return to our example: this web log file, however it is named, or referenced, is filled with automatically-generated information from the Web server program, which runs in the background.[22] The *format* of each line is invariable, since it's generated automatically, and begins with the date in a particular format (e.g., 01/3/96), followed by other

information, terminating in the name of the file requested and the number
of bytes served. Then the command:

```
egrep umich $weblog
```

will find and display every line in the file web.log containing the string
"umich".[23] There may be very many of these, and one may only want
to know how many, so the output of egrep may be piped to wc -1[24]:

```
egrep umich $weblog | wc -1
```

which simply provides the number of lines found, instead of a listing of
all of them. This works for more complex strings, too, though one is
well-advised to use quotation marks to delimit the search string. If, for
example, one wanted to count how many requests were made for a given
file, say "FAQ", on a given day; the command would be:

```
egrep '01/23/98.*FAQ' $weblog | wc -1 [25]
```

Since "." matches any character and "*" matches any number of the
preceding character, ".*" comprises a regular expression idiom that
matches any string at all, and "01/23/98.*FAQ" thus matches any string[26]
containing the date and the file name, in that order.

We alluded above to the analogs to the ablative (source) and dative
(goal) cases, with reference to the input or output of a command on the
command line, i.e., whatever the user types after the Unix prompt.[27] It
is worth looking at the command line in some detail, since it is the principal linguistic structure of Unix, analogous to the Sentence level in
natural language. The basic syntactic structure is

```
command [-switches] [arguments]
```

That is, verb, plus optional (marked) adverbials, plus optional noun
phrases; some command verbs are intransitive, some are transitive, some
are bitransitive, and some vary in the number of arguments they take.
These linguistic analogies are reasonably straightforward: virtually every
Unix command is, as the name suggests, an imperative verb, directing
some action to be taken; the arguments, like nouns, refer to a person,
place or thing, generally a user, a ***path*** or ***directory***, or a string or file,
respectively; and the switches, like adverbials, specify optional modes and
manners in which the action is to be performed.

Commands are not always simplex; they may be conjoined or
embedded, and there can be quite intricate flow of information from one
to another, as we have seen. Concatenation of commands is straightforward: to instruct Unix to perform several commands, one merely separates
them with semicolons; when the RETURN key is pressed, each is
performed in order.

```
cd ~/News; trn; cd
```

changes the current directory to one's own News directory (which is used by news readers like rn, trn, or tin), invokes trn, and returns to the ***home directory***[28] when trn exits. These are coordinately conjoined clauses, unlike the subordinate complement clauses[29] produced by input/output redirection, where each successive command depends on a previous one.

Or, using the ***backquote convention***, whole commands may function as nouns, like complement clauses[30], with the output of the complement command functioning as the argument of the matrix command. Quoting a command inside backquotes "` ` `" runs that command in the background and then uses its output as the argument for the main command, so that:

```
finger `whoami`
```

first runs the whoami program, which returns the current user's login name, then uses that string as the argument for finger, which provides information about a user from their name.

Unix is a ***multi-user, multi-processing*** system. This means that several (on larger systems, several hundred) people can simultaneously use the same machine, and each of them can, in theory, run several processes simultaneously.[31] With such complexity, it is obvious that there are a lot of people, places, and things to refer to, and Unix has a file and directory system that accommodates this. The basic unit in Unix, as in most computer systems, is the file, which is by default a text file. Each file resides in some directory, and every user has their own home directory, usually named for their login ID.

Thus, if my login is jlawler, my home directory on a given Unix system might be /usr/jlawler, while hdry's home directory would be /usr/hdry. A file named wordlist in my home directory has a full ***pathname*** of /usr/jlawler/wordlist, and it would be accessible from anywhere on the system with that name. Most Unix systems use a special referential convention to the effect that "~jlawler" means "jlawler's home directory", while "$HOME" is an indexical, referring to the current user's (first person singular) home directory. Finally, one always has a current directory, which is thought of (and referred to) in locative terms: i.e., one is "in" /usr/hdry and "goes to" it with the cd command: cd /usr/hdry. Files referred to without a pathname, i.e., by the name of the file alone (e.g, wordlist) are interpreted as being in the current directory by default. Thus, for anyone who is in my home directory, "wordlist" is sufficient; for someone in /usr/hdry, "~jlawler/wordlist" is necessary; and I can always refer to it as $HOME/wordlist, no matter what directory I'm in.

Directories may contain other directories, and references to them are simply concatenated with the directory separator slash "/". A file wordlist that was in a ***subdirectory*** lists under a subdirectory English under

my home directory would have a fully-specified pathname of /usr/
jlawler/English/lists/wordlist, and other users could reference it
this way, or as ~jlawler/English/lists/wordlist. The concept of
hierarchical directories originated in Unix, but it has spread to most
modern systems. Users of DOS will be familiar with this convention,
although DOS uses backslash "\" instead of slash as a directory separator; in Macintosh usage, directories are called "folders", and colon ":"
is used in pathnames.

Unix filenames are normal ASCII strings of varying lengths[32], and may
contain any alpha-numeric character, and a number of non-alpha-
numerics. They may (but need not, except for special purposes) end with
an extension of a period followed by a short string denoting the file type.
Thus, C program code files end in .c, *HTML* files accessed by Web
*browser*s end in .html, and compressed tar archive files end in .tar.z.
Some programs require special extensions on filenames, but most Unix
tools do not, though they are often defaults.

In natural languages, imperative forms are almost always regular,
frequently based on simple verb roots unless elaborated by a politeness
system. In dealing with machines politeness is not an issue, hence the
lack of verbal inflection *per se* in Unix. There is, however, an elaborate
clitic system, called *switch*es.[33] By way of example, let us examine the
common Unix command ls, which displays file names and information,
like the DIR command in DOS. The online manual entry for ls (the
Unix command to display it is man ls) starts this way:

```
LS(1)      UNIX Programmer's Manual
NAME
   ls — list contents of directory
SYNOPSIS
   ls [ -acdfgilqrstulACLFR ] name
```

Figure 5.4   Top of man page for ls command: man ls | head

The heading shows that the ls command is in part 1 of the Manual
(most ordinary commands are there); the next part gives its name (in
lower case) and its purpose. The "synopsis" then gives all the possible
switches, each a single character, that it may take. The square brackets
signal that they are optional; the hyphen character precedes any switch
markers, which may be concatenated, in any order. The rest of the man
page then details the operation of ls; in particular, the operation of ls
with each switch is discussed separately.

For instance, here is what it says about the -t, -s, and -r switches:

```
-t   Sort by time modified (latest first) instead of by
     name.
-s   Give size in kilobytes of each file.
-r   Reverse the order of sort to get reverse alphabetic
     or oldest first as appropriate.
```

Figure 5.5   From man page for `ls` command: effects of *-t, -s,* and *-r* switches

This means that `ls  -rst`[34] will present the names of the files in the directory name[35], with their sizes, sorted by time, most recently modified files last. Each of the other letter switches listed in the Synopsis does something different; further, what each does is context sensitive, in that it may vary if used with some other switch, like the combination of -r with -t, which changes the sort order from reverse alphabetic to reverse temporal.

`ls` has 18 switches in this dialect, which is a larger degree of modification than most Unix commands have. Each command has a unique set of switches, however, most of which are only infrequently needed. The syntax ranges from extremely simple to rather complex. Below are some syntactic synopses of other Unix commands. Underlining indicates variables to be supplied by the user, and square brackets optional ***element***s – switches separately bracketed require separate "-" prefixes. Vertical bar "|", like linguists' curly brackets, requires a choice among elements.

In each of these, the switches may be expected to have a different meaning. All this might seem a large burden to place on the user, and it would indeed be excessive, were it not for the facts that:

- a complete list with glosses is always available via the man command
- some, at least, of the switches are mnemonic (in English): -time, -reverse, -size
- one need never learn any switch more than once, since any useful configuration can be made into an ***alias*** or ***script*** with a name chosen by (and presumably significant to) the user; thus `ls  -rts` can be renamed, say, reversedate with the command

```
alias reversedate ls -rts
```

Any command, or sequence of commands, can be given a name, thus making it into an idiom, or a little program. This facility is provided by the Unix ***shell***, the tool that coordinates the other tools by interpreting commands. There are two principal shells, and each provides a different facility for command formation. csh, the "C-shell",[36] provides ***alias***es; it is principally used interactively, where it identifies itself with a "%"

rev: reverse the order to
characters in each line   **rev [_file_]**

cp: copy files   **cp [-ip] _file1_ _file2_**

mv: move or rename files   **mv [-i] [-f] [-] _file1_ _file2_**

head/tail: give first/last few
    lines of a file   **head/tail [-_count_] [_file_]**

mail: send and receive mail   **mail [-v] [-i] [-n] [-s _subject_]**
                       [_user_ . . .]

uniq: remove or report   **uniq [-cdu [+|-n] [_inputfile_**
    adjacent duplicate lines   **[_outputfile_]]**

diff: display line differences   **diff [-bitw] -c[#]|-e|-f|-n|-h]**
    between files   **_file1_ _file2_**

spell: report spelling errors   **spell [-blvx] [-d _hlist_] [-h _spell_**
          hist] [-s _hstop_] p+_localfile_] [_file_]

Figure 5.6   Synopses and syntax of selected Unix commands

prompt. sh, the "Bourne shell",[37] is used mostly to interpret files
containing ***shell scripts***; it has fewer interactive features, but when it is
being used interactively, it identifies itself with a "$" prompt.[38]

The command reversedate could be either an alias (as in the example
above), or a shell script. Generally, simple commands like this are more
likely to be made into aliases, since the process is easier, and doesn't
involve creating and activating a file. Of course, to make an alias permanent, it is necessary to record it; each csh user has a file called .cshrc[39]
that may be customized in a number of ways, including a list of their
aliases. One of the first aliases some users put in .cshrc is something
like the following:

```
alias define 'edit $HOME/aliases;unalias *;alias -r
$HOME/aliases40
```

which allows them to define new aliases on the fly.[41] A good rule to
follow is that any command one notices oneself typing more than a few
times should become an alias with a mnemonic name; and to keep track
of these, it is also useful to have a few aliases whose purpose is to remind
oneself of one's previous aliases. The Unix tool which is helpful here;
which define, for instance, will return the following information:[42]

```
define — aliased to: edit $HOME/aliases;unalias *;source
$HOME/aliases
```

egrep can be used to advantage as well, to refresh one's memory about previous lexicography. Suppose you have several aliases for ls with various switches, but you don't recall all of them; Figure 5.7 shows how to print each line in .cshrc containing the string "ls ".[43]
by means of the following alias:

```
alias definitions "egrep \!* $HOME/aliases "
```

"\!*" is the C-shell code for a command parameter, i.e., whatever appears on the command line after the alias; in this example, it is translated by the shell into the string "ls " (note the space), and passed on to egrep, which dutifully searches $HOME/aliases[44] for lines containing this string and prints the result.

Of the various aliases in Figure 5.7, dates shows multi-column output sorted by time, oldest last, and pipes the output to a file viewer that shows only a screen at a time; this is useful for directories with a large number of files. ll and lc both produce a "long directory", with all details of each file printed on a separate line; lc is sorted by time of last edit, most recent first. The last alias, whichls, uses the backquote convention; which finds executable programs, scripts, or aliases anywhere in the user's path, but it returns only the name and location, and not the size, date, or any other information. If one wants more information, one can then use ls to find it; but it's often convenient to combine the steps, as here.

By contrast with an alias, a shell script:

- is interpreted by the Bourne shell sh (aliases are interpreted by csh, the C-shell; this means that aliases and scripts use somewhat different conventions)
- consists of a file and resides on disk, like other Unix programs (aliases are loaded from a file when csh starts at login and are thus in-memory commands)
- is generally longer and more complex than an alias, which is usually a short sequence of commands or a mere synonym for a single command

```
% definitions 'ls '
alias dates     'ls -sACFt | more'
alias dir       'ls -alF'
alias lf        'ls -sF'
alias ll        'ls -l'
alias lc        'ls -lc'
alias whichls   'ls -l `which \!*`'
```

Figure 5.7   Operation of the *definitions* alias

As an example of a shell script, consider a problem one often encounters: making a simple change in multiple files. This could be done individually with an editor, making the change by hand in one file, loading the next file and making it by hand again, etc. But this is not only wasteful of time but also prone to error, and Unix provides better facilities for such tasks. Suppose the files in question are all HTML files in a single directory on a Web server, and that what needs to be done is to change a **URL** link that may occur several times in each file (or may not occur at all) to a new address, because the server that the URL points to has been renamed (this particular task is likely to be with us for some time).

A two-step process will serve best here: first, a shell script (call it `loopedit`) to loop over the files and edit each one with the same editing commands, and a separate file (call it `editcmds`) of editing commands. This has the benefit of being reusable, since subsequent editing changes can be made with the same script merely by changing the contents of `editcmds`. The Unix `cat`[45] tool will print any file on the screen, so we can see the files:

```
% cat loopedit
#!sh
for i in *.html
  do
   ex - $i < editcmds
  done
```

Figure 5.8a   The *loopedit* script, with commands in *editcmds* file (Figure 5.8b)

The first line invokes the sh shell to interpret the script (one gets to specify the language and dialect). The next line (a "`for`" statement) instructs the shell to carry out the line(s)[46] between the following "`do`" and "`done`" markers once for each file ending in "`.html`",[47] just as if it were typed at the keyboard. At each successive iteration of the command, the shell variable "`i`" is to be set to the name of each successive file in the set of those ending in "`.html`". The fourth line is the command itself; it runs the ex line editor (using ex's silent switch "`-`" that tells ex not to print its usual messages on the standard output for each file, unnecessary with multiple files), and the name of each file (referenced as the value of `i`, or `$i`) as its argument. ex is further instructed by the input redirection (ablative) marker "`<`" following the argument to take its next input – the commands themselves – from the file `editcmds`.

The contents of editcmds can be similarly displayed:

```
% cat editcmds
g/www.umich.edu\/\~/s//www-personal.umich.edu\/\~/g
wq
```

Figure 5.8b   The editcmds file, input to *ex* on the loopedit script (Figure 5.8a)

There are only two lines necessary; the first makes the changes, and the second saves ("writes") the file and quits. The second line is trivial, but the first is fairly complex.[48] There are several technical wrinkles, due to peculiarities of ex commands and of URL syntax, that render it more complex than usual; this makes it a good example of a number of things, and worth our while parsing out character by character below.

First, let us examine the precise change to be made. URLs begin with the address of the server to be contacted; in the case of the University of Michigan, there are several, all beginning with "www.". As the Web has grown, it has become necessary for some Web pages to be moved to different servers to equalize the load. In particular, at the University of Michigan, personal Web home pages, which are named using a tilde convention similar to the Unix home directory convention, have had to be moved from the server having the address "www.umich.edu" to a special server for such pages only, with the address "www-personal.umich.edu". Thus Eric Rabkin's home page, which used to have the URL "www.umich.edu/~esrabkin/", can now be found at the URL "www-personal.umich.edu/~esrabkin/", and this change must be made for thousands of URLs in many Web pages. The change should only be made to personal pages, however; other (e.g., departmental) pages, which are not named with the tilde convention, remain on the original server and retain the "www.umich.edu" address.

We therefore need to search for all lines in a file that contain the URL address string "www.umich.edu/~", and to change each occurrence of this string on each of these lines to "www-personal.umich.edu/~". That is what the first line does. The "s" (for "substitute") command in ex has the syntax s/re_1/re_2/, where re_1 and re_2 are regular expressions; it substitutes re_2 for re_1, and is thus a variant of the *Structural Description : Structural Change* transformation notation that generative linguists put up with for over a decade. s//re/ is a zero pronominal reference, and substitutes re for whatever the last search string has been; in this case, that has already been specified by the preceding search (the slash-delimited regular expression beginning the line). In the event of a search failure, the "s" command will not execute. However, this particular command has a special twist: slash "/" and tilde "~" are themselves both meaningful characters to ex, and thus cannot be searched for directly.

Slash is used to delimit search strings,[49] and in order to search for slash itself in a string, or for strings containing it, it must be **escape**d with a backslash "\" literal prefix. I.e., "\" quotes the next character literally, so that the string "\/" means "the character '/' "; the slash will not be interpreted by ex as a string delimiter. Similarly, unescaped tilde implicitly refers to the last replacement string (re_2) used in a previous "s" command (just as unescaped ampersand "&" refers to the search string (re_1) of the current "s" command), and to the empty string if there have been no previous "s" commands, which will be the case in this script. So the actual string we must instruct ex to search for is

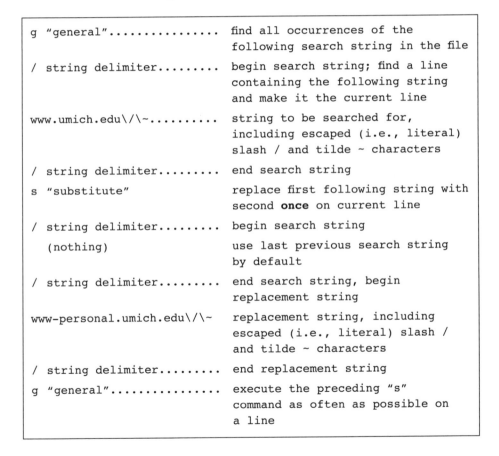

g "general"...............	find all occurrences of the following search string in the file
/ string delimiter........	begin search string; find a line containing the following string and make it the current line
www.umich.edu\/\~..........	string to be searched for, including escaped (i.e., literal) slash / and tilde ~ characters
/ string delimiter........	end search string
s "substitute"	replace first following string with second **once** on current line
/ string delimiter........	begin search string
(nothing)	use last previous search string by default
/ string delimiter........	end search string, begin replacement string
www-personal.umich.edu\/\~	replacement string, including escaped (i.e., literal) slash / and tilde ~ characters
/ string delimiter........	end replacement string
g "general"...............	execute the preceding "s" command as often as possible on a line

Figure 5.8c   Parse of the edit command in *editcmds* file (Figure 5.8b) interpreted by *ex* in the *loopedit* script (Figure 5.8a)

"www.umich.edu\/\~", with both slash and tilde escaped,[50] and the replacement string is "www-personal.umich.edu\/\~".

The two "g", for "general", commands, one at the beginning and one at the end, refer to two different contexts. The initial "g" instructs ex to find all lines in the file with an occurrence of the following search string, and to execute the command following on those lines where it is found, while the final "g" refers only to the (line-oriented) "s" command, and instructs ex to perform all possible substitutions on the indicated line; this covers the case where there is more than one occurrence of the string on the line. Without the suffixal "g", the "s" command could only be executed once on any line.

With these files in place, the only thing remaining is to activate loopedit as an *executable* (i.e., program) file with the chmod[51] command. From then on it works the same as any Unix program. One need hardly add that, with several hundred Unix tools available to be used, singly or together, plus dozens of specialized sublanguages for instructing them, shell scripts offer unlimited possibilities for automated text processing to every Unix user. For instance, the LINGUIST List is edited, distributed, archived, abstracted, and put on the Web via a large suite of Unix scripts that depend on tools like the ones discussed in this chapter.

5.5   EDITING AND FORMATTING

The Unix toolbox always includes an editor, actually several editors, of several different kinds. Editors are programs that create and change the contents of ASCII files. They may do many other things as well, and some, for instance emacs, can become an entire environment. An editor is a significant part – the part that connects keyboard, screen, and disk – of the usual microcomputer wordprocessing programs; the usual metaphor is a typewriter, without paper, but with a memory. A word-processor is a large complex program with many capabilities; the usual metaphor is a typewriter that not only has paper, but also a print shop, an art studio, a type foundry, and a reference library. Wordprocessors are used to produce actual printed pages, while an editor need only fool around with bits and bytes, not fonts and footnotes. An editor is thus usually much smaller and faster, because it is a tool that only does one thing and doesn't try to do others.

They are also especially useful in Unix, because Unix was originally invented by programmers for programmers, and its editors, though mostly used for ordinary writing, are designed to be especially useful for programmers. In order to make a shell script or save an alias, for instance, one must use an editor. Which one? That is a semi-religious matter for many. The choices include:

- **pico**, the screen editor that is a part of the pine e-mail package. Many people have found it easy to use, and the editor is available separately from e-mail. Furthermore, pico's key commands are a subset of the standard key commands for:
- **emacs**, the most powerful and flexible editor in the computer world. It can be found on most Unix systems in academia, though not always in business. It is the product of the Free Software Foundation and must be given away free. Though it is not simple to install, nor to learn completely, it is thoroughly programmable (in Lisp) and can do almost anything with ASCII text. emacs' main competitor is:
- **vi**, universally pronounced /viyáy/, which, growing out of a short tradition of line editing, was the first screen editor available on Unix, and, as part of the standard Unix distribution, may be found on every Unix system, along with its relatives:
- **ex** and **edit**, essentially command-line versions of vi (they become vi with the "v" command); and **ed**, the first Unix line editor, still a functional tool within its limitations.

All of them work, but they all work differently. In this chapter, I use the ex line editor, both as a least common denominator, and because it is the editor I use myself by choice for most simple file editing tasks like adding or modifying aliases, mail names, text Web pages, and writing small scripts. It is fast and convenient for these tasks, and can easily be automated. Thus the details of the editing in the transcriptions here are independent of the rest, in that the editing could have been done visually.

But it's irrelevant, from the standpoint of the Software Tools philosophy, or of Unix, which tools you use, as long as they work, because all of the tools work together. There is thus a wide choice of programs available for virtually any task, and editors are no exception. Indeed, editors are so important to programmers that they are constantly improving them, often on their own time, for glory; and since programming glory involves efficiency and power, among other things, this leads to some very interesting tools.

There is an important class of wordprocessing tool program, called a text formatter, which is also usually part of a wordprocessor, but may be used as a separate tool in combination with an editor. Examples are T_eX and LaT_eX, programs used by many scientists to produce technical text, and the Unix programs roff (for "run off") and troff (for "typesetter runoff"), all of which implement special printing instructions from special **tag**s or commands embedded in a text file. Formatters and embedded commands are common with file structures that follow **SGML** or HTML, or some equivalent **markup** scheme, like Web browsers (see Chapters 1, 4, and 6 in this book for further discussion of markup, T_eX, and SGML). In all of these, the "stream and pipe" metaphors of information flow control via tool programs can easily be discerned. Separate formatter programs are not as widely used in ordinary writing as previously, since the locus of most text construction has moved to microcomputers with full-featured wordprocessing programs with built-in formatting; but they are still a common type of program, one of the larger class called *filters*.

5.6   FILTERS

As mentioned above, a filter program is one that takes input (prototypically textual input) from some source, performs some regular transformation on it, and sends the resulting output to some terminus. This may be sequential, like the speculum example, or interactive, like a Web browser interpreting HTML code; but frequently enough filters employ regular expressions, used in special filter languages, to specify their transformation.

Regular expressions are far more powerful than simple string search examples would suggest. Besides "." and "*", there are a host of other special inflections with special senses, as in any synthetic morphology:

- "?" means 0 or 1 of the preceding character, so "s?" means that "s" is optional
- "+" means a string of **one** or more of the preceding characters ("*" is **zero** or more)
- "|" indicated alternation, so "to (day|morrow)" matches either today or tomorrow
- "[A-Z]" matches any single character from the ASCII range between "A" and "Z"
- "[^AUZ]" matches any character **except**"A", "U", and "Z"
- "[^A-Z]" matches any character **except** an uppercase letter, so
- "[A-Za-z0-9]" matches any single alphanumeric character, while
- "[A-Za-z0-9]*" matches any string consisting only of alphanumerics, and
- "[^0-9]*" matches any string that does not contain numeric characters
- "$" means the end of a line, and "^" means its beginning, so "^$" matches an empty line

---

Figure 5.9a   Simple examples of regular expressions and the strings they match

Special characters intended to be used literally, rather than interpreted like this,[52] are preceded by "\", thus "\. " matches a period with two spaces afterward, and "\\" matches a single (literal) backslash.

Some other examples of regular expressions, all working with egrep (and all delimited with quotes):

´ .*is?tic(|al(|ly) ´.......any word ending (note the spaces) in -itic, -istic, -itical, -istical, -itically, or -istically.

´ [A-Z][a-z]* ´.......any Capitalized word (note the spaces).

´ [A-Z][a-z]*[A-Z][a-z]+ ' . . . . any CapiTalized word containing one other CapiTal.

´^́[^]*$ ´ . . . . a complete line containing no spaces (* matches empty line, + doesn't).

´^́[A-Z].*\.$ ´ . . . . . . a complete line beginning with a Capital and ending with a period.

´ spr?[^\.?,:;!]*[\.?,:;!]´.......any wording beginning with sp- or spr-; this expression specifies that the string must begin with a space, and may not **contain** period, question mark, comma, colon, semicolon, or bang, while it must **terminate** with one of them, or with a space, making it suitable for searching in normally punctuated text.

´ [A-Z][A-Za-z]* [A-Za-z]*: ?([Tt]he|[aA]n?) [A-Z]?[a-z]* of .*´
...a specification for certain styles of academic title like Regular Titles: An analysis of technical paper nomenclature.

Figure 5.9b Complex examples of regular expressions and the strings they match

Besides egrep, many other Unix tools can use these regular expressions. The text editors ed, ex, vi, and emacs, for example, can perform very complex string manipulations based on regular expressions. In addition, the text filter languages sed,[53] awk[54], and perl[55] make extensive use of regular expressions. sed, from "stream editor", is the simplest filter tool. It can do the same things as ex, but operates on the entire text stream with predetermined instructions. It is useful for repetitive editing tasks; since these are character-based editors, sed is best at character-level manipulations. awk is a more complex language, based on the concept of the word instead of the character, but still oriented toward sequential operation on each line in a filter operation. awk is somewhat more like a conventional programming language, and one can write quite complex programs in it, but is simple enough for useful short programs to be written on the fly. It works best for formatting repetitive and relatively predictable text data. perl is a general-purpose programming language oriented toward text handling, which is very widely used on the Internet, especially the Web. It is very powerful and efficient, and, though relatively easy to learn, is more complex than awk, and does not presuppose the filter metaphor so literally.

5.7   UNIX RESOURCES FOR USERS

There are hundreds, probably thousands, of books on Unix in press. Since it has not changed in its basics since the 1970s, even books published a long time ago can still be useful. Rather than attempt to survey this vast and variable market, I will point to a few standard references (many of which can be found in used book stores).

I have already mentioned the various books by Brian Kernighan and assorted co-authors; they remain standard, even though their examples show signs of aging in some environments. The single best source of printed information (both on Unix, and on regular expressions and their use in filters as well) for sophisticated beginners remains the first four chapters of Kernighan and Pike's classic (1984) *The UNIX Programming Environment*, which treat much the same topics as this chapter. This is pretty condensed stuff, but admirably clear; Kernighan is not only the *k* in *awk*, and one of the creators of Unix, but also one of the best writers in information science.

For those curious about how software is designed and developed, Brooks (1995) explains a great deal about the mistakes that can be made and the lessons that have been learned. For the historically-inclined, Salus (1994) covers the territory very well. Raymond (1996) is the latest installment of an online lexicographic project called the *Jargon File*; it contains a lot of good linguistics and ethnography, and some wonderful metaphors. Other books of historic and ethnographic interest include Kidder (1981), Levy (1984), Libes (1989), and Stoll (1989).

Regular expressions are covered in every book on Unix. They are especially well treated in books on filter languages. A good source for all of these is the set of books from O'Reilly and Associates (the ones with the strange beasts on the cover); they publish good manuals on sed and awk, regular expressions, Perl, and many other topics, centered on Unix and the Internet.

When evaluating a Unix book for reference purposes, look for a thick book with a good index and multiple appendices. Like good linguistics, it should give copious examples of everything, and say what each is an example of. A good check for the index (a vital part to any reference grammar) is to see if it's easy to find out how to refer to command-line arguments in a C-shell alias – you should be able to find the arcane formula (\!* or \\!*) without looking hard. Check the index also for mentions of useful commands like sed, ls, head, sort, uniq, rev, and awk. Check the table of contents for a separate section on regular expressions near the beginning of the book; there should also be discussions (ideally, entire sections) on aliases and customization, as well as shell programming in both the Bourne shell and the C-shell. Both vi and emacs should be treated in detail, with examples, and commands for both should be listed in detail.

Marketing hype about how the book makes Unix easy, even for those unwilling to attend to details, is extremely suspect, just as it would be if it were encountered on a linguistics book; one needs reference grammars as well as phrasebooks.

For technical reference, the official source is the Unix edition of the *Bell System Technical Journal* (1979, 1987), and Bell Laboratories' *Unix Programmer's Manual* (1979), which is largely a collection of standard man pages. (The online man system always provides the most up-to-date and deictically-anchored – and terse – Unix information available.) Stallman (1993) is the standard reference on the editor emacs, by its designer and author; the result is comprehensive, though as always the author of a program is not necessarily the best possible author of its manual. There are a vast number of Web and Usenet resources – see the online appendix at

   http://www.lsa.umich.edu/ling/jlawler/routledge/

NOTES

1 *Unix* (or UNIX) is a registered trademark (at press time, it was a trademark of the Open Group) whose provenance and ownership, along with the traditions and variations of its use, is part of its history as a language, in much the same ways that, say, *Indo-Germanic* is a term with roots in the history of linguistics, and of the study of the Indo-European language family. This point having been made, we do not hereinafter use the ™ symbol with the word *Unix*. For the etymology of *Unix*, see Salus (1994).

2 All of these proper names are also registered trademarks; hereinafter we do not distinguish trademarks from ordinary proper nouns.

3 My models in this sketch, to the extent practicable, are the excellent language sketches in Comrie (1987).

4 This has recently changed with the licensing of the Mac OS to other manufacturers.

5 This team did not rest on its Unix laurels. They have been working on a successor, and it is now being released under the whimsical name Plan 9.

6 Technically, this is a pervasive metaphor theme, with accompanying social movement, rather than a philosophy *per se*. Software Tools and Unix predate modern metaphor research and terminology by about a decade.

7 So-called because it was the successor of the B programming language.
8 Kernighan and Plauger: *The Elements of Programming Style* and *Software Tools* (both 1976), and *Software Tools in Pascal* (1981); Kernighan and Ritchie: *The C Programming Language* (1978); Kernighan and Pike: *The Unix Programming Environment* (1984).
9 See Section 5.6 of this chapter on *filters* for example.
10 See Section 5.3 of this chapter for further discussion of the *stream* metaphor. Note that *pipe* and *filter* are usefully coherent with it.
11 The **standard input** (and **output**) are abstract *streams* that are associated with every Unix program by the OS. They are the ablative source (and dative goal) of any filter program. The unmarked (default) standard input is the keyboard (and the unmarked standard output is the screen) unless they are redirected; i.e., unless overtly referenced with a pipe "|", as in

```
egrep umich.edu' $web.log | wc -l
```

or a case marker (<, >), as in

```
mail jim@somewhere.edu < job.talk
```

12 Besides being a genuine acronym, *bit* is also a remarkably apposite English name for the smallest possible unit of information.
13 /'æski/ in American English; an acronym of American Standard Code for Information Interchange.
14 This is certainly as true (and mnemonically as useful) as the rough equivalences of one meter with one English yard or of one liter with one English quart.
15 This byte is also expressible as number "6A" in **hexadecimal** (base 16) notation. "A" is a digit in Hexadecimal notation, representing the number after "9", which is called *ten* in Decimal notation. The capital letters "A–F" are single Hexadecimal digits representing Decimal "10" through "15", respectively; Decimal "16" is written "10" in Hexadecimal. It is customary to add "H" after writing a Hexadecimal number (e.g., "6AH") to indicate the base; but there are other conventions as well, such as "$6A", with sources in a number of languages.
16 But not all. This is the source of much frustration (see note 17), and explains why communication programs like `telnet` include provisions to use either BS or DEL as the destructive backspace character.
17 With one exception. No. 127, DEL, is at the very end of the chart. This is binary "1111111" and represents an original convention in (7-hole) paper tape, an early input medium. If one made a mistake in punching the tape, one simply punched everything out and it was skipped. This later became a standard in the early Unix community for keyboarding; thus the Back Space key on many workstation keyboards produces no. 127, DEL (^? or *Delete*). This has not been completely integrated with the other early convention of using no. 8, BS (^H or *Back Space*), that persists in most microcomputer applications.
18 Again, early conventions have resulted in variation. In DOS and Windows ASCII files, each text line is terminated by a cluster consisting of no. 13, CR (^M, or *Carriage Return*, which originally returned the teletype print head to the left margin without advancing a line), immediately followed by no. 10, LF. In Mac ASCII files, the standard newline character that terminates lines is CR alone, and in Unix it is LF alone.
19 Or roughly 60 Kilobytes (KB). The *kilo-* prefix, normally denoting 1000, refers in computing context to 1024, which is 2^{10}. Similarly, *mega-* is 1,048,576 (2^{20}),

rather than 1,000,000. While this is not standard metric, it rarely causes confusion.

20 One important qualification must be made here. Text files in word-processing programs (Unix or elsewhere) are not Standard ASCII files, and rarely mark individual lines with anything; on the contrary, most use newline to end paragraphs only, preferring to reformat lines on the fly. In fact, each wordprocessor has its own proprietary *file format*, in which control characters and High ASCII characters are used to code information peculiar to the particular program that writes (and expects to read) the file. In general, one may assume that any two wordprocessors' files are incompatible unless special steps, like *format* translation or translation to a common interlanguage, such as *Rich Text Format* (*RTF*), have been taken. Virtually all wordprocessors, however, have the capability to save text as a standard ASCII file, in some cases with or without line breaks specified, and this format is universally compatible.

21 The apl programming language is an example of a polysynthetic computer language, for instance.

22 The usual metaphor is that programs like those that serve files on the Web (httpd), respond with personal information on the finger command (fingerd), or make *ftp* connections (ftpd), etc, are *d(a)emons*, whence the suffixal -d in their names. Daemons are invisible slavery programs that run only in the background, checking every so often to see if what they're looking for has come in, responding to it if it has, and going back to sleep. This metaphor refers to Selfridge's (1958) "Pandemonium" model of perception, which is fairly close to the way many net programs work.

23 Note that the argument immediately after egrep on the command line is interpreted as a regular expression, while the one following that is interpreted as a file name; we have here a system of subcategorization that specifies the lexical class and morphological properties of verbal case roles. The string to be matched by egrep need not be quoted (though it may be). However, one is well advised to "single-quote" complex search strings containing space and other special characters, to avoid unexpected misinterpretations.

24 From "word count"; wc counts lines, words, and characters; the optional -l, -w, and -c switches say which.

25 It is also possible to have Unix supply the current data in the appropriate format as the string (thus making the command indexical), by means of the backquote convention (see below):

```
egrep `date +%d/%h/19%y` $weblog | wc -l
```

26 As a matter of fact, it will match the longest such string in the line, if there is any ambiguity in the match.

27 The prompt is usually "%" (possibly with other information, like the name of the machine), and sometimes "$".

28 cd (from "change directory") changes the directory location to the one specified; when issued without an argument, it defaults to the user's home directory.

29 With the usual Western "narrative presupposition" to the effect that the conjuncts occur in the order they are mentioned. In this case, of course, it is not so much a presupposition as a performative.

30 In particular, they are very reminiscent of conjunctive embedded questions of the form

I know who Bill invited

where in fact what I know is the answer to the question "Who did Bill invite?"

31 Any Unix command, for instance, can be run "in the background", i.e., simultaneously, by suffixing "&" to it.

32 The length of filenames was one of the major differences between BSD Unix and System V; Berkeley filenames could generally be longer, and this caused problems in adapting programs.

33 Sometimes called options. These are generally adverbial in nature.

34 Or the commands ls -r -st, or ls -rs -t, or ls -t -r -s, etc. Switches need not be concatenated.

35 In case *name* is not specified (as it isn't in the command in the previous line), *ls* assumes the current directory is intended. This is an example of the Software Tools philosophy in action: instead of requiring literal compliance with the syntax, make the defaults useful.

36 So called because it incorporates many features of the C programming language.

37 Named after its inventor. sh was an earlier shell, superseded for interactive use by csh: however, its simplicity has made it the default choice for shell programming.

38 Others include ksh, the "Korn Shell", which combines features of sh and csh, and tcsh, an improved csh.

39 The period prefix is obligatory; most Unix programs use such *dot files* containing customizations of preferences. The ls command does not display dot files unless instructed to with the -a switch.

40 The three successive commands separated by semicolons respectively: (a) edit the user's aliases file, presumably to insert a new alias; (b) remove all current aliases; (c) reload the presumably modified aliases.

41 Provided this is where their aliases are: the following command should be the last line in the dot file .cshrc:

```
alias -r $HOME/aliases
```

This will load the alias file when the shell starts, e.g., at login.

42 Besides aliases, which will also locate any executable files (shell scripts or programs) matching a name that are in the user's *path*. As such, a command like which foobar answers the question: "If I type foobar, will anything happen?"

43 Note the final space, to restrict the match to commands. Quotes are used to disambiguate strings whenever necessary, as with spaces and special characters, but they are not necessary with simple strings. There is a principled pragmatic difference between single and double quotes in Unix.

44 Each user's dot and customization files are located in their home directory, to which cd returns when invoked without arguments, and which is contained in the system variable $HOME.

45 From "catenate", since the tool will concatenate multiple files named as arguments.

46 There can be many lines between do and done, but we need only one for such a simple task.

47 Thus, by default, lying in the current directory; this also applies to editcmds. This means that editcmds should be in the same directory as the files to be edited, and that that should be the current directory. loopedit, however, need not be there, since as an executable script it can be located anywhere in the user's *path* (the series of directories searched by the shell to find programs to be executed). ex itself resides in a system directory, where it is accessible to (but not modifiable by) ordinary users.

48 And in fact took a couple of tries to get right. However, once debugged it can be saved and reused indefinitely, a major feature of the Software Tools philosophy.

49 As in this command. Although any character may function as a string delimiter in an "s" command, slash is most common. Using a different character for the "s" command would eliminate one pair of backslashes in this command. However, slash is the canonical delimiter for searching and may not be changed in that sense.

50 Actually, we could do without the escaped slash in the search string. Since any string containing "www.umich.edu" followed by a tilde is acceptable, we could simply use a period, which will match any character, instead of an escaped slash in the search string: "www.umich.edu.\~". Indeed, the periods in "www.umich.edu" will match any character, too; the fact that they are intended to match literal periods is entirely coincidental. However, in the replacement string, period is not interpreted, while slash is, so the escaped slash is necessary there.

51 From "change modifiers", a reference to the executability of the file. The command that activates loopedit as a program is chmod u+x loopedit, which means that the user adds executability to the file's properties. If this seems difficult to remember (and it is hardly intuitive), an alias renders it more memorable: alias activate chmod u+x.

52 There are other possible interpretations; for instance, the ex editor has a special meaning for slash "/". See above for examples.

53 From "stream editor". sed can do the same things as ed, but operates on the entire text stream with predetermined instructions, instead of interactively. It is useful for repetitive editing tasks.

54 An acronym of "Aho, Weinberg, Kernighan", the authors of the program. awk is more powerful than sed, and is designed specifically for use as a text filter, especially for repetitively-formulated files.

55 An acronym of "Practical Extraction and Report Language". Perl is a full programming language, oriented towards manipulating large texts. It is widely used on the Web for CGI scripts; a very simple example is the Chomskybot, whose URL is: http://stick.us.itd.umich.edu/cri-bin/chomsky.pl; the URL of its Perl script is: http://www/lsa.umich.edu/ling/jlawler/ fogcode.html. I do not consider Perl much further here, except to point out ways of learning it easily, by automatic translation.

Chapter 6

Software for doing field linguistics

Evan L. Antworth and J. Randolph Valentine

In his introduction to Bloomfield's posthumous grammar of Menomini (Bloomfield, 1962), Charles Hockett recounts Bloomfield's stratagem for the documentation of the endangered languages of North America: as linguists each of us should take a vow of celibacy, not teach, and dedicate the entirety of our summers to fieldwork, and our winters to collating and filing our data, year after year. With such dedication, Bloomfield speculated, we could each hope to do an adequate job of documenting three languages over the course of our professional lives. Upon being reminded of this anecdote not too long ago, a frustrated Algonquianist remarked, "Yes, and now that we have computers, it's down to *two* languages apiece!" Computers certainly present a mixed blessing: at the same time that they allow us to perform tasks such as querying and sorting the reams of data that we typically gather in extended periods of fieldwork, they also structure the ways in which we address these data, and often become petulant intermediaries that distance us from the very languages which we seek to describe. The amount of time required to learn the intricacies of software can have a significant impact on our time. Yet, properly used, computers can provide us with the means of documenting languages at a level of detail and sophistication that would have made Boas swoon.

Most linguists use computers mainly for general academic use such as preparing manuscripts with a word processor or communicating with colleagues via e-mail. In recent years, however, we have begun to see software that is intended for specifically linguistic tasks: speech analysis, **corpus** management, grammatical parsing, text analysis, and language comparison. This chapter is a survey of such linguistic software that is suitable for doing field linguistics. The focus will be on readily available, low cost software products that run on personal computers, especially portable computers.

6.1 HARDWARE AND OPERATING SYSTEMS

A perennial problem facing anyone wanting to use a computer is, "which kind of computer should I choose?" The bad news is that we still must live with competing computing platforms, such as DOS, Windows, Macintosh, NeXT, and Unix. The good news is that there is a conceptual convergence among these platforms in favor of a graphical user interface driven with a mouse. This at least makes it possible for a program to run on more than one platform and still have a very similar look and feel. In choosing which computer to use, here are some considerations.

- First choose the software that best meets your needs, and then choose the computer that runs it. No matter how powerful or popular or expensive a particular computer is, if it doesn't run the software you need to do your work then it is of limited usefulness to you. Let software drive your decision as to which computer to use, not ideological arguments about the best hardware architecture and operating system design.

- Buy the power that you need for the software you are going to run today, rather than buying expensive features for the future. Research on price versus performance trends in personal computers has shown that today's top-of-the-line computer costs only half as much two years later. Rather than buying a $4000 computer today (when you need only half its power), you can buy a $2000 computer today and buy the $4000 computer in two years for $2000 when you really do need the power. The net result is that you have spent $4000, but have two machines instead of one. (For substantiation of this recommendation, see Simons, 1992 and Rettig, 1992.)

- If you work with languages other than English, and particularly languages that use non-Roman scripts, choose a computer that has adequate multilingual capability. Computers with *operating system*s that are graphics-based (*GUI*s), such as the Macintosh, have offered better multilingual support than computers that are *character*-based, such as the IBM PC. However, with the advent of Windows (which is graphics-based) for IBM compatibles, the gap is narrowing. Because the whole area of multilingual support is changing so rapidly, you should carefully investigate what is currently available before making a major purchase.

- Consider your local computing community. If most of your colleagues use computer *X*, and you use computer *Y*, then it will be more difficult to share your work and expertise with them and vice-versa.

- Choose a computer for which you can most readily obtain local repair and technical support. This is particularly important if you work in third world countries. If you must use a computer in a country where no reliable local service is available, then establish a service contract with a company in your home country that will repair your computer and ship it back to you. If you are going to be doing time-bound research it is probably best to stick with name-brand, reliable machines, because a single repair cycle from a remote location could leave you without a computer for much of your fieldwork.

- Purchase a portable or laptop computer only if you genuinely need it. Compared to desktop computers, laptop computers are more expensive, less expandable, and have poorer screens and keyboards. If you travel a lot, work in more than one place, or intend to do fieldwork, a portable computer is invaluable. But if you generally work in just one place, a desktop computer will provide a superior working environment. Some portables allow the attachment of external monitors and keyboards. If you work with more than one computer, you will have to give some attention to file management, to avoid a proliferation of versions of the same file on your different computers.

6.2   GENERAL-PURPOSE VERSUS DOMAIN-SPECIFIC SOFTWARE

Traditionally linguists used notebooks and index cards to record and organize their field observations. Today, most field linguists use a portable computer and the electronic analogs of the notebook and index cards: a word processor and a database management system. While these software tools are in many ways superior to their predecessors, most general purpose word processors and database programs are not well-suited to the special needs of linguistic work. For instance, word processing in English is reasonably well-supported, but multilingual word processing remains a challenge. Most database programs require that all data fit into fixed length fields, but lexicographic and textual data have no easily fixed length. Sorting data in languages other than English often requires a sorting sequence different from that of English – a capability not provided by most general purpose software. Worse yet, general-purpose software offers no direct way to represent linguistic entities such as multilinear phonetic and phonological representations, syntactic trees, semantic networks, and discourse structures. For these reasons it is usually better to use software that is domain-specific: software specifically developed with linguistic applications in mind. The major part of this chapter is devoted to such domain-specific linguistic software. Unfortunately, though, adequate linguistic software still does not exist for many tasks, thereby forcing the field linguist to use general-purpose software. The next section lists a number of criteria to consider when you are evaluating a given piece of software, particularly general-purpose software, though the same criteria apply also to domain-specific software.

6.3   CRITERIA FOR EVALUATING SOFTWARE

The discussion in this section is organized around three major tasks (or categories of tasks) performed by field linguists: data collection and management, analysis, and description (or presentation). The nature of each task is described and criteria for evaluating software relevant to that task are itemized.

6.3.1   Data collection and management

A field linguist's first task is data collection. Each day of fieldwork brings the linguist a veritable flood of new sounds, words, sentences, and texts. To manage this data, the field linguist needs a linguistic database system. Like general database systems, a linguistic database system must provide facilities for entering new data, editing existing data, sorting and searching the database, and retrieving data. But the unique requirement of a linguistic database system is that each type of linguistic structure should have a means of representation that is appropriate to its intrinsic nature. For instance, phonetic and phonological data should be representable as phones, phonemes, suprasegmentals, and so on; morphological data should be representable as words, morphemes, roots, affixes, and so on; syntactic data should be representable as sentences, phrase structure trees, grammatical relations, and so on. Unfortunately, most of our present software does not go very far beyond representing all data structures as linear strings of characters. We must look to the next generation of software to provide a comprehensive solution to the problem of linguistic representation (see Chapter 1).

Here are some desirable features to check for when evaluating a database management system.

- **Variable length fields** – The vast majority of database systems require fixed length fields which can eat up substantial amounts of storage space. For example, if one wishes to include example sentences with some entries in a lexical database, each entry in the lexicon will have to include a field containing as much space as the longest sentence likely to be used in the *corpus*, regardless of whether or not the entry actually contains an example sentence. If one dedicates 100 characters to such an example sentence field, every 10 entries will collectively require a kilobyte of storage, and every 10,000 entries, collectively a megabyte.
- **Multilingual support** – Can the database program handle fields in different languages? Can it switch languages within a field? Can it handle non-Roman scripts, and if so, can you mix scripts within a single field?
- **User-defined alphabet and sorting sequence** – Can the user fully define which characters are alphabetic? Can the user define a sorting sequence? (see Chapter 4).

- **Domain-specific data types** – Does the database program permit only character strings and numeric data or can the user define complex data types such as multilinear phonological representations and syntactic trees?
- **Programmable** – Can the user write *script*s to manipulate the database?
- **Reliability** – How safe is the database from internal corruption, and can corrupted databases be salvaged?
- **Ease of use** – Can the database be used by nonexperts who may wish to use your materials derivatively to address local needs, such as the development of vernacular educational materials?

6.3.2 Analysis

The second major task of field linguistics is analysis (which of course is not limited to field linguistics). No computer software will do linguistic analysis for you, but it can help you to formulate and test your analysis in two ways. First, you can use software to explore and manipulate the data in your database. This helps in quickly finding data that supports or refutes a hypothesis. Here are some of the typical tasks done to explore and manipulate data.

- **Sorting** – Sorting a data set according to a particular criterion groups all the bits of data that go together, thereby allowing a pattern to emerge. As noted above in connection with database programs, a sorting program for linguistic use must permit the user complete control over definition of the alphabet and sorting sequence. Ideally, sorting operations should be sensitive to data types; phonological representations may be sorted quite differently from syntactic representations.
- **Searching** – Often one has a particular hypothesis in mind and wants to search a data set for specific data items that will confirm or disconfirm the hypothesis. Searching software must permit abstract pattern matching, not just finding literal forms. For instance, most word processors permit you to search for a literal string such as "phoneme"; but very few word processors permit you to search for a pattern such as "any word containing only sonorants." Searching and pattern matching must also be sensitive to data types; for instance, one might want to search analyzed sentences by looking for those that contain more than one overt noun phrase.
- **Concordancing** – Producing a concordance of a text requires a combination of sorting and searching; thus concordance software is subject to the criteria mentioned above. A good concordance program should also be able to handle the type-token problem; for instance, if you

want to concord lexemes, then you need to be able to consider inflected forms such as *saw* and *seen* as instances (tokens) of the lexeme (type) *see*. You also need to distinguish *saw* as an instance of the verb *see* from *saw* as an instance of the noun *saw*.

- **Counting** – Retrieval software should be able to produce various types of statistical analysis of the data such as frequency lists (of both types and tokens).

The second way that you can use software to aid the analysis process is to test or model the analysis by applying it to a corpus of data. Using the computer to model and test analyses could lead to a new era of empirical accountability! Since computer software tends to lag behind theoretical developments in linguistics, you should not expect to find software that fully models the latest theoretical advance in phonology, morphology, or syntax. Be prepared to make some theoretical compromises for the benefit of having the computer automatically test your analysis against data. Here are some of the typical tasks done to test and model (note that they are all domain-specific rather than general-purpose).

- **Testing phonological rules** – A program that applies phonological rules to a corpus of data is very useful for developing a basic phonological analysis.
- **Morphological parsing** – A program to parse words into their component morphemes is invaluable for languages with complex morphological structure, both to model and test a morphological analysis and to provide inflectional information required for syntactic analysis.
- **Syntactic parsing** – A syntactic parser can be used not only to model and test an analysis but to do practical tasks such as syntactically tagging a text.
- **Interlinear analysis of text** – Possible interlinear annotations include phonological representations, morpheme glosses, word glosses, and syntactic categories. The process of providing explicit annotations for a text forces the linguist to consistently apply his or her analysis of the phonological, morphological, and syntactic systems of the language.

6.3.3   Description

The third major task of field linguistics is description, or presentation, of the data and analysis for others to review and use. Good software will make it easy for you to transfer examples from your database and analysis files to your word processor for inclusion in a research paper. For instance, if you plan to use both a word processor and a database program together, consider these points when making your choice.

- Choose software that supports transfer of data. If you already use a certain word processor and now want a database program, choose one that supports exporting the data in a *format* the word processor can import. For modest amounts of data in the Windows and Macintosh environments, this often can be achieved simply by copying to and pasting from the system clipboard. In a DOS environment, it might require explicit export and import of the data via an interchange format. In many cases, though, if you want fine control over the formatting of text output from a database program, you will have to know how to write programs to embed the word processor's formatting codes in the output from the database.

- If you are using a system that supports fonts and scripts (such as Windows and the Macintosh), check to see if the word processor and database program can use the same fonts or scripts and that the data are displayed and printed identically. Many database programs have comparatively poor font and script capabilities, though they often make claims otherwise.

- Check to see if you can directly "copy and paste" data from one program into another, or whether you have to export data from one program to a file and then import that file into the other program. Can you transfer both text and graphics?

When choosing a word processor or other document processing system for producing manuscripts, consider these points:

- Does it handle multilingual documents? Does it support fonts for languages other than English? Does it support non-Roman scripts, including right-to-left text editing if required? Does it allow you to mark text for exemption from English spelling checking, so that it isn't applied to your non-English example sentences? Can you define which characters are alphabetic and which are not?

- Does it support style sheets? Rather than directly formatting each paragraph (font, line spacing, indents, tabs, and so on), many word processors keep style and formatting information separate from the text itself. This permits the writer to change the style of the document for various publishers by simply choosing a different document style sheet, rather than reformatting every paragraph of the document.

- Does it support character styles, that is, can you assign styles to formatting strategies for such things as citation and emphasis, so that when a publisher requires a different format for these items, you can make the required changes by simply changing the formatting specification of the style rather than having to make the changes individually?

- Is it a batch formatting system or a WYSIWYG (What You See Is What You Get) system? Virtually all common commercial word processors are WYSIWYG systems, where the document appears on the screen just as it will look when printed (or as closely as possible). A system of document preparation on laptop computers using Microsoft Word (a WYSIWYG word processor with style sheets) is described in Kew and Simons (1989). While such systems are adequate for most purposes, very complex documents are better handled by batch formatting systems. In such systems, formatting is done by placing codes directly into the stream of text; the final appearance of the document cannot be seen until it is printed (see Coombs, Renear and DeRose, 1987). One widely used batch formatting system specifically designed for academic writing is called LaT$_e$X (Lamport, 1986); it is based on a typesetting system called T$_e$X (Knuth, 1986). The power of T$_e$X can also be harnessed to do very domain-specific tasks; for example, Kew and McConnel (1990) describe a system for typesetting interlinear text based on T$_e$X.

In the future, we look for systems that will seamlessly integrate a language corpus with a descriptive grammar. In a visionary article, Weber (1986) describes the "reference grammar of the future" which will be an "online, interactive, information management system, built around a *corpus*" (p. 30). These same concerns are taken up by the CELLAR system described by Simons in chapter 1 of this book. One experimental program, called Rook, is available now (see Section 6.4.4 below). It enables the linguist to incrementally and interactively build up a descriptive grammar while annotating texts.

6.4   A CATALOG OF LINGUISTIC SOFTWARE

This section contains the major part of this chapter: a catalog of specific pieces of software for doing field linguistics. Most, though not all, of the software is domain-specific rather than general-purpose software. The section is divided into subsections corresponding to subdomains within linguistics:

- data management
- speech analysis and phonetics
- phonology and morphology
- syntax and grammar description
- lexicon
- text analysis
- language survey and comparison

For specific information on each program described below (including name of developer and vendor, price, reviews, and so on), see the online appendix at http://www.lsa.umich.edu/lig/jlawler/routledge/

6.4.1   Data management

This section describes four pieces of software that fall into the category of general data management tools: Shoebox, askSam, HyperCard, and Xbase systems. The first three would mainly be used for managing lexicon, texts, and grammar, but are general enough to also be used for other types of information such as anthropological notes. Xbase systems are not well suited to textual manipulation, but arguably offer more power than any of the other software for lexical work. Of these three pieces of software, the first is domain-specific and the other three are commercial, general-purpose software.

6.4.1.1   *Shoebox*

Shoebox is a database program designed for field linguists to manage their lexicon and to interlinearize text. While Shoebox can be used to manage nearly any kind of textual data, its most common use for field linguists is in managing a lexicon and text corpus. The metaphor of index cards in a shoebox is translated as a database file composed of records. Records are displayed on the screen and can be modified with a built-in *editor*. The content of a record can either be free-form text or data in fields or a combination; Shoebox does not force uniformity among the records of a database. The database can be sorted on any field. The sorting order can be defined by the user and supports multigraphs. By referring to its primary sort field, any record can be located and displayed nearly instantly. A *filter* function permits the user to select only records that match specified criteria. For example, in a lexical database you could choose to look at only verbs or only transitive verbs, assuming you have coded that information. Shoebox permits the user to have multiple database files open at once in a multidocument window. For example, you could have your lexicon, texts, syntactic examples, anthropological notes, and bibliography all available at once.

Shoebox also has a built-in function for producing interlinear text. It uses a lexicon file to semiautomatically gloss words and morphemes in a text.

Shoebox supports TrueType fonts. Its output capabilities include draft printing of any part of a database and exporting to an *RTF* file which can be read by word processors such as Microsoft Word.

6.4.1.2   *askSam*

askSam is a free-form textbase program for DOS and Windows. It can be used for data management, word processing, and text retrieval. An askSam file is comprised of records. A record can contain unstructured

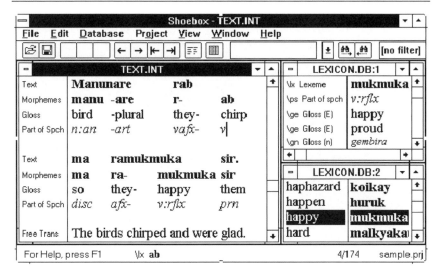

Figure 6.1   A record in Shoebox

text, structured fields, or a combination of both. A number of powerful text and data retrieval tools are available including wild-card operators, Boolean expressions, and proximity searching. Data in fields can be sorted, formatted, and output in reports. askSam also supports multiple file access, thus providing relational capabilities. askSam for Windows has impressive text-formatting capabilities, and is very easy to use. The program supports graphics. Its comprehensive text formatting capabilities and retrieval capabilities make it ideal for researchers whose data consist primarily of prose. The program also has *hypertext* capabilities, making it useful for presenting data. There is an electronic publisher version which can be used to build hypertext presentations that can be distributed royalty free. Thus it should be given serious consideration in the development of materials for classroom use.

6.4.1.3   HyperCard

HyperCard has been described by its author as an "electronic constructor kit." It is fundamentally a programmable database system that can handle text, numerical data, sound, and graphics. Its basic metaphor is a stack of cards which contain fields of data. The user interface relies on buttons and menu commands. Underlying HyperCard is a *script*ing language called HyperTalk. Numerous books about HyperCard and HyperTalk programming are available; for example, Goodman (1990) and Winkler and Kamins (1990). Many existing HyperCard applications are available at low or no cost (see for example Rook, described below in Section

```
File: IFUGAO                                            1 80   13 01
EDIT RECORD     <Ctrl-Enter> done                       STREAM
<Esc> undo   <Enter> row 20, after   <PgUp> before   <PgDn> after   TAB SET 5

\lx t~abaw
\px n
\sn Lynx rufus
\gl A wild cat living in forested areas.
\ie cat, wild
\ex Hay inal~ahan di punhit~uwan nan t~abaw.
\tr The forest is the place where wild cats live.
\rg p~uha
\sc 2.1
\li punt~abawon
\ps v
\co T do sth. stealthily.
```

Figure 6.2   Lexicon record in askSam (MS-DOS version)

6.4.4.2). But the user who learns to control cards, fields, buttons, and scripts has the capability to build nearly any computer application he or she desires. For the field of linguistics, where relatively little off-the-shelf software exists, this is a powerful asset.

6.4.1.4   *Xbase database systems*

Provided one is willing to devote some time to learning their idiosyncrasies, Xbase database management systems such as dBase IV and FoxPro represent powerful general purpose applications that can be used to great advantage in some kinds of linguistic work, particularly list-oriented tasks such as the compilation of simple lexicons. These programs have elaborate *index*ing capabilities far beyond those offered by Shoebox or HyperCard, and rich programming languages with well-developed *command* sets for working with text *string*s. Their multilingual capacities are, however, very modest, and the way in which they deal with freeform text is controversial, involving the storage of such text in a file separate from the main database file, which can be overlooked when files are copied. One problem with much DOS-based software is that there is a tendency to use some character slots for program-internal functions, which can cause problems if you use a font that happens to have characters defined in the same positions, since they will either be *filter*ed out on import, or misinterpreted as commands to be carried out rather than text. Also, the learning curve for mastering these programs to a degree to really exploit their power is precipitous, and unless one stays with it,

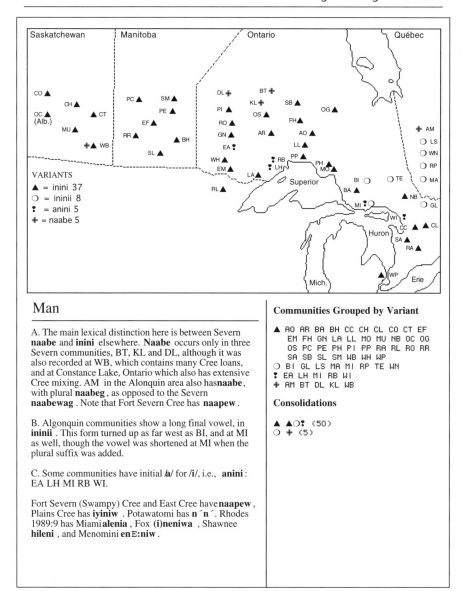

The map contains the following labels and text:

Saskatchewan | Manitoba | Ontario | Québec

CO ▲   CH ▲   PC ▲   SM ▲   DL ✚   BT ✚
OC ▲ (Alb.)   ▲ CT   PE ▲   PI ▲   KL ✚   SB ▲   OG ▲
MU ▲   EF ▲   RO ▲   OS ▲   FH ▲
✚▲ WB   RR ▲   ▲ BH   GN ▲   AR ▲   AO ▲   ✚ AM
SL ▲   EA ⁝   LL ▲   ○ LS
WH ▲   ⁝ RB   PP ▲   ○ WN
EM ▲   ⁝ LH   PH ▲   ○ RP
VARIANTS   LA ▲   MO ▲   ○ MA
RL ▲   Superior   BI ○   ○ TE

VARIANTS
▲ = inini 37
○ = ininii 8
⁝ = anini 5
✚ = naabe 5

BA ▲   ▲ NB
MI ⁝○   ○ GL
WI ⁝
Huron   CC ▲ ▲ CL
SA ▲
RA ▲
▲ WP
Mich.   Erie

Man

A. The main lexical distinction here is between Severn **naabe** and **inini** elsewhere. **Naabe** occurs only in three Severn communities, BT, KL and DL, although it was also recorded at WB, which contains many Cree loans, and at Constance Lake, Ontario which also has extensive Cree mixing. AM in the Alonquin area also has **naabe**, with plural **naabeg**, as opposed to the Severn **naabewag**. Note that Fort Severn Cree has **naapew**.

B. Algonquin communities show a long final vowel, in **ininii**. This form turned up as far west as BI, and at MI as well, though the vowel was shortened at MI when the plural suffix was added.

C. Some communities have initial **a/** for /i/, i.e., **anini**: EA LH MI RB WI.

Fort Severn (Swampy) Cree and East Cree have **naapew**, Plains Cree has **iyiniw**. Potawatomi has **n´n´**. Rhodes 1989:9 has Miami **alenia**, Fox **(i)neniwa**, Shawnee **hileni**, and Menomini **enE:niw**.

Communities Grouped by Variant

▲ AO AR BA BH CC CH CL CO CT EF
  EM FH GN LA LL MO MU NB OC OG
  OS PC PE PH PI PP RA RL RO RR
  SA SB SL SM WB WH WP
○ BI GL LS MA MI RP TE WN
⁝ EA LH MI RB WI
✚ AM BT DL KL WB

Consolidations

▲ ▲○⁝ (50)
○ ✚ (5)

Figure 6.3   Dynamic dialectological map produced in HyperCard

this arcane knowledge is easily forgotten. Many linguists hire Xbase experts to produce simple systems for data entry and formatting. The fact that these databases are commonly used in the business world also weighs in their favor, in that they tend to be priced well, be updated often, and have good data integrity.

6.4.1.5   *LinguaLinks*

LinguaLinks is an electronic performance support system designed to help field language workers. The full product has two parts: data management tools and a library of reference materials. The data management tools (which are based on CELLAR; see Chapter 1) include tools for lexical database management, interlinear text analysis, phonological analysis, and ethnographic database management. The reference materials include books on linguistics, language learning, anthropology, literacy, and socio-linguistics. The entire package requires a Windows system, a Pentium processor, and 32 megabytes of memory. A second product, LinguaLinks Library, contains only the reference materials and will run on any Windows or Macintosh system.

6.4.2   Speech analysis and phonetics

One of the basic tasks of field linguistics is phonetic transcription. A number of phonetic or IPA fonts are now available, including the SIL Encore fonts.

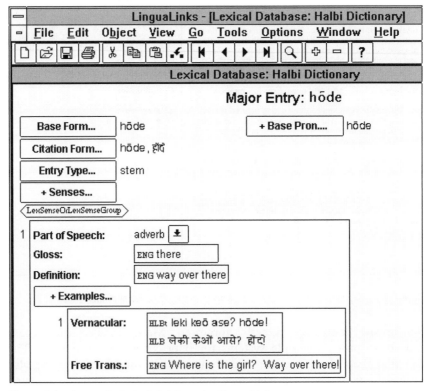

Figure 6.4   A sample lexical database in LinguaLinks

Three programs related to speech analysis and phonetics are also described here: CECIL, Signalyze, and FindPhone. The CECIL program is intended for field use. Signalyze is an excellent, if pricey, speech analysis tool, which can also be immensely useful in the field. FindPhone is useful for doing basic distributional analysis of phonetic forms.

6.4.2.1 *SIL Encore fonts and Encore IPA fonts*

The SIL Encore fonts are available in two packages: the full Encore fonts (commercial) and the Encore IPA fonts (freeware).

- The SIL Encore fonts are a complete package of over 1300 phonetic characters and linguistic symbols that can be used to create customized, scalable fonts in either PostScript Type 1 or TrueType formats. The SIL Encore glyph library has a complete Roman-based glyph set for linguistic applications in three font families (SIL Doulos, SIL Sophia, and SIL Manuscript) in four type styles (regular, bold, italic, and bold italic) available in Macintosh or Windows platforms. A free Windows TrueType font compiler is included with the Windows TrueType package. With Mac or PostScript you will need a third party font manipulation package, such as FontMonger or Fontographer to build your customized font.
- The SIL Encore IPA Fonts are a set of scalable IPA fonts containing the full International Phonetic Alphabet with 1990 Kiel revisions. Three typefaces are included: SIL Doulos (similar to Times), SIL Sophia (similar to Helvetica), and SIL Manuscript (monowidth). Each font contains all the standard IPA discrete characters and nonspacing *diacritic*s as well as some suprasegmental and punctuation marks. Each font comes in both PostScript Type 1 and TrueType formats and is available in Macintosh or Windows platforms.

6.4.2.2 *Keyboard remapping programs*

To facilitate typing text using nonstandard fonts such as IPA fonts, consider using a utility program that modifies the behavior of the keyboard. With such a utility it is possible to remap keys (make them generate characters other than the standard ones), to combine sequences of keystrokes into single characters, and to generate multiple characters from a single keystroke. Two such keyboard remapping programs are KeyMan (for Windows) and SILKey (for Macintosh).

6.4.2.3 *CECIL*

CECIL (which stands for Computerized Extraction of Components of Intonation in Language) is a system for doing acoustic speech analysis, mainly tone and stress analysis (see Hunt, 1988). It is intended for use in a field situation using a DOS or Windows portable computer. The DOS version uses a battery-powered speech box (sound digitizer) is used for recording and playback, while the Windows version uses a standard Windows sound card. The software performs graphical displays of waveform, fundamental frequency (pitch), and amplitude (stress), as well as spectrograms and spectra. It also supports a language learner's mode in which traces of the learner's attempt to mimic a recorded utterance are superimposed on the traces of the original recording. Utterance length is limited to 3.3 seconds at a 19,500 Hz sampling rate.

6.4.2.4 *Signalyze*

Signalyze is an interactive program for the analysis of speech, and can work with 8- or 16-bit sound. It contains a large set of signal editing, analysis and manipulation tools. With Signalyze, you can measure duration, amplitude, and frequency, make beautiful 250 color or greyscale spectrograms, extract pitch, slow down or speed up speech. You can easily obtains numeric measurements pertaining to the duration of a speech sound, the frequency from a spectral peak, the amplitude differences between two vowels, and so on. Signalyze has extensive labeling facilities, coded for up to nine levels (segment, syllable, etc.); labels can apply to points or segments of text, and may be saved as tab-delimited text files. Signalyze thus represents an invaluable tool for field research, aiding in transcription and analysis. You can listen to a given sample over

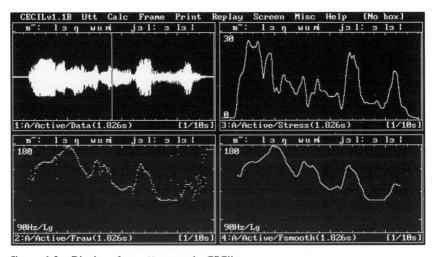

Figure 6.5 Display of an utterance in CECIL

and over, slowing it down to hear difficult material better; you can easily compare two samples to determine their relative phonetic properties; the ease of pitch tracking invites analysis of important aspects of prosody often overlooked in phonological analyses; different portions of discourse of can easily be queued up to observe varying patterns of cadence and amplitude. The sound samples Signalyze produces can easily be saved as sound files and used in derivative presentations by importing them into programs capable of playing sounds, such as HyperCard or Microsoft Word. While Signalyze is a little expensive for individuals, there are excellent departmental and institutional rates.

6.4.2.5   FindPhone

FindPhone is an interactive, menu-driven program for DOS that performs distributional analysis of phonetic data transcribed in IPA (see Hunt, 1992 and Bevan, 1993). A built-in editor facilitates maintenance of a

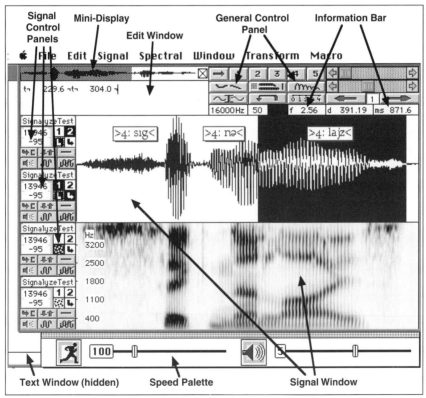

Figure 6.6   Display of an utterance in Signalyze

phonetic database in which each transcribed utterance is represented as a record. An utterance record can also contain any number of other fields such as gloss, grammatical category, reference number, and so on. The database can then be searched according to patterns defined by the user; for example, the pattern #pV will return all utterances containing an utterance-initial [p] followed by any vowel. Phonetic class symbols such as C (for consonants) and V (for vowels) can be defined by the user. Features such as stress, pitch, and syllable boundaries can be included in search patterns or can be ignored. The results of a search can be viewed on the screen, formatted and saved to a file, or printed.

6.4.3   Phonology and morphology

Although syntactic parsing of English and other economically important European languages has received great attention in recent years, morphological parsing has largely been left to those working in agglutinative languages who cannot sidestep morphological analysis. This is borne out by the heritages of the programs described below: AMPLE was initially developed for Quechua and PC-KIMMO is an implementation of a system first applied to Finnish.

```
pʰ/i_#      wom'pʃipʰ           bracelet                              L023
pʰ/i_#      wa'zipʰ             meat                                  L034
pʰ/ə_#      sɛ'ʔəpʰ             seed               .                  L038
pʰ/a_#      ʔe:'βapʰ            mother                                L062
pʰ/i_#      wonindʒn̩'tʃipʰ     lime                                  L151
pʰ/e:_#     se:pʰ              axe                                   L155
pʰ/i_#      wo'tsipʰ            pith                                  L157
pʰ/ə_#      saʔa'ʔəpʰ          hiccup                                L166
pʰ/i:_#     ʃi:pʰ              day                                   L192
pʰ/e:_#     se:pʰ              land                                  L217
pʰ/ɪ_#      ji'jɪpʰ            smoke                                 L223
pʰ/i_#      sa'ʔipʰ            grandfather                           L231
pʰ/ə_#      məpʰ               heel                                  L239
pʰ/i_#      san'dipʰ           thigh                                 L240
pʰ/i_#      jɪ'nipʰ            nose.ring                             L246
pʰ/i_#      wɛ'ʔipʰ            heap                                  L250
pʰ/i_#      jijɪrɪ'ʔipʰ        sweet.potato                          L282
pʰ/a:_#     wa:pʰ              rib                                   L286
pʰ/i_#      won'dipʰ           necklace                              L326
pʰ/ə_#      pjɛ'ləpʰ           cat                                   L329
pʰ/ə_#      sa:'βəpʰ           arm                                   L358
Results (28)
↑ ↓      | PgUp PgDn Home End | Line:      1 |          | Help: F1 | Exit: Esc
```

Figure 6.7   Results of a search in FindPhone

6.4.3.1   AMPLE and STAMP

AMPLE and STAMP are components of a practical system for doing machine translation of texts between closely related languages or dialects. AMPLE does the morphological analysis (parsing) of an input text and STAMP does transfer and synthesis of the text into a target language. AMPLE can also be used by itself for purely linguistic purposes, namely, to model and verify a morphological analysis of a language. An AMPLE description consists of a lexicon which lists all stems and affixes and a set of rules that specify morphotactic structure. AMPLE has a strong item-and-arrangement view of morphology, but is able to handle phenomena such as reduplication and infixation. AMPLE works strictly at the phonological surface level. Rather than modeling phonological rules, all allomorphs of a lexical item must be explicitly listed in the lexicon. A preprocessor called PHONRULE applies phonological rules to underlying lexical forms and generates all the allomorphs to be inserted into the lexicon.

6.4.3.2   PC-KIMMO

PC-KIMMO is a new implementation for microcomputers of a program named after its inventor Kimmo Koskenniemi, a Finnish computational linguist (see Koskenniemi, 1983 and Karttunen, 1983). Its main practical use is to build morphological parsers for natural language processing systems, but it can also be used to model and test a phonological and morphological analysis of a language. PC-KIMMO is based on Koskenniemi's two-level model of morphology, where "two-level" refers to the underlying (lexical) and surface levels of phonological representation. In this model phonological rules apply simultaneously and can refer to both underlying and surface environments. The result is that there need be no rule ordering, no intermediate levels of derivation (just two levels), and rules can be run in either direction: underlying to surface or surface to underlying. In addition to a set of phonological rules, a PC-KIMMO description includes a lexicon of all stems and affixes. The structure of the lexicon enforces a simple system of morphotactic constraints. Version 2 of PC-KIMMO added an optional word grammar component that can return full parse trees and feature structures.

PC-KIMMO can also be applied to other tasks, such as analyzing and tagging texts. See Antworth (1993) for a description of using PC-KIMMO to produce morphologically tagged interlinear text.

6.4.4   Syntax and grammar description

Most software applicable to syntax comes from the field of natural language processing where the main concern is syntactic parsing (see

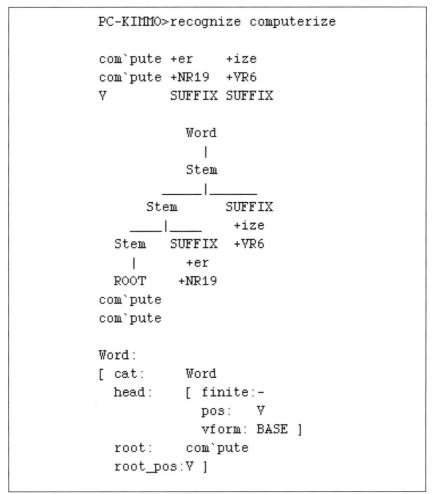

Figure 6.8   Sample word parse in PC-KIMMO version 2

Chapters 7 and 8). However some software is available that is intended for modeling syntactic analysis, namely PC-PATR. For the field linguist developing a syntactic corpus and grammar description, there is Rook for the Macintosh and Shoebox's grammar outline for DOS.

6.4.4.1 PC-PATR

PC-PATR is a syntactic parser for DOS, Windows, Macintosh, and Unix. It is based on the PATR-II formalism (see Shieber, 1986). A PC-PATR grammar consists of a set of rules and a lexicon. Each rule consist of a context-free phrase structure rule and a set of feature constraints, that is,

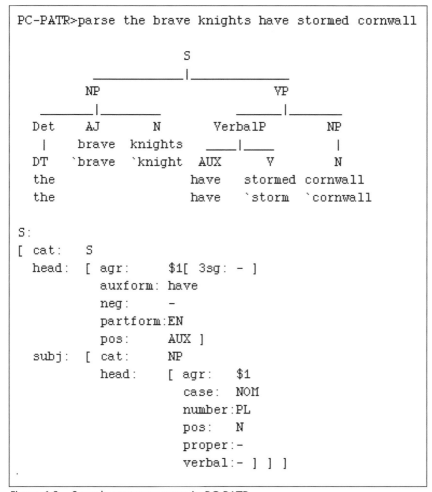

```
PC-PATR>parse the brave knights have stormed cornwall

                           S
              _____|_____
             NP                          VP
         ____|____               ____|____
    Det    AJ      N          VerbalP        NP
     |    brave  knights      ___|___        |
    DT   `brave  `knight    AUX      V        N
    the                     have   stormed  cornwall
    the                     have   `storm   `cornwall

S:
[ cat:    S
  head:   [ agr:       $1[ 3sg:  - ]
            auxform:  have
            neg:       -
            partform:EN
            pos:       AUX ]
  subj:   [ cat:       NP
            head:      [ agr:     $1
                         case:   NOM
                         number:PL
                         pos:    N
                         proper:-
                         verbal:- ] ] ]
```

Figure 6.9   Sample sentence parse in PC-PATR

unifications on the feature structures associated with the constituents of the phrase structure rules. The lexicon provides the items that can replace the terminal symbols of the phrase structure rules, that is, the words of the language together with their relevant features. PC-PATR is especially good for modeling basic syntactic analysis.

6.4.4.2   Rook

Rook is a system for authoring descriptive grammars in HyperCard for the Macintosh. Rook is a tool for interactively and incrementally developing a grammar description based on an interlinear text corpus (see also

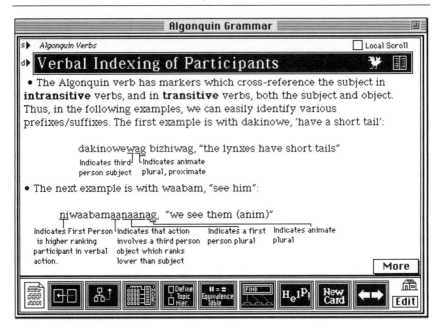

Figure 6.10   Sample grammar card in Rook

IT, Section 6.4.6.1). The resulting on-line descriptive grammar exploits the capacity of the computer to provide instant access to cross-referenced topics, text examples, explanations of morpheme glosses, and so on.

6.4.5   Lexicon

For field linguists developing a lexicon or bilingual dictionary of a language, data management programs such as Shoebox, askSam, Hyper-Card, and Xbase database systems are suitable (see Section 6.4.1). Multi-Dictionary Formatter and MacLex are two programs specifically designed for lexical work.

6.4.5.1   Multi-Dictionary Formatter

Multi-Dictionary Formatter for DOS is a set of programs that work together with Shoebox and a word processor such as Microsoft Word to structure, manipulate, format, and print dictionaries.

6.4.5.2   MacLex

MacLex is a Macintosh program for managing dictionary files in SIL's "Standard Format" (used also by Shoebox). It provides a full-screen editor for lexical entries as well as find and replace functions. Lexical files can be sorted according to a user-defined sorting order (including multigraph handling). MacLex also has a facility for reversing entries.

6.4.6   Text analysis

Under the general rubric of text analysis falls several types of programs. *IT* and Shoebox are tools for producing annotated interlinear text. Many programs for searching text and producing concordances and word lists are available, such as TA, Micro-OCP, MonoConc and TACT for DOS and Conc for Macintosh. For more on text analysis, see also Chapter 4 of this book.

6.4.6.1   IT (Interlinear Text processor)

IT (pronounced "eye-tee") is a software package for producing annotated interlinear texts. It performs two main tasks: (1) it maintains the vertical alignment of the interlinear annotations, and (2) it stores all word and morpheme annotations in a lexical database thus enabling semi-automatic glossing. *IT* supports up to 14 levels of aligning text annotations and up to 8 different freeform (nonaligning) annotations. The interlinear text file produced by *IT* is a plain **ASCII** text **file** that is accessible to other text-processing software. It is also portable between the DOS and Macintosh versions of the program. Here is the text file for one sentence from a text glossed with *IT*:

```
Unuunua                        sulia       tee    wane si   kada 'e
unu-unu             -a         suli -a      tee    wane si   kada 'e
RDP-tell.a.story    -NMZR      about-3s.O   one    man  PARTV time 3s.G


kasia        tee baru.
kasi -a      tee baru
build-3s.O   one canoe


The story about when a man built a canoe.
```

The first line is the original text. The second line is the morphemic representation which breaks the words into morphemes. The third line glosses each morpheme. The line below the interlinear text provides a free translation.

Interlinear text files produced by *IT* can be searched and concorded using other text analysis software including Conc (for Macintosh). An interlinear text corpus can be formated and prepared for professional typesetting using ITF, the Interlinear Text Formatter (see below).

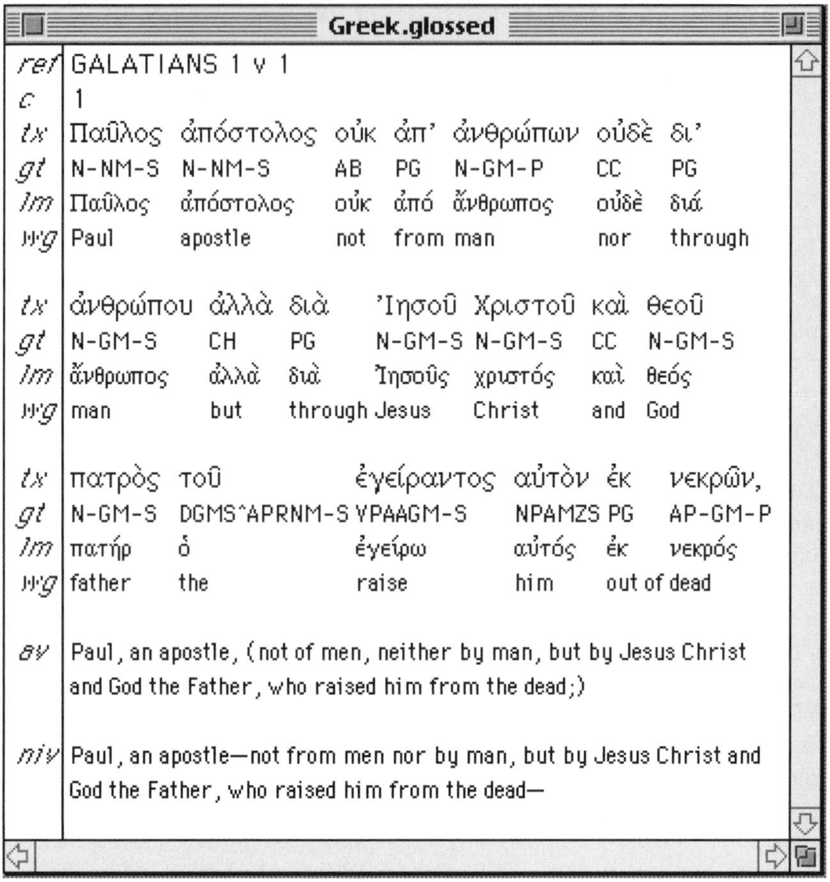

```
┌─────────────────────────────────────────────────────────────────┐
│ ▦▦▦                    Greek.glossed                       ▦▦ │
├─────────────────────────────────────────────────────────────────┤
│ ref│GALATIANS 1 v 1                                           ⇧ │
│ c  │1                                                            │
│ tx │Παῦλος  ἀπόστολος  οὐκ  ἀπ’  ἀνθρώπων  οὐδὲ  δι’             │
│ gt │N-NM-S   N-NM-S     AB   PG   N-GM-P    CC    PG             │
│ lm │Παῦλος  ἀπόστολος  οὐκ  ἀπό  ἄνθρωπος  οὐδὲ  διά             │
│ wg │Paul     apostle    not  from man       nor   through        │
│    │                                                             │
│ tx │ἀνθρώπου  ἀλλὰ  διὰ    ’Ιησοῦ  Χριστοῦ  καὶ  θεοῦ            │
│ gt │N-GM-S    CH    PG     N-GM-S  N-GM-S   CC   N-GM-S          │
│ lm │ἄνθρωπος  ἀλλὰ  διὰ    ’Ιησοῦς χριστός  καὶ  θεός            │
│ wg │man       but   through Jesus   Christ   and  God            │
│    │                                                             │
│ tx │πατρὸς  τοῦ          ἐγείραντος  αὐτὸν  ἐκ   νεκρῶν,         │
│ gt │N-GM-S  DGMS^APRNM-S VPAAGM-S    NPAMZS PG   AP-GM-P         │
│ lm │πατήρ   ὁ            ἐγείρω       αὐτός  ἐκ   νεκρός          │
│ wg │father  the          raise        him    out of dead          │
│    │                                                             │
│ bv │Paul, an apostle, (not of men, neither by man, but by Jesus Christ │
│    │and God the Father, who raised him from the dead;)           │
│    │                                                             │
│ niv│Paul, an apostle—not from men nor by man, but by Jesus Christ and │
│    │God the Father, who raised him from the dead—                │
│                                                              ⇩ │
│ ◁                                                         ▷ ▣ │
└─────────────────────────────────────────────────────────────────┘
```

Figure 6.11   Annotation window in Macintosh *IT*

6.4.6.2 ITF (Interlinear Text Formatter)

ITF (Interlinear Text Formatter) is a software package that formats interlinear texts for publication (as for producing a monograph of annotated
texts). It is based on the T$_e$X typesetting language (Knuth, 1986). ITF
works with interlinear text produced by *IT* and Shoebox. A program is also
provided that converts output from AMPLE (a morphological parser) into
the format required by ITF. ITF can format an arbitrary number of aligning annotations with up to two freeform annotations. A number of page
layout options are available, including placing a free translation at the bottom of the page or in a column down the side of the page. The ITF T$_e$X
macros can be used with either T$_e$X 2.9 or T$_e$X 3.0. A LaT$_e$X (Lamport,
1986) style is provided as well as the plain T$_e$X formatting definitions.

6.4.6.3   Shoebox

Shoebox (see Section 6.4.1) has a built-in text interlinearizer which is very similar to *IT*. It has the advantage over *IT* that its lexicon is readily available to the user. However, *IT* is more flexible and robust than Shoebox's interlinearizer.

6.4.6.4   TA

TA (for Text Analysis) is a set of DOS programs that perform basic text manipulation tasks including generate *word list*s from text, automate word segmenting in texts, generate concordances of texts, sort, *filter*, and *format* lexical files, and make reversals of lexical files. Some of these functions expect the data to be encoded in SIL's "Standard Format" (also used by Shoebox). The TA package is especially suitable for those with limited computing resources.

6.4.6.5   Micro-OCP

Micro-OCP is a batch-oriented concordance program for DOS. It is based on the mainframe version of the Oxford Concordance Program (OCP). Micro-OCP produces word lists (list of words with frequency of occurrence), indexes (list of words with references), concordances (KWIC, or keyword-in-context, style), and vocabulary statistics. A number of sorting options are supported, including sorting by frequency, word length, and word ending. Subsets of text can be selected for processing or marked for omission. Alphabets for several languages are included and other alphabets can be defined by the user. Multigraphs of up to eight characters can be used. Words can be retrieved that match a pattern containing *wildcard* characters. The execution of the program is controlled by a file that contains a script of commands. The output of the program can be sent to the screen, printer, or disk file.

6.4.6.6   MonoConc

MonoConc is an interactive concordance program for Windows. It supports loading multiple files, word and phrase searching with wildcard characters, and frequency counts.

6.4.6.7   TACT

TACT is an interactive DOS program for doing full-text retrieval, concordancing, and content analysis. A text is first prepared by marking reference units in it and then is converted into a TACT database. TACT offer several views of the database, including a word list with frequencies, a one-line KWIC concordance (which TACT calls an index), a KWIC concordance that shows several lines, distribution graphs, and collocations. The entire text can also be viewed. Specific words can be collected into a named category or theme; for instance, inflected forms of a word or a set of synonyms can form a category which is then referred to in more complex searches.

6.4.6.8   Conc

Conc is a concordance program for the Macintosh. Whereas most concordance programs are mainly intended for literary analysis, Conc has been specially designed for linguistic analysis. It exploits the Macintosh interface and is fully interactive. Conc produces keyword-in-context (KWIC) concordances of texts. A KWIC concordance consists of a list of the words in the text with a short section of the preceding and following context of each word. The sorting order is defined by the user. Conc also produces an index of the text, which consists of a list of the distinct word forms in the text, each with the number of times it occurs and a list of the places where it occurs. Conc displays the original text, the concordance, and the index each in its own window. If the user clicks on a word or entry in any of the three windows, the other two windows automatically scroll to display the corresponding word or entry. Concordances can be saved, printed, or exported to plain text files.

The user can restrict which words will be included in or excluded from a concordance. The user can choose to omit words of more/less than *n* letters, omit words occurring more/less than *x* number of times, or omit words explicitly listed. The user can choose to include all words, include words explicitly listed, or include words that match a pattern. A pattern can include devices to match any character, match zero or more characters, match one or more characters, match classes of characters, match at the start of a word, match at the end of a word, and so on (this is essentially a grep pattern, or **regular expression**).

In addition to flat text files, Conc also does concordances of multiple-line interlinear texts produced by the *IT* program. It can produce either a word concordance or a morpheme concordance (if the interlinear lines include morpheme decomposition). An interlinear concordance can be limited to selected lines (fields). By designating a primary and secondary field, Conc can produce a concordance of the correspondences between these two fields (for instance, morpheme and gloss).

In addition to word (and morpheme) concording, Conc can also produce a concordance of each letter in a text or body of phonological data. Pattern-matching facilities are also available in letter concordances, so the user can specify search patterns that will have the effect of retrieving, say, words containing intervocalic obstruents.

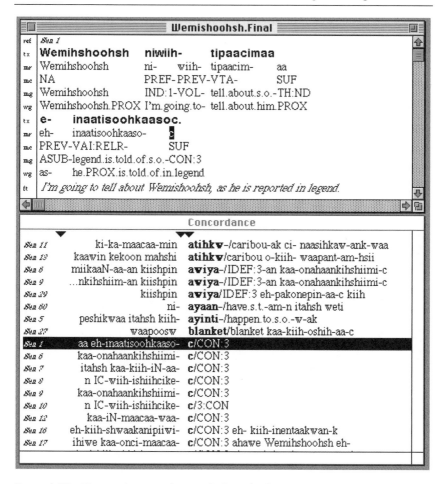

Figure 6.12 Text and concordance windows in Conc

6.4.7 Language survey and comparison

While various general purpose database management programs and statistical analysis programs could be used for tasks associated with language survey and comparison, there is at least one domain-specific program, namely WORDSURV.

WORDSURV is a menu-driven program for DOS that was developed to aid in the management and analysis of language survey word lists. Typically a language surveyor collects a word list (such as the Swadesh word list) in several dialects in an area. The word lists are then compared to determine the amount of shared vocabulary and the genetic relationships among the dialects. WORDSURV assists this labor-intensive process in several ways. First, it provides a printed copy of the word list that includes all of the linguistic forms that have previously been collected for each gloss. This makes it easier for the surveyor to elicit possible cognates on the spot. Second, WORDSURV automates the process of comparing several word lists to determine shared vocabulary. Third, WORDSURV supports more rigorous types of analysis: a phonostatistic analysis measures phonological divergence between dialects, and the COMPASS analysis (Frantz, 1970) measures the strength of phoneme correspondences in proposed cognates. Lastly, WORDSURV can output data in a format suitable for printed reports. WORDSURV is useful not only for doing language surveys in the field, but also for doing comparative reconstruction.

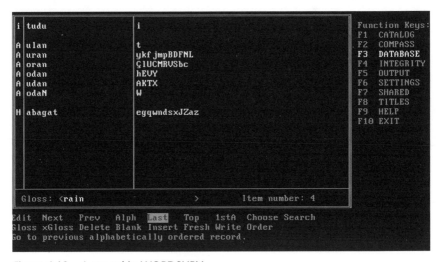

Figure 6.13   A record in WORDSURV

Chapter 7

Language understanding and the emerging alignment of linguistics and natural language processing

James E. Hoard

7.1 OVERVIEW

The potential impact of natural language processing (NLP) has been widely recognized since the earliest days of computers. Indeed, even as the first electronic computers were becoming a reality, Alan Turing imagined a symbolic processing system – one with true artificial intelligence – that could converse with a person in a way that could not be distinguished from a conversation one might have with a real person. Turing, in his famous article (1950), called his thought experiment the Imitation Game. Nowadays, it is called the Turing Test. While no computer program has so far come even remotely close to passing the Turing Test for intelligence, and none will be able to do so at any date in the future that we can reasonably predict, NLP programs that do "understand" language – albeit to a far lesser degree than Turing imagined – will be able to perform many useful and valuable tasks for the foreseeable future. Among them are these:

1 **Grammar and style checking** – Providing editorial critiques of vocabulary usage, grammar, and style – improving the quality of all sorts of writing – especially the readability of complex technical documents.
2 **Machine translation** – Translating texts, especially business and technical texts, from one natural language to another.
3 **Information extraction** – Analyzing the meaning of texts in detail, answering specific questions about text content. For many kinds of text (e.g., medical case histories) that are in a well-bounded domain, systems will extract information and put it into databases for statistical analyses.
4 **Natural language interfaces** – Understanding natural language commands and taking appropriate actions, providing a much freer interchange between people and computers.
5 **Programming in English** – Enabling the use of carefully controlled, yet ordinary, human language to program computers, largely

eliminating much of the need for highly-specialized and arcane computer "languages".

6 **Modeling and simulation** – Enabling computer modeling and simulation of all manner of real-world activities and scenarios where symbolic information and symbolic reasoning are essential to success.

This informal overview of language understanding and NLP is divided into four sections. Section 7.2 examines the changing relationship between NLP and linguistics and advances the thesis that the need for language understanding to meet the goals of NLP will have a profound effect on the objectives of linguistics itself and on what qualifies as good linguistic theory and practice. To illustrate this thesis, Section 7.3 discusses the scope of language understanding, outlines some fundamental criteria that must be satisfied before any adequate language understanding semantics can be achieved, and offers some suggestions about how one might go about satisfying them. The essential point is that the semantics of natural language has a logic of its own, which must be dealt with on its own terms, as part of linguistics proper. Section 7.4 outlines some considerations about approaches to and components for constructing working NLP systems. Section 7.5 discusses the design and implementation of a grammar and style checker that can determine the senses in which words are being used. (Space limitations preclude taking up any of the other application areas listed above.) The promise of NLP technology is just beginning to be felt in the commercial marketplace. As its commercial impact grows, the effect of NLP on academic linguistics will produce a profound enlargement in its scope and objectives and greatly influence the work of its practitioners. The shift will be, in brief, one that places the present focus on language description, including the concern for language acquisition and linguistic universals, within the much larger (and to my mind, much more interesting) context of language understanding.

7.2 THE CHANGING RELATIONSHIP BETWEEN LINGUISTICS AND NATURAL LANGUAGE PROCESSING

Traditionally, work in NLP has been viewed as quite peripheral to linguistics. The relationship was one where NLP received the benefits of linguistic theories and methods, and, at best, imposed perhaps a few requirements on linguistics. Before 1990, commercial and industrial NLP systems were, indeed, few and far between. The entire spectrum consisted of a few machine translation (MT) systems and the odd natural language database query system. Everything else was too primitive or too experimental to have any noticeable impact. The MT systems were non-general and essentially atheoretic, having been built up over a number of years by an accretion of specialized lexicons and procedural code. (See Kay,

Gowron, and Norvig, 1994, for an overview of MT systems, of approaches to MT, and for a refreshing discussion of translation as a process of negotiation across languages and cultures.) The database query systems had to be tailored to particular databases and had very limited utility. In this period, NLP did, of course, draw on other disciplines extensively. These areas included computer science, mathematics, and the cognitive sciences. Computational linguistics also played a large role here, since it was the principal source of parsing algorithms and of symbolic processing strategies.

In the mid-1980s, however, a change in the NLP-linguistics relationship started to accelerate. The change came about as NLP practitioners attempted to develop fieldable systems with sufficient coverage to address real-world problems in an acceptable fashion (one which adds value to the users). Constructing robust NLP systems both for grammar and style checking and for information extraction exposed linguistic theories and methods to testing and validation of unprecedented complexity and comprehensiveness. In both areas it quickly became clear that a premier problem is ambiguity resolution (or disambiguation). Systems like these, which are intended to cover a very wide range of inputs, must have comprehensive lexicons and grammars. Yet, the broader the lexical and grammatical coverage, the larger is the potential ambiguity of language analyses produced by the system. That is, in analyzing input text, a robust NLP system must arrive at a preferred interpretation (syntactic, semantic, and/or pragmatic) before any useful action can be taken. The feedback to linguistics was now not just of requirements expressed from a distance, but reports of results (or the lack thereof), and NLP now came to the fore as the arena where linguistic theories and methods are to be tested and validated.

There is now a growing tendency to ensure that linguistic theories are computationally effective. Three examples will serve to illustrate the changing situation: (1) Fraser and Hudson's work on inheritance in word grammar (Fraser and Hudson, 1992) is indicative of the trend to add computational and NLP support to theoretical work already well underway (Hudson, 1984; 1990). (2) Similarly, Harrison (1988) supplies a full parsing algorithm for generalized phrase structure grammar [GPSG] (Gazdar, Klein, Pullum, and Sag, 1985). (3) In contrast, for head-driven phrase structure grammar [HPSG] (Pollard and Sag, 1987; Pollard and Sag, 1994), now perhaps the most common theoretical framework used in NLP, the development of computational methods was a concern from the beginning. As is the case for HPSG, we can expect in future that linguistic theory and computational algorithms will be developed in tandem and that testing and validation over large-scale problems will be not just "in scope" but, indeed, both customary and mandatory from the outset.

Clearly, testing and validating a (putative) comprehensive set of linguistic rules formulated within some given theory, over a representative domain, is a very difficult task. Success criteria need to be agreed on; and there is no obvious way these can be independently established to everyone's satisfaction. Moreover, different acceptance criteria will be needed depending on the particular language component the rules address and on whether the rules are being evaluated as a stand-alone system or as part of some larger system with which they interact. Evaluating results within a single framework is difficult enough. The evaluation problem is compounded when cross-theory comparisons are attempted. This is a most difficult area, since even agreeing on terminology equivalents that can serve, in part, to bridge theoretical differences, is arduous. (See Neal and Walter, 1991; Harrison, *et al.*, 1991; and Neal, Feit, Funke, and Montgomery, 1992, for some initial contributions to this topic.) The evaluation of comparative system performance is likely to remain both *ad hoc* and not very satisfactory for many years. What can be said now for both within-a-theory comparisons and for cross-theory comparisons is this: While coverage *per se* is the paramount issue (what is correctly analyzed and what is not), so is robustness (the ability of a system to deal with unexpected input), space and time complexity (the resources required for the coverage obtained), extensibility, adaptability, and maintainability.

The trend toward software implementation and large-scale testing and validation in linguistics, driven by NLP application development, ensures that the very objectives of linguistic research will be broadened and deepened. The objectives of linguistic theory before the 1980s were aimed largely at accounting for language structure, not language understanding. The efforts centered on syntax and phonology, with emphasis on language descriptions (synchronic and diachronic), structural universals, language acquisition, and sociolinguistics. Work on semantics, pragmatics, and discourse analysis was a secondary concern. Considering language as a functional system of communication was on the periphery. Given the ambiguity of linguistic expression generally and the fact that people normally interpret verbal and written communication correctly (they "get it right"), this is surprising. It's not that linguists were unaware of ambiguity. Rather, the inclusion of such examples as "time flies like an arrow" and "the shooting of the hunters" in the linguistic literature seemed to be motivated by a requirement to illustrate that one's theory provided a distinct structure (a representation) for each interpretation. That is, the motivation served the needs of descriptive linguistics, and the real issue – how pervasive ambiguity is resolved in everyday language use – was not addressed. And ambiguity is pervasive, arising at all linguistic levels (phonetic, phonological, morphological, lexical, syntactic, semantic, pragmatic), and all of these occur in concert, as it were, in ordinary discourse. The NLP and computational linguistics literature, in contrast, is chock-full of articles on resolving ambiguity – with numerous approaches and methods proposed for disambiguation, both statistically based and knowledge (rule) based. This situation will not hold. Traditional academic linguistics will indeed need to "get with the program" and broaden its objectives. The change is inevitable and will take place quite quickly, since the people who contribute to linguistics research will be, more often than not in coming years, the very same people who also do work in computational linguistics and NLP.

The development of computational linguistics and the emergence of NLP enables linguists to develop and test theories using large amounts of data. Indeed, it demands and compels them to do so. In brief, linguistics must expand its horizons, augmenting a traditional agenda that is largely limited to descriptive linguistics and representation issues to the much larger – and vastly more difficult – objective of language understanding.

7.3 UNDERSTANDING LANGUAGE

7.3.1 Meaning, interpretation, and speakers' intentions

The overall goal of natural language processing is to get computers to understand our language, where "our language" is, of course, any language we happen to speak. To anyone who has attempted to design and implement a natural language processing system (or even to anyone who, as a thought experiment, has contemplated doing so), it is obvious that the sheer complexity of language dictates that the goal is at once audaciously difficult and necessarily long-term. No one could hope to get computers to "understand our language" without grounding the enterprise in linguistics, both theory and practice, for that is where the inner workings of language are investigated and described. Many other disciplines have much to contribute to the enterprise. Among them are computer science, mathematics, psychology, philosophy, and cognitive science. Of these, computer science has been the most important, because that is where the methods and limits of computability have been extensively explored and where software engineering methods have been developed. At the intersection of these two disciplines, computational linguistics has flourished and has taken on a vigor of its own. From the 1960s into the 1990s, computational linguistics developed primarily through the work of computer scientists interested in string manipulation, information retrieval, symbolic processing, knowledge representation and reasoning, and natural language processing. Only from the mid-1980s has the linguistic community begun to interact and participate in the development of computational linguistics in a significant way.

The NLP community has been especially interested in analyzing text-based inputs and outputs, primarily because computers readily accept text inputs in standard orthographies, not inputs in a phonetic alphabet (without special provision). Nor, of course, do computers readily accept voice inputs. Using text inputs is also standard practice in linguistics among those who study syntax, semantics, pragmatics, and discourse theory. NLP is complementary to and has much to contribute to the success of speech recognition, speech synthesis, and pen (handwriting) recognition technologies, but, from the NLP point of view, these are extended capabilities.

What do we mean by "understanding" when we talk of language understanding? What would it take to convince us that our computer understands language? It is hard to say precisely, since there is no exact formulation of what we mean by ordinary human understanding of language. The gap between what people do with language in their "native" state – as a matter of course – and what computers can do is profound. In their "native" state, computers accept strings of **character**s as inputs. These character strings have absolutely no meaning or significance to the computer. Any understanding of character strings as natural language is external to the computer and is done at present only by the people who enter the strings, manipulate them (with one sort of application program or another), view them on screen, and print them out.

Now, as a first approximation to language understanding, we would say that a computer understands language if it could represent the meaning of a text (which could be as short as a single sentence) in such a way that it could draw the same conclusions that people do. The kinds of inferences that we would expect our computer to make would include at least the immediate, or shallow, kind. For example, suppose we learn that *Max died on Tuesday*. We can immediately conclude that: *Max died. Max is dead. Max is no longer living. Something happened to Max. Something happened. Someone died. Max used to be alive. Max is not alive now. Max lived up to Tuesday. Max was alive last Monday. There was a death.* – and so forth. Such inferences are shallow in the sense that we draw them immediately from the content of the input text sentence, and we use no information to form our conclusions of the sort that ranges beyond the text we are given. Deeper inferences depend on the extensive knowledge we all have about our culture in general and on any particular knowledge we might have about Max. For instance, we could reasonably conclude, on the basis of cultural expectations, that there will be, in all likelihood, a funeral or memorial service for Max and that the time and place will be announced in the local newspaper. Suppose we also know that Max was the president of the town bank. Then we can conclude that the bank is now without a president, at least temporarily. If we know that Max was married to Abigail, we know that Abigail has been widowed. Given everything people know about the world and what goes on in it, deep reasoning about events and situations that arise can be carried out at will and for as long as one wishes. The number of conclusions we can draw and their significance is open ended.

It seems highly unlikely that one can make a principled distinction between shallow and deep reasoning, claiming that the first is characteristic of and intrinsic to language (and to language understanding) while the second involves general reasoning that goes far beyond language (and far beyond language understanding). Certainly, inferences that apparently follow directly from the meaning of words and their actual use in sentences and discourse seem more basic, even different, from those that follow from broader knowledge of the world. The problem is that it is difficult to see where one sort of reasoning ends and the other begins, for knowledge of the meaning of words is, so far as we know, of the same kind as any other sort of knowledge.

However it is that meaning is represented and that inferences are drawn, for people or for computers, one essential point to keep in mind is that meaning and interpretation are not at all the same thing. In the words of Barwise and Perry (1983:37) "meaning underdetermines interpretation" (see also Barwise, 1989:61ff). Sperber and Wilson (1988:141) go even further, proclaiming that "the linguistic structure of an utterance grossly underdetermines its interpretation."

Consider the following sentences, which, clearly, do not have the same meaning:

1) Dan turned on the power.
2) Dan threw the switch.

They could easily, however, have the same interpretation, for one possible interpretation for 1) – and also for 2) – is this:

3) Dan pushed upward a lever that is inside the electrical power box on the outside of his house, thereby completing the circuit that supplies his house with electrical power.

Now suppose, however, Dan works for the power company and that the intended interpretation of 1) – and also for 2) – is:

4) Dan reset a large circuit breaker at a substation.

Just as easily, the speaker who uttered 2) could have intended the interpretation to be:

5) Dan physically threw a switch, say, an electrical switch, across the room.

There is clearly a semantic difference in the meaning of "throw" that contributes significantly to the interpretation of 2), in some actual context of use, as 3) or 4), on the one hand, and as 5), on the other. Suppose, though, that the intended interpretation of 2) is 3). Even so, we have underdetermined the situation, since the utterance does not describe the kind of switch nor exactly what Dan did. The actual situation, which we might know through observing Dan, could be this: Dan reached out with his right arm and moved the lever on the main switch upward, using the thumb and index finger of his right hand, thereby completing the electrical circuit and turning on the power to his house. The point is that whatever we take the semantic representation of a sentence to be (or its several semantic representations if it is ambiguous), we have only accounted for its meaning (or its several meanings), not for its actual interpretation in the context in which it is used. In sum, the overt and essentially explicit (or public) meanings of utterances serve as the input to interpretation (a further cognitive endeavor). Any factual correspondence between an interpretation (a mental representation) and the real world (a real–semantic interpretation) is necessarily indirect.

For Barwise and Perry, "Reality consists of situations–individuals having properties and standing in relations at various spatiotemporal locations" (1983:7). That is, situations are states of affairs that are grounded in space and time. Following Pollard and Sag, we will refer to states of affairs as circumstances, where "roughly speaking, circumstances are possible ways the world might be; they are the kinds of things that obtain or do not obtain, depending on how the world is" (1987:86). The circumstance of "Dan's turning on the power" becomes a situation when it is grounded as in utterance 1) at some past time and at some unspecified location. Clearly, to account for situations and circumstances adequately a language understanding system must implement a theory of pragmatics, discourse, and verbal communication. Such a theory must account for a host of phenomena, including those of reference, dialogues, narratives, and discourse relations. The problem of reference is twofold. First, within language, the rules of anaphoric reference must be delineated. Second, the formulation of an adequate theory of reference that holds between language descriptions of things, circumstances, and situations and the actual objects and states of affairs in the real world is also very much at issue. A theory of reference in the second sense stands outside the theory of linguistic semantics, although it very much depends on it.

By and large, the rules of anaphora are not well understood. In particular, the rules for referring to circumstances are not adequately formulated. For example, what is the precise description of *that* in the following pair of sentences?

6) John broke his leg last year.
7) I sure hope that doesn't happen to me.

Evidently, the anaphoric interpretation of *that* requires a procedure that extracts "break" and its complement structure from the situation, generalizes it to a circumstance, namely, "X breaking X's leg", and substitutes "my" for X. The interpretation of *that* is, then, the circumstance "my breaking my leg" (which is embedded in the circumstance of "that not happening to me", which is embedded in the situation that is the complement of "hope").

While Barwise and Perry's theory of Situation Semantics provides a principled way of describing the information that language communicates – through situations (and situation types), circumstances (and circumstance types), and the relations among situations and circumstances – it does not provide a theory of communication. And, hence, there is no way within the theory of Situation Semantics to constrain the determination of speaker's intention, which is the goal of language understanding. For a theory of communication we turn to Relevance Theory, as presented by Sperber and Wilson (1986).

Sperber and Wilson's basic thesis is that a "principle of relevance" governs "ostensive–inferential" communication. The relevance principle is: "Every act of ostensive communication communicates the presumption of its own optimal relevance" (1986:158). Ostensive–inferential communication occurs when: "The communicator produces a stimulus which makes it mutually manifest to communicator and audience that the communicator intends, by means of this stimulus, to make manifest or more manifest to the audience a set of assumptions {I} (1986:155). The presumption of optimal relevance has two parts:

1 The set of assumptions {I} which the communicator intends to make manifest to the addressee is relevant enough to make it worth the addressee's while to process the ostensive stimulus.
2 The ostensive stimulus is the most relevant one the communicator could have used to communicate {I}" (1986:158).

For Sperber and Wilson, the language understanding task:

> . . .is to construct possible interpretive hypotheses about the contents of {I} and to choose the right one. In different circumstances and different cognitive domains, the task . . . may be carried out in different ways. In some cases, it is best carried out by listing all the possible hypotheses, comparing them, and choosing the best one. In others, it is better carried out by searching for an initial hypothesis, testing it to see if it meets some criterion, accepting it and stopping there if it does, and otherwise repeating the process searching for a second hypothesis, and so on. (1986:165).

Kempson (1988b:12ff.) briefly discusses some of the similarities and differences between Situation Semantics and Relevance Theory, pointing out that apparent conflicts about the nature of cognitive representations may not be as deep as they seem. Kempson concludes that "the theory of situations does not preclude a system of mental representations"

(1988:14). This being so, we are free to use the constructs of Situation Semantics as part of the cognitive language of thought that is at the core of determining speakers' intentions and of language understanding. As Kempson says: "It is the language of thought that is semantically interpreted, not the natural language expressions. Put crudely, it is our beliefs which are directly about the world we live in, not the sentences of our language" (*ibid*:10). In short, the interpretation task for language understanding requires determining first the meaning of utterances and then the (apparent) intended interpretation of the utterances. Now, it might be the case that the representation of utterance meaning (linguistic semantics expressions) is quite different in kind than the representation of internal cognitive interpretations (propositional semantics expressions). It is a thesis of Section 7.3.2 that this is not so and that a single representation system will suffice for expressing semantic meanings and interpretations.

7.3.2   Basic linguistic elements of language understanding systems

There are a number of basic linguistic elements and capabilities which any model of language understanding must provide, whether we view it as linguistic theory *per se* or as a basis for language understanding systems. To the extent that a given language model fails to satisfy these requirements (in principle or in practice), it is to that extent inherently insufficient for one or another NLP task. It is convenient to separate the capabilities into three categories, one for phonology, morphology, and syntax, one for semantics, and one for pragmatics and discourse. Within all three, there are manifold opportunities for alternative approaches. Since ambiguity is the norm for natural language, and it is the norm at all levels, a fundamental challenge for any language understanding system is to confront ambiguity and resolve it.

Figure 7.1 shows the conceptual architecture of an information extraction system, suitable for extracting information from (online) texts, that contains a language understanding system as its principal subsystem. (The modules of the Sentence and Discourse Analyzers constitute the language understanding subsystem.) The Preprocessor handles such chores as separating out formatting codes and the like from the basic text stream and segmenting longer texts into pieces appropriate for analysis and information extraction. The Data Extractor contains a set of queries and the rules for applying them. Information extraction is useful whenever there are large numbers of relatively short texts in some domain, the things that go on in that domain share a number of attributes, and it is desirable to "reduce" the goings on to standardized database records. For example, newswire articles on product offerings and sales (in some industry), financial takeovers and mergers, and stock market trends are suitable domains. Other uses for information extraction include tracking maintenance and repair reports, quality assurance reports, and military tactical messages. (Nicolino (1994) describes a Boeing prototype message processing system which extracts information from military tactical messages, then uses the information to drive a "situation awareness" display. With such a system, a field commander could monitor an entire military operation in near-real time as reports of it arrived and were processed. See also Chinchor, Hirschman, and Lewis (1993) and Chinchor and Sundheim (1993) for a description and evaluation of a number of message processing systems.)

7.3.2.1 *Phonology, morphology, syntax*

Phonology, morphology, and syntax are concerned with the form of language, i.e., with all the tokens of language and with all their permissible concatenations (groupings and arrangements as constituents). Getting a computer to recognize natural language tokens is not as easy as one might suppose, even for a language like English for which the morphology is sparse and all the occurring forms can either be listed or can be easily computed. First, groups of characters and the spaces between them, as they are ordinarily represented in the standard orthography, are only loosely correlated with the morphemes and other lexical units. (The English orthography seems to be typical in this respect). The roots and affixes of inflections, derivations, and compounds must be recognized by some combination of rules and lists. Then, too, multi-word combinations

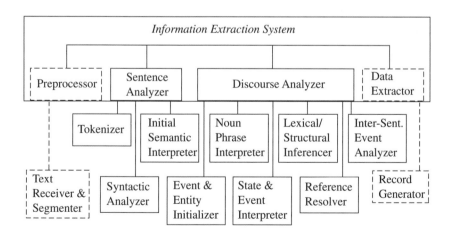

Figure 7.1 Overall information extraction architecture

abound. Here are some typical examples: *Las Vegas, Las Cruces, Ingmar Bergman, Ingrid Bergman, De Witt Clinton, Bill Clinton, Vannevar Bush, George Bush, roll back, roll bar, roll call, landing gear, landing strip, bevel gear, pinion gear, slow motion effects, personal effects, liquid assets, liquid crystal display.* Moreover, the list of single-word and multi-word lexical items is unbounded. New proper nouns and multi-word lexical items are constantly added to languages and are regularly encountered in language use. A language understanding system must be prepared to deal with new tokens and combinations of tokens on demand. It is also worth noting that, when punctuation is taken into account, tokenization must be considered on more than one level. For example, one cannot be sure, *a priori* and in isolation, whether *fig.* is an abbreviation for *figure*, whether it represents the word *fig* followed by a sentence-ending period, or whether, indeed, it represents an abbreviation for *figure* at the end of a sentence, where, by convention, only a single period is used. Ambiguity is clearly the norm at the lexical level.

For languages like Arabic, Hebrew, Turkish, and Finnish, which have very complex morphologies, tokenization is a major problem. Some number of (morpho)phonological rules may apply to any given form, and analyzing (i.e., tokenizing) surface forms can lead to an exceptionally large search space as the rules that have been applied are "undone" to determine the underlying base forms. Because until quite recently the vast majority of the work in computational linguistics has been done on English and similarly "isolating" European languages, computational phonology is an underdeveloped field. It is now receiving much more attention. See especially Koskenniemmi, 1984; Kaplan and Kay, 1994; Maxwell, 1994; Bird, 1995, and Kiraz, 1996.

If one's language understanding system can map character strings into possible tokens, then, given syntactic information about the tokens (part-of-speech and constituent membership possibilities, in particular) we would expect that a comprehensive grammar and a parser could together produce syntactic analyses of sequences of tokens into constituent phrases, clauses, and sentences. (A syntactic parser is an algorithm for applying a grammar to a sequence of tokens. More generically, a parser applies a set of pattern-matching rules to a set of concatenated symbols. A syntactic parser is, then, a particular sort of parser, as is a morphological parser.) When a token sequence is sanctioned by the grammar, a parse, i.e., a description of the sequence, is produced by the parser. There is no guarantee, of course, that the sequences the parser and grammar sanction are actually grammatical. Grammaticality judgments are external to the parser-grammar. Here again the inherent ambiguity of natural language asserts itself. A sentence of twenty words can have dozens, even many dozens, of parses when the analysis is based on syntactic (part-of-speech and constituency) information alone. From this perspective, it does not much matter what syntax formalism one chooses for the grammar. It could be one based on GPSG, HPSG, categorial grammar, tree-adjoining grammar, or some other coherent formalism. The important thing is that the grammar produces (surface) syntactic parses for the actually occurring sequences of tokens. In short, the parser and grammar must together recognize and provide an analysis of the actually occurring sequences of lexical items that speakers of the language agree are acceptable. If the language understanding system is robust, its parser and grammar must handle lexical sequences that, while not completely acceptable, are nonetheless interpretable by speakers of the language. (For example, in the new era of word processing software, writers frequently produce "sentences" with double articles when rewriting and editing text. Readers are obliged to ignore one of the extra tokens to interpret them successfully.)

7.3.2.2   Semantics

The semantic interpretation capabilities of any language understanding system depend ultimately on the semantic theory that it implements (however imperfectly). We judge the adequacy of a semantic theory according to at least the following criteria (see Hoard and Kohn, 1994): (1) Partial intentionality, (2) Real-world validity, (3) Multi-valued logic, (4) Inferencing rules, (5) Semantic operators, (6) Coherence conditions, (7) Connectivity, (8) Generalized quantification, (9) Non-arbitrary relation to syntax, (10) Intentionality, (11) Higher-order constructs, and (12) "Amalgamation". Each of these attributes has its functional counterpart in the actual language understanding systems of real language users. They must eventually find functional expression and implementation in one fashion or another in computer-based language understanding systems.

1   **Partial intentionality** – A language understanding system must achieve its understanding of a verbal or text input in finite time and with finite resources. Real-time understanding is a highly desirable goal for a computer-based language understanding system. It is, after all, what people are very good at. To meet a real-time objective a language understanding system must provide semantic representations of sentences (actually, of connected discourses) in no worse than linear time as a function of sentence length, and it must do so with a well-bounded amount of memory ("calculation space"). This is not to say that people are computers or use a computer program to understand language. The criterion merely states that any simulation of language understanding using computers must model human capabilities at least to this extent.

2   **Real-world validity** – Semantic representations must have an overt and explicit character that describes the real world and is consistent with it. The representations must fix (or determine) the semantic

interpretations and provide one (and only one) possible meaning for any given semantic representation.

3   **Multi-valued logic** – To describe the real world of language use, a semantic theory (and a language understanding system) needs at least three truth values, namely, *yes* (true), *no* (false), and *don't know* (indeterminate). These three truth values are required for both open-world and closed-world universe-of-discourse assumptions.

4   **Inferencing rules** – Being able to draw conclusions that are compatible with the real world and with the knowledge at one's disposal is fundamental to how people use language, and to both semantic theory and to language understanding systems. The conclusions one can draw are of at least two different kinds. The first can be called the *means* relationship and is the basis for being able to conclude that *X means Y*. On p. 202, for example, we concluded that *Max died* implies *that Max is no longer living*. We did this in part on the basis of the *means* relationship, since, informally, *X dies means that X stops living*. The second relationship can be termed *is covered by* and is the basis for concluding that, say, *Sam built a dory* entails that *Sam built a boat*, for a dory is a kind of boat (i.e. *dory is covered by boat*). Note that we need at least these two kinds of relationships, since we cannot claim either that *dory means boat* or that *boat means dory*.

5   **Semantic operators** – The operators (or relations) that a semantic theory provides are the basis for deciding how the morphemes in any given sentence are joined to form semantic structures. For instance, in the simple sentence *John loves Mary* we can ask what John's relationship and Mary's relationship is to *loves*. Possible answers are that John is the "cognizer" of *loves*, the one who has a particular cognitive attitude, and that Mary is in the "range" of his cognitive attitude. Neither the exact nature of the semantic operators ("cases", "valences", and/or "thematic roles") that a theory may provide, nor their number, is at issue here. We do, however, postulate a closed set of primitive semantic operators over which semantic structures can be formed. A semantic theory must make substantive claims about how language combines morphemes into semantic structures, admitting some relationships among morphemes and disallowing others, or we cannot construct accounts of situations and circumstances whose real-world validity can, even in principle, be verified.

6   **Coherence conditions** – To distinguish possible from impossible semantic representations requires, in addition to semantic operators, a set of well-formedness conditions. The set of constraints on combinations of semantic relations provides for the incoherence of such putative sentences as: *John smiled Mary a watch* (too many complements for *smiled*), *On Wednesday John loved Mary on Tuesday* (two conflicting temporal expressions), *In New York Bob read the book in*

Boston (two conflicting locative expressions), and *Mary knows John swiftly* (manner expression incompatible with a cognitive verb).

7   **Connectivity** – All the morphemes in a sentence contribute to its meaning and must be accounted for in the semantic representation of the sentence. There are no "sentences" like *John read the book the*, which have "stray" elements (in this example an extra *the*) not integrated into the whole. In those cases when the meaning of a sentence does not result by composition from the meaning of its semantic constituents, we invoke the notion of an idiom to explain the anomaly.

8   **Generalized quantification** – While the semantics of mathematical proofs can make do with just a universal quantifier and an existential quantifier, human language has an unlimited number of quantifiers. These encompass such variable value quantifiers as *few, many,* and *some,* as well as fixed-value quantifiers like *two, between three and five,* and *half.* Then, too, natural language quantifiers also include temporal expressions such as *frequently, once, occasionally,* and *always.*

9   **Non-arbitrary relation to syntax** – The relation between syntax and semantics is not arbitrary, but systematic. Any viable semantic theory will have to provide a consistent and effective means to map a syntactic structure to a corresponding semantic representation and from a semantic representation to a corresponding syntactic structure. Because semantic and syntactic structures are of different kinds, there can be no isomorphism.

10 **Relativistic intentionality** – Not only are semantic representations but partial descriptions of reality, they are also relative. Total and neutral descriptions of the world using language are impossible, in principle. Any use of language always reflects someone's viewpoint and emphasizes some aspects of a situation to the neglect of others. Different languages use different constructs and devices to describe reality; what is obligatory in the sentences of one language can be absent in another. Furthermore, there is no clear delineation between literal and metaphoric expression. While a semantic theory can provide representations of coherent and meaningful structures, both utterances and the intended interpretations of these utterances, it cannot provide a neutral representation, for the intended interpretation is inevitably a cognitive, mental structure that is determinable only in the context of actual use within a particular language community.

11 **Higher-order constructs** – Any adequate model of semantics must be able to make higher-order generalizations about language constructs. For instance, verbs that have a cause complement, can have a manner modifier, i.e., if *The fish swam off* is coherent, so is *The fish swam off quickly.*

12 **Amalgamation** – A semantic theory must be self contained – a notion for which the term "amalgamation" suggests itself. There cannot be

any "meta-language" statements of some sort or other that somehow stand outside the semantic theory and "interpret" it. Statements about semantic theory, if they are meaningful, will necessarily be adequately represented by semantic structures that are expressible within the semantic theory itself. Otherwise, they would themselves need interpretation, and that would require yet another (incomplete) theory of semantics, and so on, endlessly. It follows that pragmatic interpretations and the representation of discourse relations can also be expressed in the same semantic theory used for representing the meaning of individual sentences.

While detailed discussion of these twelve baseline attributes is beyond the scope of this paper, we need to introduce some of the fundamental notions of Cognitive Grammar (Langacker, 1987) and the Relational Logic model of semantics (Hoard and Kohn, 1994) as background to the discussion of a grammar and style checking system.

One of the most salient distinctions in natural language is that between complements and modifiers. The distinction is due to the essential asymmetry among meaningful elements as they are actually used in linguistic constructions. In Langacker's terminology (1987:298ff.), the elements of a sentence are dependent (D) or autonomous (A). The autonomous elements are those that are cognitively (and semantically) complete, requiring no obligatory elaboration by other elements. The autonomous elements are things (and syntactically, nominals). Dependent elements are cognitively incomplete and cannot stand alone in ordinary language use. They require elaboration and appear in construction with at least one other linguistic element. The dependent elements are relationals (and form such syntactic classes as verbs, adverbs, adjectives, articles, conjunctions, and prepositions). Further, a profile is defined as the entity designated by a semantic structure, and the profile determinant is the component in a construction whose profile is inherited by the composite structure. For example, *girl* is the profile and the profile determinant in *the clever girl*. That is, *girl* is an autonomous element in *the clever girl*, and both *the* and *clever* are dependent elements. The modifier relation is defined as follows: In a construction with autonomous element A and dependent element D, if A is the profile determinant, then A is the head of the construction, and D modifies (is a modifier of) A. Consider now the prepositional phrase *with the clever girl*. In this case, D is the profile determinant. The complement relation is defined as follows: In a construction with autonomous element A and dependent element D, if D is the profile determinant, the head of the construction is D, and A complements (is a complement of) D. Similarly, there are other relationship types where one dependent element modifies another dependent element (as in *walk fast* and *very tall*), one autonomous element modifies another autonomous element (as in *customer service* and *shake roof*), and one dependent element complements another dependent element (a circumstance complements a situation).

In Relational Logic (RL), semantic structures are represented by directed, acyclic semantic graphs. Relational operators are the edge labels, and morphemes are the nodes. We show the modifier relationship, as in 8a), with a semantic graph that displays D above and to the right of A. The complement relationship is shown, as in 8b), with A displayed below and to the right of D. Diagrams 8c), 8d), and 8e) show schematically relationships where both elements are of the same kind, with one of them being the profile determinant in the construction. As indicated in the semantic graphs, some operator (given here as *op*) always sanctions the relationship between the elements in a construction.

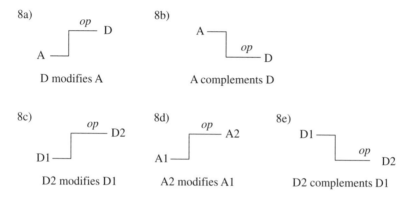

8a) *op* D

A

D modifies A

8b) A

op D

A complements D

8c) *op* D2

D1

D2 modifies D1

8d) *op* A2

A1

A2 modifies A1

8e) D1

op D2

D2 complements D1

Examples of semantic components are given in 9). The operators sanction (in part) the linking of linguistic elements to form components. The operator names suggested in 9), and elsewhere in this paper, are plausible, but in no sense definitive. They are *ag(ent)*, *att(ribute)*, *man(ner)*, *kind*, and *id(em)*. The *idem* operator links situations to circumstances. In 9), it links the situation node, denoted by S, with *love*.

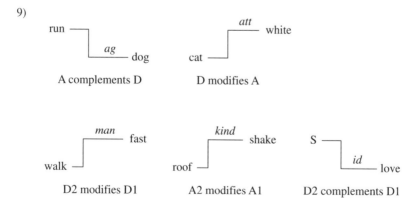

9)

run

ag dog

A complements D

att white

cat

D modifies A

man fast

walk

D2 modifies D1

kind shake

roof

A2 modifies A1

S

id love

D2 complements D1

The semantic graph for the sentence *John loves Mary* is given in 10a) and 10b). The root of a semantic structure is denoted by the situation node, S (which is indexed in a multi-situation discourse). Here, S is linked to the circumstance "John's loving Mary", which is headed by *love*.

10a)   10b)

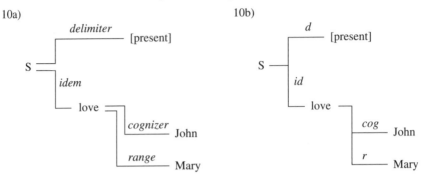

The two complements of *love* – *John* and *Mary* – are linked to it by the *cog(nizer)* and *r(ange)* operators, respectively. The present tense morpheme is linked with the *d(elimiter)* operator to S and is displayed above and to the right of the S-node as a situational modifier. For convenience, and without loss of generality, in depicting semantic graphs, we use the abbreviations for the operator labels and superimpose the common portions of independent edges (as shown explicitly in 10a)), drawing them as shown in 10b).

The semantic graph in 11) gives the semantic representation for *Mary kissed John on the cheek in the park*, showing how the semantic representation accounts for the circumstance of "Mary's kissing John on the cheek" (with its internal locative modifier) and situates it in the past and "in the park" (an external modifier). The operators introduced in 11) are *loc(ation)* and *u(ndergoer)*. Note that the delimiter operator sanctions the situating of nominals with determiners (just as it sanctions the situating of verbs with tenses).

11)

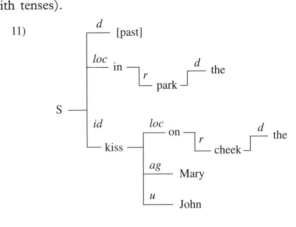

The completeness and closedness of semantic representations in RL guarantees a path between any two morphemes in a sentence. For instance, in example 11) the path from *Mary* to *cheek* goes through *kiss* and *on*; the path between *Mary* and *John* goes just through *kiss*; and the path from *park* to *John* goes through *in*, S, and *kiss*. Note that the explicit (and initial) semantic representation of the sentence does not indicate whose cheek was kissed. It is, in fact, part of the meaning of kiss that the agent does it with the lips, that the default location for the under-goer is also the lips, and that an explicit internal modifier location is that of the undergoer. In short, we infer that it is John's cheek that was kissed.

Example 12) gives the semantic representation for *Jill – this will amaze you – managed to solve the problem*, a sentence which illustrates both a situation embedded in a situation and a circumstance embedded in a circumstance. (The operators introduced in this example are *dis(junct)*, *m(odal)*, and *asp(ect)*.) The disjunct is a modifier of the matrix sentence, while the "solving" circumstance is a complement of the "managing" circumstance. The "solving" circumstance has an understood agent (indi-cated with Δ) that we infer is *Jill*.

12)

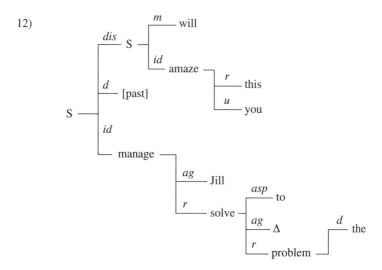

The incorporation into RL semantic representations of such basic cogni-tive distinctions as that between dependent and autonomous elements and between modifier and complement is a step toward a linguistic seman-tics with real-world validity. RL semantic representations require semantic operators – one for every edge – to sanction semantic components, with no morpheme appearing in any semantic graph without explicit sanction, and with no morpheme being left out of account. Hence, on the presump-tion that every morpheme makes some contribution to the meaning of the sentences in which it appears, RL provides a principled approach to explaining the cognitive basis of semantic coherence and connectedness. Indeed, RL offers some hope of accounting for why a sentence is traditionally described as a "complete thought" and of illuminating such concepts as "the language of thought", for we will use RL semantic graphs both for what is explicitly stated and for everything inferred from what is stated. Among the inferences will be, whenever the inferencing is successful, a representation of the speaker's intentions. In any case, representing all semantic structures with the very same RL semantic graphs is, clearly, a large step toward amalgamation.

Natural language inferencing is not at all like that for mathematical logic. In propositional logic and predicate logic, a set of logical operators permit joining components into well-formed formulas, and inferencing proceeds from the (given) truth values of components to the (derived) truth values for whole statements. That is, in mathematical logic, inferencing proceeds from the bottom up. In natural language it is the other way around. Inferences are made from the top down, from the presumed truth value of the whole to the derived truth values of both explicit components and of inferred semantic structures. The fundamental reason is that the function of language is to communicate. Recall Sperber and Wilson's presumption of optimal relevance: the speaker intends to make something manifest that is both optimally relevant and worth the addressee's while to process. It follows that the basic assumption we have as we process language is that what we hear or read is justified. Sperber and Wilson (1988:139) phrase this basic assumption in terms of "faithfulness", asserting that "every utterance comes with a guarantee of faithfulness, not of truth. The speaker guarantees that her utterance is a faithful enough interpretation of the thought she wants to communicate".

Relational Logic uses the value t ("true") to indicate that the speaker's utterances are guaranteed to be justified (or faithful). For example, if someone states that "Max is tall and wears a mustache", we assign the entire statement the value t and deduce a) that "Max is tall", and b) that "he wears a mustache" also have the value t. The truth values in RL are t ("true" or "yes"), f ("false" or "no"), and t/f ("indeterminate" or "unknown" or "don't know"). The necessity for at least three values is simply illustrated by the problem posed in answering such questions as: "Do they grow a lot of coffee in Venezuela?" to which a truthful answer, based on all the knowledge at one's disposal, could be "yes", "no", or "I don't know". RL has general, relational mechanisms for inferring logical and structural relationships among sentences and sentence components, for inferring valid, meaningful sentences and semantic components from speakers' utterances, and for inferring valid conclusions from a posed query relative to a knowledge base of natural language messages. In the next several paragraphs we examine some of these inference mechanisms.

To illustrate how natural language deduction works, we consider first the implicative and negative implicative verbs (Karttunen, 1971). For implicative verbs (like *manage*), if the whole sentence is true, then so is the complement of the verb. The truth of *John managed to let out the cat* implies that *John let out the cat*. On the other hand, if it is false that *John managed to let out the cat*, then it is false that *John let out the cat*. Finally, if we do not know whether or not *John managed to let out the cat*, then we do not know whether *John let out the cat*. For negative implicative verbs (like *forget*), if the whole sentence is true, then the complement of the verb is false; if the whole sentence is false, then the complement is true; and, if the whole sentence is indeterminate, then the truth of the complement is unknown. For example, if it is true that *John forgot to phone his mother on her birthday*, then it is false that *John phoned his mother on her birthday*; if it is false that *John forgot to phone his mother on her birthday*, then it is true that *John phoned his mother on her birthday*; and, if we do not know whether *John forgot to phone his mother on her birthday*, then we do not know whether or not *John phoned his mother on her birthday*. Truth tables for implicative and non-implicative verbs and their complements are given in 13) and 14). The truth table for a negative element (like *not*) and what it modifies is given in 15). This table is just like that for the negative implicatives (hence, the "negative" label).

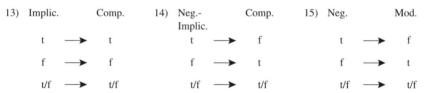

13) Implic.		Comp.	14) Neg.-Implic.		Comp.	15) Neg.		Mod.
t	→	t	t	→	f	t	→	f
f	→	f	f	→	t	f	→	t
t/f	→	t/f	t/f	→	t/f	t/f	→	t/f

The semantic graph in 16) of *Jill managed to solve the problem* shows the application of the truth table in 13) for implicative verbs. The truth value of the situation, indicated by **t** on the *id*-operator edge, is inferred to be true for the circumstance headed by *solve*.

16)

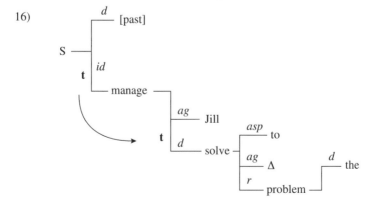

A circumstance inherits the situators of the situation in which it is embedded. This circumstance inherits, therefore, the past tense situator of *manage*, and we infer the truth of the sentence *Jill solved the problem*, whose semantic graph is given in 17).

17)

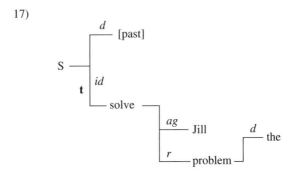

Truth values propagate through complex semantic structures. Sentences with a negative and an implicative and those with a negative and a negative implicative give straightforward inferences. For example, *Jill didn't manage to solve the problem*, whose semantic graph is shown in 18), implies that *Jill didn't solve the problem*. Similarly, *John didn't forget to phone his mother* implies that *John phoned his mother*.

18)

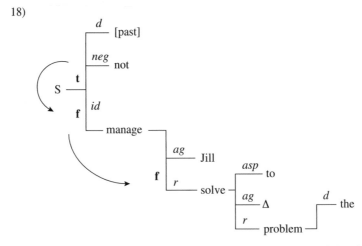

There are, of course, many verbs (like *believe*, *imagine*, and *hope*) that are non-implicatives. For non-implicative verbs, the truth value of their complements is indeterminate (t/f) regardless of the truth value of the dominating semantic component. For example, whatever the truth value of *Bob believed that Jill managed to solve the problem*, we do not know whether or not *Jill managed to solve the problem* or whether *Jill solved the problem*. In fact, once a t/f-value is encountered in any complex semantic structure, at the topmost situation or anywhere below it, then all truth values from that point in the structure are indeterminate. That is, neither a t-value nor an f-value can ever be inferred when the dominant value is a t/f-value.

7.3.2.3   *Pragmatics and discourse*

From a language understanding perspective, any theory of pragmatics and any theory of discourse are just subparts of a theory of communication, a way of accounting for how it is that a speaker's intentions are formulated, organized, interpreted, and understood. Grice (1975, 1981) proposed a theory of cooperation among the participants in a discourse or dialog. Sperber and Wilson's theory of relevance encompasses and supersedes Grice's pioneering work and attempts an overall framework for understanding verbal (and other) communication. The task for pragmatics and discourse analysis is to take the explicit linguistic semantics representation of utterances and to derive the intended interpretation. Given our goal of amalgamation, we can think of this as a conceptual or propositional semantics representation. While pragmatic analysis makes use of real-world information at every turn, there is, obviously, no guarantee that the interpretation arrived at actually obtains in the real world.

(1)   Pragmatics

Pragmatics is concerned with the use and interpretation of language in context. Determining the intended interpretation of language requires real-world knowledge; and, typically, it requires a lot of knowledge. The sorts of information that language users bring to bear include information about the basic vocabulary, say, the most commonly used ten to twenty thousand English words in their most common senses. This knowledge is shared with the larger English-speaking community. Alongside this general stock of information, there is a seemingly endless array of domain-specific vocabularies and of special senses of common words. Jargons include those associated with occupations (e.g., law, stock trading, military, medicine, farming, academe), technologies (automobiles and trucks, computing, airplanes, and economics), individual companies and regions, and sports and outdoor activities (baseball, tennis, fly fishing, duck hunting, and mountain climbing). One should not ignore, either, the role of history, since terminology varies and changes over time, and what is well known and understood in one era may be virtually unknown to most people in another. (Even widespread vocabulary of recent vintage can quickly fall into disuse. For instance, key-punch cards, key-punch machines, and key-punch operators are no longer evident, and knowledge of this phase of the history of computing is rapidly fading.)

Knowledge of vocabulary presupposes that one knows how to use it. That is, it presupposes that one knows how the vocabulary is used to organize and characterize events into typical scenarios and topics. It is, in fact, one's experience and expectations about "goings on in the world", including their description, that enable language interpretation to proceed at all.

How is all this knowledge organized? Certainly, taxonomies and concept hierarchies play a role. Knowing that X "is covered by" Y is one basic kind of vocabulary knowledge. So is knowing that X is associated with Y, X is a part of Y, and X is the opposite or antonym of Y. Concept hierarchies are "tangled", since a given term can participate in a number of relationships. The organization of vocabulary terms in *Roget's Thesaurus*, with its relatively flat and shallow hierarchy of many categories, is very much in accord with prototype theory (see, for example, Rosch, 1978; Tversky, 1986). Not very surprisingly, basic-level (English) vocabulary items like *dog, bird, chair, tree, water, dirt, white, red, talk, walk, eat, drink*, and *sleep*, which are eminently suited for the human scale of experience and interaction with the environment, are in the middle of the hierarchy. Basic terms like *chair* typically have superordinate terms (such as *furniture*) and subordinate terms (like *rocking chair* and *recliner*). Basic-level terms typically have a best exemplar, a "cognitive reference point" that forms the basis for inferences (Rosch, 1983). For example, the robin is about the size of the prototype bird. Hence, a chickadee is a small bird, and a raven is a large bird. Then, too, terms can be modified in such a way as to cancel temporarily some of their prototypical attributes. Thus, there is no contradiction in speaking of a dead bird, in noting that some birds are flightless, or in using the word *bird* to designate the figurine of a bird. Basic-level terms do not necessarily have a single prototype. The word *tree*, not in any case a botanical concept, has three basic prototypes – broadleaf, conifer, and palm. Depending on one's life experience, one or two of the three types might be more cognitively salient than the other two. One recent and important effort to organize and categorize English vocabulary is WordNet, an on-line lexical reference system organized in terms of lexical concepts that reflect human cognition and lexical memory. The overall organization of the WordNet database is described in G. Miller, *et al.* (1990); nouns and lexical inheritance properties in G. Miller (1990); adjectives in Gross and K. Miller (1990); verbs in Fellbaum (1990); and computer implementation in Beckwith and G. Miller (1990).

Whatever one knows about words and what goes on in the world, it is nonetheless true that new words and old words in new uses are constantly encountered. What language users do to determine the meaning of new items must be explained by linguistics and functionally duplicated by a NLP system, which will also be confronted with "unknown words". At least in part, we can capitalize on the fact that speakers and writers are sensitive to the expectations of addressees, usually provide implicit definitions of items that they believe their audience will not be familiar with, and fail to give descriptive clues about items they believe their intended audience should be familiar with. For example, given the expectation that virtually every adult American knows that Canada is the country immediately to the north of the United States, it is highly unlikely that a news story would contain "In Canada, the country to the north of the United States, ..." On the other hand, it is quite likely that a news story about Burkina Faso would identify it as a West African country – on the reasonable assumption that most Americans do not know what Burkina Faso is, let alone where it is. Appositives are one of the favorite mechanisms for introducing the meaning of unknown words: "Abra Cadabra, the Foreign Minister of ... ," "Abra Cadabra, the oil-rich province of ... ," "Abra Cadabra, the new software program from ..." The point is that NLP systems, like ordinary language users, must exploit whatever is available in any discourse to ferret out the meaning and categorizations of new items.

Much of the recent work in cognitive grammar seeks to explain the pervasiveness of metaphor and metonymy in language. (See especially Lakoff and Johnson (1980), Lakoff (1987), Johnson (1987), MacCormac (1985).) In essence, the view that has emerged is that human thought and reason have a rich conceptual structure, one that necessarily and characteristically supports and demands the use of figurative language. As Lakoff (1987:xiv) puts it:

- Thought is *embodied*, that is, the structures used to put together our conceptual systems grow out of bodily experience and make sense in terms of it; moreover, the core of our conceptual systems is directly grounded in perception, body movement, and experience of a physical and social character.
- Thought is *imaginative*, in that those concepts which are not directly grounded in experience employ metaphor, metonymy, and mental imagery – all of which go beyond the literal mirroring, or *representation*, of external reality. It is this imaginative capacity that allows for "abstract" thought and takes the mind beyond what we can see and feel. ...
- Thought has *gestalt properties* and is thus not atomistic; concepts have an overall structure that goes beyond merely putting together conceptual "building blocks" by general rules.

Basic-level concepts like chairs, birds, and dogs have gestalt properties. While such concepts clearly have internal structure, the wholes seem to be altogether more cognitively salient and basic than the parts.

Martin (1992) presents a proposal for implementing a computer-based capability for understanding metaphors. Martin's approach provides an explicit representation of conventional metaphors and a mechanism (metaphor maps) for recognizing them. For example, to understand "How do I kill this [computer] process?", it is necessary to map "kill" onto "terminate". Similarly, "How do I open up this database application?" requires that "open up" be mapped onto "start".

Another vexing problem is that of polysemy (related word senses), which is to be distinguished from homonymy. Homonomy refers to cases of accidental identity, such as the word *pen* (writing instrument or enclosure). Similarly, *bank* has a number of distinct and homonymous meanings, as in such noun compounds as *river bank* and *savings bank* and such verb uses as *bank money, bank a plane, bank a fire*. The various meanings of *bank* are not nowadays felt to be systematically related, although they may have been at an earlier time. For polysemy, where the various senses of a word do seem to be systematically related, the major research issue is the establishment of criteria for determining the number of senses. Two criteria that indicate different senses are (1) the systematic use of a word in different relational operator configurations and (2) the systematic co-occurrence of a word with words from different parts of the concept hierarchy. From a Relational Logic perspective, in the first case the arc labels are different, while in the second, the nodes characteristically have different "fills". For example, two senses of *open* are indicated for *John opened the door* and *The door opened*, since in the first use the relational operators are cause and undergoer, with relational structure $open(c{:}X, u{:}Y)$, while, for the second, the single operator is just the undergoer, and we have $open(u{:}X)$. Similarly, for *teach* we note such examples as *Mary taught algebra*, with the relational structure $teach(c{:}X, r{:}Y)$, *Mary taught Bill*, with $teach(c{:}X, u{:}Y)$, and *Mary taught Bill algebra*, with $teach(c{:}X, u{:}Y, r{:}Z)$. Our pragmatic expectations about what can fill a given node largely determine ambiguity resolution. In the preceding example, the knowledge that *algebra* is a subject and that *Bill* is a personal name is the basis for determining which of the two transitive relational structures is intended. For prepositions, which typically have many senses, it is often the object of the preposition that enables ambiguity resolution. For instance, in *on Tuesday*, and *on the table*, the temporal and (one of the) locative senses of *on* are disambiguated by the choice of object. Brugman (1981) examined the large range of senses for *over*, including its use as a preposition, particle, and adverb. (This work is discussed at length in Lakoff, 1987:418ff.) The senses of *over* include "above-across" (*fly over*), "above" (*hang over*), "covering" (*cloud over*), "reflexive" (*turn over*), "excess" (*spill over*), and various metaphorical senses (*oversee, overlook*). Brugman shows that the numerous senses of *over* are, indeed, systematically related. Disambiguating the uses of *over* in these few examples depends on the category of what *over* modifies: *fly, hang, cloud, turn,* and *spill* are in different parts of the concept hierarchy.

The senses and uses of words are not static. New uses occur with great frequency and are to be expected. For example, recent new uses of the word *word* include *word processor* (a computer application program for authoring and editing text), *Microsoft Word* (a word processing product), *Word Grammar*, a theory of grammar, and WordNet, an on-line lexical database. Evidently, new word senses are easily acquired in context, and disambiguation depends on noting part of speech, relational semantic structure, and the co-occurrence of words from different parts of the concept hierarchy (including specific items, as in these examples). For both people and for NLP systems, then, learning new vocabulary and new senses of existing vocabulary items is a major concern. Yet, linguistics has paid almost no attention to this area.

(2) Discourse

A theory of discourse understanding must encompass interactive dialogs, short text messages (including memos and letters), narratives, and extended texts of the sort that typify expository writing. The theory of discourse structure advanced by Grosz and Sidner (1986) has been particularly influential. Grosz and Sidner propose that discourse structure is composed of three distinct, but interrelated, components: linguistic structure, intentional structure, and attentional state. Viewed as linguistic structure, a discourse consists of an assemblage of discourse segments. The segments consist of utterances (written or spoken), which are the basic linguistic elements. While the organization of discourse segments is largely linear and hierarchical (since discourses consist for the most part of topics and subtopics), the discourse model also provides for segments embedded in other segments, and for asides, interruptions, flashbacks, digressions, footnotes, and the like. The intentional structure component accounts for the purposes and aims of a discourse. Each discourse segment must have a purpose. Further, the originator of a segment must intend that the recipient(s) recognize the intention. As Grosz and Sidner say: "It is important to distinguish intentions that are intended to be recognized from other kinds of intentions that are associated with discourse. Intentions that are intended to be recognized achieve their intended effect only if the intention is recognized. For example, a compliment achieves its intended effect only if the intention to compliment is recognized . . ." (1986:178) Although apparently formulated quite independently, Grosz and Sidner's insistence that discourse intentions be manifest agrees wholly with Sperber and Wilson's theory of Relevance. Much recent work (e.g., Asher and Lascarides, 1994) continues to investigate discourse intentions. The attentional state, the third component of Grosz and Sidner's discourse model, refers to the "focus spaces" that are available to the participants in a discourse as the discourse unfolds. "[The attentional state] is inherently dynamic, recording objects, properties, and relations that are salient at each point in the discourse. . . . changes in attentional state are modeled by a set of transition rules that specify the conditions for adding and deleting spaces" (1986:179). The development of a framework for modeling the attentional state, called centering, has been developed since the mid-1980s by Grosz, Joshi, and Weinstein (1995). Another important issue is how, in third person narratives, the reader (or listener) recognizes that the point of view is shifting from the narrator to one or another of the characters. Wiebe (1994) discusses at length the mechanisms that underlie understanding and tracking a narrative's psychological point of view.

While Grosz and Sidner discuss only linguistic utterances and linguistic structure as a discourse component, it is obvious that discourses can contain many other sorts of elements and segments (which may be linguistic in part). Among them are, in spoken discourse, virtually anything that can be pointed to as a deictic element. In written texts these elements and segments include figures, drawings, pictures, graphs, and tables. In the newer discourse structures that use electronic multimedia, various graphics, video, and sound elements can be included in a discourse. That is not to say that everything one might link together on-line and electronically, no matter how sensibly, forms a discourse. Quite the contrary. For instance, in preparing an on-line version of a technical manual, one could provide a link from every mention of every technical term to its definition in a technical glossary. None of these links or definitions would be part of the discourse; they would be included as a convenience, merely for ready reference.

Within a discourse segment, the discourse coherence relations among the situations are often implicit and involve such notions as cause, consequence, claim, reason, argument, elaboration, enumeration, before, and after. (See Sanders, Spooren, and Noordman (1993), for a recent discussion and proposal.) On the other hand, many transitions within a discourse structure, especially changes and transitions from one segment to another, are often made overt through the use of "clue word" or "cue phrase" expressions that provide information at the discourse level. These expressions include *incidentally, for example, anyway, by the way, furthermore, first, second, then, now, thus, moreover, therefore, hence, lastly, finally, in summary,* and *on the other hand.* (See, for example, Reichman (1985) for extended discussion of these expressions, and Hirschberg and Litman (1993) on cue phrase disambiguation.) Anaphora resolution has also been the subject of much work in NLP. Representative treatments are given in Hobbs (1978), Ingria and Stallard (1989), Lappin and Leass (1994), and Huls, Bos, and Claasen (1995). In NLP, discourse referents (i.e., discourse anaphora) have themselves been much studied (see Webber (1988), and Passonneau (1989)). Lastly, ellipsis is yet another topic that is at once a prominent feature of discourse structure and very important to language understanding. A recent treatment is found in Kehler (1994).

Needless to say, no language understanding system currently available (or "on the drawing board") has anything even remotely close to a complete implementation of the linguistic elements outlined above. The full range of linguistic and cognitive phenomena to be covered is so incredibly complex that it is arguable whether linguistic theory and its near relatives that treat communication are at all mature enough to support the development of a semantic representation and inferencing capability satisfactory for linguistic semantics and for pragmatic interpretation in context. Nevertheless, the development of NLP capability is proceeding at a rapid pace, sometimes in reasonable accord with one or another linguistic theory, but often exploiting representation schemes, analysis methods, and inferencing techniques developed in computer science for other purposes.

7.4   LINGUISTICALLY-BASED AND STATISTICALLY-BASED NLP

The purpose of an NLP system largely determines the approach that should be taken. Broadly speaking, there are two major approaches one can take to NLP implementation, namely, linguistically (i.e., knowledge) based and statistically based. For text analysis, if one's purpose is to build a system for very accurate, detailed information extraction, an objective that requires language understanding, then only a linguistically-based approach will serve. A comprehensive linguistically-based approach requires, however, full lexical, morphological, syntactic, semantic, pragmatic, and discourse components. These are not easy to come by. Less ambitious goals for text analysis – for instance, finding out what very large numbers of documents are "about" – can make excellent use of statistical methods.

Singular value decomposition (SVD), one such statistical method (see Berry, Dumais, and O'Brien, 1995), is a promising technique for achieving **conceptual *index*ing**. Conceptual indexing, which correlates the combined occurrence of vocabulary items with individual text objects (typically a few paragraphs in length), enables querying and retrieval of texts by topic – in accord with what they are "about". The objective is not language understanding; rather, it is to achieve robust text indexing and information retrieval that does not depend on the presence in a text of particular vocabulary items.

SVD is, like many other statistical techniques, a practical means for investigating and analyzing large corpora. The goals for large corpora analysis are many. In addition to conceptual indexing, they include: finding instances (in context) of interesting and/or rare language phenomena; determining the frequency with which language phenomena occur; discovering linguistic rules, constraints, and lexical items; and constructing bilingual dictionaries and/or ascertaining translation quality (by aligning texts, one a translation of the other). Two special issues of *Computational Linguistics* (March, 1993; June, 1993) were devoted to large corpora analysis. (See especially the introduction by Church and Mercer (1993).) In sum, from a linguistic point of view, statistical techniques are not ends in themselves, but are tools to get at knowledge about language or the world. Large corpora analysis techniques, in particular, give several different sorts of results of direct interest to linguists. Among them are: (1) using conceptual indexing of a large number of short texts (or long texts segmented into suitable "chunks"), to select texts on particular topics for some linguistic purpose or other, (2) culling example sets of some linguistic phenomena from very large collections of text, and (3) finding bilingual equivalents of lexical items in (presumably) equivalent contexts.

For natural language understanding applications *per se*, statistical methods can augment – and complement – rule-based systems. For instance, since any system will, in operational use, repeatedly encounter new (i.e., "unknown") lexical items, an automatic part of speech tagger can be used to make a best guess as to the correct part of speech of the unknown item. Further, no semantic lexicon will be complete, either; and an automatic semantic tagger can make a best guess as to the category in which an unknown term is being used (minimally, "person", "place", or "thing") or can suggest the sense in which a known word is being used. For instance, if we encounter, "He introduced that idea several lectures ago", a semantic tagger could suggest that "lectures" is being used as a temporal expression. (The literature on statistical methods for language analysis is burgeoning. See, for example, Kupiec (1992); Charniak (1993); Pustejovsky, Bergler, and Anick (1993); Merialdo (1994); Brill (1995); Roche and Schabes (1995); Mikheev (1996).)

7.5 CONTROLLED LANGUAGE CHECKING

To meet the needs of users of technical documentation, especially those whose native language is not that in which the materials are written, a highly desirable goal is to restrict the vocabulary and grammatical structures to a subset of that which would ordinarily occur. Codifying the restrictions systematically defines a controlled language standard. One of the best-known is Simplified English, developed by AECMA (Association Européenne des Constructeurs de Matériel Aérospatial) (AECMA, 1986; 1989), and mandated by the Air Transport Association as the world-wide standard for commercial aircraft maintenance manuals. The general English vocabulary allowed in Simplified English (SE) is about 1500 words, only about 200 of which are verbs. Except for a few common prepositions, each of these words is to be used in one, and only one, prescribed meaning. Aerospace manufacturers are to augment this highly restricted core vocabulary with technical terms. (Boeing adds over 5000.)

SE grammatical and stylistic restrictions are wide ranging. For example: the progressive verb forms and the perfective aspect are not allowed; the past participle is allowed only as an adjective; the passive voice is not allowed in procedures (and is to be avoided in descriptions); singular count nouns must be preceded by a determiner; noun groups should not contain more than three nouns in a row (long technical terms should use a hyphen to join related words); sentences in procedures should not be longer than 20 words, those in descriptions no longer than 25 words; verbs and nouns should not be omitted to make sentences shorter; instruction sentences cannot be compounded, unless the actions are to be done simultaneously; paragraphs should have no more than six sentences, and the first sentence must be the topic sentence; warnings should be set off from other text.

While manuals that conform to SE are easy to read, the many restrictions make writing them extremely difficult. To meet the need of its engineer writers to produce maintenance manuals in SE, Boeing developed a syntax-based Simplified English Checker (SEC) (Hoard, Wojcik, and Holzhauser, 1992). Since its introduction in 1990, the Boeing SEC, which contains a grammar of roughly 350 rules and a vocabulary of over 30,000 words, has parsed about 4 million sentences. Random sampling shows that the SEC parses correctly over ninety per cent of the sentences it encounters, detects about ninety per cent of all syntactic SE violations, and reports critiques that are about eighty per cent accurate (Wojcik, Harrison, and Bremer, 1993). The critiques suggest alternative word choices for non-SE terms (e.g., "verb error: result; use: cause") and note grammatical violations of the SE standard (e.g., too many nouns in a row). The SEC does not attempt to rewrite text automatically. Nor should it, since the author's intentions are completely unknowable to the SEC (and to any other syntax-only analysis system).

Even though Boeing's SEC is the most robust grammar and style checker of its type, it does not detect any semantic violations of the SE standard. To do so requires a meaning-based language checker, as depicted conceptually in Figure 7.2, that adds to the current SEC's Syntactic Analyzer and Syntactic Error Detector, an Initial Semantic Interpreter, a Word Sense Checker, and a Semantic Error Detector.

Currently in prototype, the Boeing meaning-based SEC adds knowledge of several types to the syntax-based checker. These include word senses for all the words known to the system (most words have several senses), semantic hierarchies and categorizations (especially important for technical terms), a word sense thesaurus which indicates for every word

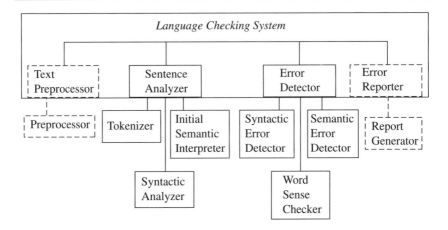

Figure 7.2   Conceptual architecture for a meaning-based language checker

sense whether it is sanctioned by the SE standard (and, if not, what alternative word is available), and semantic selection restrictions (including noun compound information and preferences that are specific to the application domain).

While the current SEC permits all the senses of an allowed SE word to pass unremarked, the meaning-based error detector makes full use of semantic graphs to find word-sense violations. For example, the verb *follow* is allowed in SE in the sense "come after", but not in the sense "obey". The sentence *Do the steps that follow*, whose semantic graph is shown in 19), uses *follow* in the "come after" sense (indicated in the graph by "follow_1"). This is determined during the analysis of the sentence by noting that the (implied) range complement of *follow* is *steps*. On the other hand, the sentence *Follow all the instructions*, uses *follow* in its "obey" sense (indicated with "follow_2" in the graph). This is determined during sentence analysis by noting that *follow* has an (understood) agent complement. Note that the transitivity of *follow* does not determine the sense. The example sentence *A reception follows the concert* has the "come after" sense of *follow*. Here, the semantic structure has *follow* with range and source complements, not with agent and range complements, as in 20. It is the difference in complement structures and in our expectations as to what can fill them that causes us to interpret *follow* as having one sense or the other.

Similarly, though the preposition *against* is restricted in SE to the sense "in contact with", the current SEC does not detect the word-sense error in *Obey the precautions against fire*. But the meaning-based checker does, suggesting that *against* be replaced with the verb *prevent*. (A possible rewrite

19)

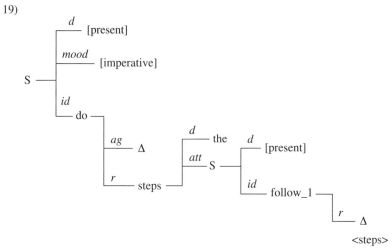

20)

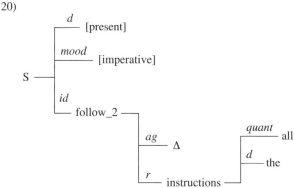

of the sentence is *Obey the precautions to prevent fire.*) Often, the meaning-based SEC can improve on the critique offered by the syntax-based SEC. For instance, the word *under* is not allowed in SE, and the current SEC suggests "below, in, less than" as alternatives – advice that is only moderately helpful. The meaning-based SEC is able to do much better by determining the (apparent) intended sense of *under* and suggesting the one most appropriate alternative for consideration as the replacement.

The ability to do true meaning-based checking has far-reaching consequences for all the application types listed at the beginning of this chapter. Obviously, being able to determine the sense in which a word is being used, as in the meaning-based SEC, will enable writers to produce materials that are far closer to that which is sanctioned by a restricted, controlled language standard like SE than ever before. But that is not the only gain. For instance, it is widely maintained that the quality of the inputs is the single most important variable in determining the quality of machine translation outputs. And, indeed, it appears that, for the foreseeable future, fully automatic machine translation will be possible only when the inputs are fully constrained by adhering to a restricted, controlled language standard. Then, too, with semantic interpretation of inputs and the ability of a system to negotiate intended meaning with users, natural language interfaces can be integrated with intelligent agent technology to provide general query capabilities (going well beyond the present ability to query a single database). Further, the ability to provide declarative knowledge bases in controlled English, for both modeling and process descriptions, and to translate the descriptions into machine-sensible underlying formalisms will greatly expand the speed with which such systems can be implemented. All of this is just to say that analyzing and controlling the meaning of the inputs to an NLP application provides a level of ambiguity resolution that identifies, reduces, and eliminates ambiguity to a degree that will give high confidence in the functioning of any system of which it is a component.

While we are clearly only at the beginning of the effort to fashion computer systems that understand language, it should be obvious that a linguistics whose objectives are broadened to include language under-standing has a large role to play. Conversely, NLP has much to offer linguistics, for real-world applications test even the most comprehensive theories of language understanding to the limit. Boeing's prototype meaning-based Simplified English Checker is an early example of such an application, one whose worth will (or will not) be borne out in actual production use when the first few million sentences submitted to it are interpreted and critiqued.

Chapter 8

Theoretical and computational linguistics: toward a mutual understanding

Samuel Bayer, John Aberdeen, John Burger, Lynette Hirschman, David Palmer, and Marc Vilain

8.1 INTRODUCTION

The nature of computational linguistics (CL) has changed radically and repeatedly through the last three decades. From the ATN-based implementations of transformational grammar in the 1960s, through the explicitly linguistics-free paradigm of Conceptual Dependencies,[1] to the influence and applications of 1980s-era unification-based frameworks, CL has alternated between defining itself in terms of and in opposition to mainstream theoretical linguistics. Since the late 1980s, it seems that a growing group of CL practitioners has once more turned away from formal theory. In response to the demands imposed by the analysis of large corpora of linguistic data, statistical techniques have been adopted in CL which emphasize shallow, robust accounts of linguistic phenomena at the expense of the detail and formal complexity of current theory. Nevertheless, we argue in this chapter that the two disciplines, as currently conceived, are mutually relevant. While it is indisputable that the granularity of current linguistic theory is lost in a shift toward shallow analysis, the basic insights of formal linguistic theory are invaluable in informing the investigations of computational linguists; and while ***corpus***-based techniques seem rather far removed from the concerns of current theory, modern statistical techniques in CL provide very valuable insights about language and language processing, insights which can inform the practice of mainstream linguistics.

There are two forces driving the evolution of this brand of CL, which we will call corpus-based CL, that we hope to emphasize in the sections to follow. The first is that the complexity and power required to analyze linguistic data is discontinuous in its distribution. Coarsely put, we have seen over and over that the simplest tools have the broadest coverage, and more and more complexity is required to expand the coverage less and less. Consider the place of natural language as a whole on the Chomsky hierarchy, for instance. Chomsky (1956) demonstrated that natural language is at least context-free in its complexity, and after a number of failed proofs, it is now commonly agreed that natural language is strongly and weakly trans-context-free (Shieber, 1985; Kac, 1987; Culy, 1985; Bresnan *et al.*, 1982). Yet what is striking about these results is both the relative infrequency of constructions which demonstrate this complexity and the increase in computational power required to account for them. For example, the constructions which are necessarily at least context-free (such as center embedding) seem fairly uncommon in comparison with constructions which could be fairly characterized as finite state; the constructions which are necessarily trans-context-free are even fewer. In other words, a large subset of language can be handled with relatively simple computational tools; a much smaller subset requires a radically more expensive approach; and an even smaller subset something more expensive still. This observation has profound effects on the analysis of large corpora: there is a premium on identifying those linguistic insights which are simplest, most general, least controversial, and most powerful, in order to exploit them to gain the broadest coverage for the least effort.

The second force driving the evolution of corpus-based CL is the desire to measure progress in the field. Around 1985 a four-step paradigm began to evolve which has motivated a wide range of changes in the field of CL; among these changes is the reliance on initial broad, shallow analyses implied by the discontinuous nature of linguistic data. This methodology, which we describe and exemplify in detail below, is responsible for introducing quantifiable measures of research progress according to community-established metrics, and has led to an explosion of new ways to look at language.

These two forces constitute the first half of our story. First through history and then through examples, we will illustrate how substantial advances have been made, and measured, in a paradigm which favors broad coverage over fine-grained analysis. We will show that the corpus-based CL commitment to evaluation has led to the insight that simple tools, coupled with crucial, profound, basic linguistic generalizations, yield substantial progress. But the story does not end there. It is not simply that linguistics informs the corpus-based, evaluation-based paradigm; the reverse is also true. We believe that the demands that large corpora impose on linguistic analyses reveal many topics for inquiry that have not been well explored by traditional linguistic methods. Abney (1996) argues that modern theoretical linguistics poorly accounts for, or fails to account for, a range of issues including the graded nature of language acquisition, language change, and language variation, as well as disambiguation, degrees of grammaticality, judgments of naturalness, error tolerance, and learning vocabulary and grammar on the fly by mature speakers. Abney further contends that current corpus-based CL approaches respond to exactly those considerations which compromise current theoretical techniques. In many cases, these approaches are born of researchers' frustration with faithful implementations of their theories: gaps in coverage and expressiveness, intolerable ambiguity, an inability to model graded distinctions of grammaticality or likelihood of use. It is with an interest in these less commonly asked questions that we invite you to read the following narrative.

8.2 HISTORY: CORPUS-BASED LINGUISTICS

Corpus-based analysis of language is hardly a new idea. Following de Saussure, the American structural linguists, from Leonard Bloomfield (1933) through Zellig Harris (1951), pursued an empirical approach to linguistic description, applying it to a large variety of languages (including Amerindian languages, Chinese, Korean, Japanese, and Hebrew) and a range of linguistic phenomena, predominantly phonology and morphology but also syntax and even discourse structure. For the structuralists, linguistic analysis required (1) an inventory of the distinct structural elements, (2) rules for the observed combinations of these elements, and (3) a procedure for discovering the units and their combinatorics via empirical observation based on systematic analysis of a corpus of utterances. The methods that the structuralists developed – distributional analysis and the study of co-occurrence data, decomposition of analysis into multiple layers of phonology, morphology, syntax, and discourse, and automatable discovery of linguistic descriptions or grammars – underlie much of the current research on corpus-based methods.[2]

Reliance on, or reference to, naturally occurring data is also taking hold in modern theoretical linguistics as well, and becoming more prevalent. Recent advocates and adherents include Birner (1994), Macfarland (1997), and Michaelis (1996); in many cases, researchers have relied on corpora to refute previously-proposed generalizations about linguistic constructions. We applaud this trend, certainly; but it is only part of the puzzle. When we talk about corpus-based linguistics today, we don't simply mean the consultation of a corpus in the course of linguistic research; we mean the commitment to robust, automatic analysis of this corpus, in as much depth as possible.

Given how old the goal of automated grammar discovery is, it is curious that it has taken approximately fifty years to make real progress in this area, measured by systems that work and methodologies that can generate reasonable coverage of linguistic phenomena. The reasons for this are partly sociological, influenced by the methods in vogue in any particular decade, but mostly technological; they include

- the ready accessibility of computational resources (fast machines, sufficient storage) to process large volumes of data
- the growing availability of corpora, especially corpora with linguistic annotations (part of speech, prosodic intonation, proper names,

bilingual parallel corpora, etc.), and increased ease of access and exchange of resources via the Internet

- a commercial market for natural language products, based on the increased maturity of computational linguistics technology
- the development of new tools, including both efficient parsing techniques (e.g. finite state transducers) and statistical techniques.

For example, the statistical technique of **Hidden Markov Model**s (**HMM**s) revolutionized speech recognition technology (Rabiner, 1989), making it possible to build robust speaker-independent speech recognizers. This technique, originally adopted by the engineering community for signal processing applications, has now been widely applied to other linguistic phenomena as well. An HMM provides a technique for automatically constructing a recognition system, based on probabilities provided by training data. An HMM consists of two layers: an observable layer and a hidden layer which is a Markov model, that is, a finite state machine with probabilities associated with the state transitions. For speech recognition, the observable layer might be the sequence of acoustic segments, while the hidden layer would be finite state models of word pronunciations, represented as phoneme sequences. Once the HMM is trained by presenting it with recorded speech segments together with transcriptions, it can be used as a recognizer for acoustic segments, to generate transcriptions from speech.[3]

Consider how this technique might be used in corpus-based CL. One of the most common tasks performed in corpus-based CL is **part-of-speech tagging**, in which lexical categories (that is, part-of-speech tags) are assigned to words in documents or speech transcriptions. It turns out that part-of-speech tags can be assigned in English with a very high degree of accuracy (above ninety-five per cent) without reference to higher-level linguistic information such as syntactic structure, and the resulting tags can be used to help derive syntactic structure with a significantly reduced level of ambiguity. For part-of-speech tagging via HMMs, the observable layer is the sequence of words, while the hidden layer models the sequence of part-of-speech tags; the HMM is trained on documents annotated with part-of-speech tags, and the resulting trained HMM can be used to generate tags for unannotated documents.[4]

The success of Hidden Markov Models for speech recognition had a major effect on corpus-based language processing research. Here was a technique which produced an astounding improvement in the ability of a machine to transcribe speech; it was automatically trained by the statistical processing of huge amounts of data, both spoken transcribed data and written data, and its performance was evaluated on a never-before-seen set of blind test data. This success had profound commercial implications, making it possible, for example, to produce medium-vocabulary speech recognition systems that required no prior user training.[5] This technique was developed in the late 1960s and early 1970s; it made its way into the speech recognition community by the mid-1970s, and into commercial quality speech recognizers by the mid-1980s. In the process, these successes also created a new paradigm for research in computational linguistics.

8.3 HISTORY: EVALUATION

Before we exemplify the corpus-based methodology and elaborate on its implications for theoretical linguistics, we want to define some terms and then trace the impact of evaluation on two communities: researchers in spoken language understanding and researchers in text understanding. When we speak of "understanding" in corpus-based CL, we intend a very limited, task-specific interpretation; roughly, we take a language processing system to have "understood" if it responds appropriately to utterances directed to it. For evaluated systems, the notion of an appropriate response must be defined very clearly in order to measure progress. Much of the work in this paradigm, then, consists of community-wide efforts to define the form and content of appropriate responses. Defining the system responses in this way has the added advantage that the internals of the language processing systems need not be examined in the process of evaluation; all that is required is the input data (speech or unanalyzed text) and the system's response. This sort of evaluation is known as a *"black box" evaluation*, so called because the language processing system can be treated as an opaque "box" whose inputs and outputs are the only indications of its performance.

There have been two major efforts aimed at the evaluation of natural language systems: one in the area of speech recognition and spoken language systems, the other in the area of text-based language understanding. The speech recognition evaluations began as part of the *DARPA* speech recognition program, and from 1990 to 1995, the speech recognition evaluations were combined with evaluation of spoken language understanding (Price, 1996). The focal point for the text-based evaluations has been the series of *Message Understanding Conferences* (*MUCs*) that have taken place every year or two since 1987 (Grishman and Sundheim, 1995), with MUC-7 scheduled for early 1998. This section briefly traces the evolution and history of corpus-based evaluation in these two research communities.

8.3.1 The Air Travel Information System (ATIS) evaluation

For speech recognition and spoken language, the push for evaluation came specifically from DARPA, the agency which funded much of the advanced research in this area. There was already a well-understood need for a corpus-based methodology, since speech recognizers rely heavily on the availability of (large amounts of) recorded speech with corresponding transcriptions and an evaluation function for automated training. Prior to the effort to evaluate the understanding aspects of spoken language interfaces, the measurement of speech recognition error had already been responsible for dramatic progress in the speech community.

To develop an automated approach to evaluating spoken language understanding, researchers chose the task of making air travel reservations. This task was chosen because it was familiar to many people, and thus promised a broad base of potential users who could act as experimental subjects for data collection to build such a language understanding system. Researchers limited the problem of language understanding for this task in some critical ways:

- Scope was limited to evaluation of spoken queries against a static database of airline information (as opposed to dynamic, unpredictable data for which the vocabulary might be unknown in advance).
- Interaction style was restricted to human-initiated queries only, since it was not clear how to automate evaluation of discourses where the language understanding system asked questions of the user as well.
- The queries were restricted to a well-defined domain of reasonable size, in order to ensure that the database provided enough coverage to ensure useful interactions.
- Evaluation was limited to a strict definition of answer correctness, based on comparison to the set of tuples to be returned from the database.

In the context of this paradigm, users were presented with a task description (for instance, "You must make reservations to visit your grandmother in Baltimore, but you must stop in Boston overnight, and due to scheduling restrictions, you must leave on a Thursday"). The users' recorded utterances, along with their transcriptions and the correct database response, form the basis of the ATIS corpus.

Despite the limitations imposed by this strategy for evaluation of understanding, this work introduced some useful candidate standards: transcription as the basis for evaluation of speech recognition (borrowed from earlier work in the speech community); development of a methodology to evaluate answer correctness based on the tuples retrieved from a database; and an annotation method to distinguish context-independent queries from context-dependent queries for evaluating the understanding of multi-utterance sequences (the latter required that the system have some model of the preceding interaction to answer correctly). In addition, the researchers undertook a highly successful collaborative data collection effort, which produced a large body (20,000 utterances) of annotated data, including speech, transcriptions, database output, and timestamped log files of the interactions (Hirschman *et al.*, 1992). Figure 8.1 shows an

```
[UtteranceID: 1]
[Timestamp: Sent speech for utterance 1 at 10:38:36]
[Begin Utterance: 1]
DO YOU HAVE ANY FLIGHTS FROM PITTSBURGH TO BOSTON ON
WEDNESDAY OF NEXT WEEK . IN THE MORNING
[End Utterance: 1]


[Timestamp: Sent sentence for utterance 1 at 10:38:56]
[Begin Query: 1]
select distinct flight.airline_flight,flight.from_airport,
   flight.to_airport,flight.departure_time,flight.arrival_time,
   flight.time_elapsed,flight.stops from flight
where flight.from_airport in ('PIT')
   and flight.to_airport in ('BOS')
   and ((flight_days like "%WE%" and flight_days not like
'NOT%')
      or (flight_days like 'DAILY'))
   and (flight.departure_time <= 1200)
[End Query: 1]


[Begin Result: 1]
```

AIRL	FROM	TO	LEAVE	ARRIVE	DURA	STOPS
US674	PIT	BOS	1200	1328	88	0
US732	PIT	BOS	710	839	89	0
US736	PIT	BOS	840	1006	86	0

```
[End Result: 1]
[Timestamp: Sent answer for utterance 1 and 10:39:00]
```

Figure 8.1   Sample ATIS log file (excerpt)

excerpt of a sample log file from the ATIS data collection efforts; it includes timestamped entries for receipt of speech input, transcription, translation into SQL (a standard database retrieval language), and system response.

These standardized evaluations resulted in a rapid decrease in the spoken language understanding error rate, showing that the research community was moving steadily towards solving the problem of getting machines to not only transcribe but also respond appropriately to what a user might say. Figure 8.2 plots error rate (log scale) against successive evaluation dates for the Spoken Language Program, using figures for the best performing system in each evaluation, processing context-independent utterances.[6] The top line (highest error rate) is a measure

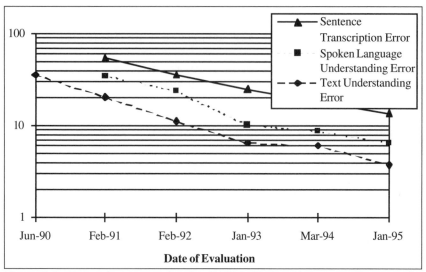

Figure 8.2 Rate of progress in the DARPA Spoken Language Program for context-independent sentences

of sentences correctly transcribed (no understanding): a sentence is incorrect if it contains one or more word recognition errors. It is clearly much harder to get all the words right in transcribing a sentence, which is why the sentence transcription error rate tends to be high; the percentage of *words* incorrectly transcribed for the ATIS task had dropped to two per cent by June 1995. The next highest line in Figure 8.2 represents spoken language understanding error rate, namely the percentage of sentences that did not receive a correct response from the database, given the speech input. The lowest error rate is text understanding error rate – given a perfect transcription as input, this is the percentage of sentences that did not get a correct database response. Not surprisingly, the text understanding error is lower than the spoken language understanding error, since processing the speech input can result in a less than perfect transcription.

Most significant, and perhaps counterintuitive, is that the understanding error rate (that is, the percentage of incorrect database responses) is lower, at every point, for both speech and text, than the sentence transcription error rate (that is, the percentage of sentences with at least one word incorrectly transcribed). This means that it is easier for the system to understand a sentence (given our definition of "understanding") than to transcribe it perfectly. In other words, perfect transcription is by no means a prerequisite for language understanding, and systems which require perfect grammatical input are at a disadvantage in this task compared to systems which do not.

8.3.2.   The Message Understanding Conferences (MUCs)

The Message Understanding Conferences evolved out of the research community's need to share results and insights about text-based language understanding. The six MUC conferences to date have been responsible for:

- the creation of an automated evaluation methodology for understanding annotated training and test data sets
- significant progress in building robust systems capable of extracting database entries from messages
- increasing the technology base in this area (participating groups have increased from six at the first conference in 1987 to sixteen at MUC-6 in November 1995).

The first three Message Understanding Conferences (1987, 1989, 1991) avoided component-based evaluation, since there was little agreement on what components would be involved, and focused on a black box evaluation methodology. The evaluation was defined at a high level. Given documents as input, a system's performance was determined by the extent to which it could produce the appropriate set of templates describing who did what to whom in a particular topic area (e.g., terrorist attacks, or joint ventures). Figure 8.3 shows an excerpt of a sample document from the MUC-4 document set about terrorist activity, along with a simplified template.

```
CLANDESTINE, 20 NOV 89 (RADIO VENCEREMOS) — [TEXT]...
SPANISH FOREIGN MINISTER LUIS YANEZ [AS HEARD] REPORTED
TODAY THAT SPAIN HAS SUSPENDED AID TO THE SALVADORAN
GOVERNMENT UNTIL THE KILLINGS OF THE SPANISH JESUITS,
WHO HAD BEEN LIVING IN OUR COUNRTY FOR YEARS, ARE
RESOLVED...
```

INCIDENT:	DATE	– 20 NOV 89
INCIDENT:	LOCATION	EL SALVADOR
INCIDENT:	TYPE	ATTACK
INCIDENT:	STAGE OF EXECUTION	ACCOMPLISHED
HUM TGT:	DESCRIPTION	"JESUITS"
HUM TGT:	TYPE	CIVILIAN: "JESUITS"
HUM TGT:	NUMBER	PLURAL: "JESUITS"
HUM TGT:	FOREIGN NATION	SPAIN: "JESUITS"
HUM TGT:	EFFECT OF INCIDENT	DEATH: "JESUITS"

Figure 8.3   Sample document and template fragment from MUC-4

Over these three evaluations, the participants defined training and test corpora, a detailed set of guidelines specifying the content of the templates for the test domains, and an automated scoring procedure. The MUC evaluations also introduced some standard terminology into the evaluation paradigm. Scores were calculated by comparing system *hypotheses* against a human-generated *key*, to produce numerical comparisons in terms of *precision* and *recall*. Precision is a measure of false positives; more precisely, it is the ratio of correct system answers to total system answers. Recall is a measure of false negatives; more precisely, it is the ratio of correct system answers to total answers in the key.

Once this basic methodology was established, the message understanding community was able to branch out in several directions, including evaluation of documents in multiple languages. The community has also been successful in decomposing the message understanding task into coherent subproblems: identifying proper names in text, identifying coreferring expressions, and gathering all the described attributes of an object or individual from its disparate references scattered through a text. Some of these tasks, such as identifying coreferring expressions, are still under development; nevertheless, it is clear that this functional decomposition, providing a layered application of linguistic knowledge, has been highly successful in defining the strengths and weaknesses of current technology, as well as opening new areas for research (e.g., tagging for coreference or for parts of speech in multiple languages).

8.4   METHODOLOGY

With this history in hand, we can now turn to a more detailed description of these corpus-based approaches to language processing. In the next few sections, we will outline and exemplify this family of approaches.

We can describe the corpus-based approach in four steps. First, we obtain and analyze linguistic data in the context of the task we choose (*information extraction*, *named entity* extraction, summarization, translation, etc.). Second, we hypothesize a procedure for producing the appropriate analyses. Third, we test this procedure, and finally, we iterate our procedure based on our evaluation. We will examine each of these steps in turn.

8.4.1   Step 1: analyze the data

Before we analyze data, we need to have data, in some computer-readable form. With the advent of powerful, inexpensive networked computing, this has become far more feasible than in the past. We now have corpora which encompass a wide range of data types (speech, text, multimedia documents), and increasingly, a range of languages. The community has also benefited considerably from well-organized efforts in data collection, exemplified by the multi-site ATIS and MUC efforts and the services and products provided by the *Linguistic Data Consortium*.

Our analysis of the data must be guided by the task at hand, whether it be transcription, translation, search, summarization, database update, or database query. The data provide us with the input; the structure of the task provides us with the output. For instance, in the ATIS task, the input is a speech signal and the output a database query. Our goal is to find a systematic, robust mapping from input to output. We may need to break that mapping down into many smaller steps, but we are still analyzing the input in terms of the desired output. In many cases, the form of the output is an annotated form of the input (for instance, a document augmented with the part of speech of each word); these annotations are drawn from a *tag set* of all possible tags for a given task.

8.4.2   Step 2: hypothesize the procedure

Based on our analysis of the data, we hypothesize a procedure that allows us to map from input to output. What matters is that this procedure can be implemented as a computer program. There are many approaches to choose among, from neural nets to stochastic models to rule-based systems. Some of these use explicit rules created by a human, some use machine learning, some are based on statistical processing. In general, the faster and more efficient the procedure, the more successful the procedure will be, because it will provide the opportunity for a greater number of iterations through the process (see Step 4 below).

8.4.3   Step 3: test the procedure

The corpus-based methodology uses data for two distinct purposes: to induce the analysis, and to provide a benchmark for testing the analysis. Our goal is to use this methodology to improve our performance on our chosen task. Therefore, the corpus-based method requires that there be a defined evaluation metric that produces a result, so that we can compare strategies or rule sets. If we cannot make this comparison, we have no reliable way of making progress, because we do not know which technique yields the better result.

We must choose our evaluation metric with care. We must believe that the evaluation metric has relevance to the task we are trying to perform, so that as our evaluation results improve, the performance of the system will improve. Furthermore, it is critical that we use new data (that is, data not used in the hypothesis phase) for evaluation, to ensure that we have created a system that is robust with respect to the kind of data we expect the system to have to handle. If we do not, we run the risk of designing strategies which are overly specific to the data we've used for training.

Finally, it is important to understand that the accuracy of our evaluation depends crucially on our accuracy in determining the "right" output, that is, our accuracy in creating the key. If any two humans performing the task in question can only agree on the "right" output 90 per cent of the time, then it will be impossible for us to develop a system which is 95 per cent accurate, because humans can't agree on what that means. So *inter-annotator agreement* among humans sets an upper bound on the system accuracy we can measure.

8.4.4   Step 4: iterate

Once we evaluate our approach, we can use standard techniques to improve our results, such as a systematic machine learning approach, or iterative debugging, or regression testing. During the iteration, we can revisit any one of the previous steps. We may need to refine our tag set, our procedure – or even our evaluation. Depending on the scope of the problem, all of these may get revised in the course of research.

In the next two sections, we describe applications of this paradigm in the domain of text-based language understanding. We will attempt to emphasize these four steps, showing how progress can be made using this technique.

8.5   EXAMPLE: SENTENCE SEGMENTATION

While the corpus-based methodology has successfully pushed progress in many areas traditionally of interest to linguists, it has also revealed many new problems which are frequently overlooked or idealized away in theoretical linguistics, yet which are essential steps for large-scale processing of language. One example of such an area is the segmentation of linguistic data into sentences, a task which can be surprisingly complex.

Recognizing sentence boundaries in a document is an essential step for many CL tasks. Speech synthesizers produce output prosody based on a sentence model, and incorrect identification of boundaries can confuse them. Parsers, by definition, determine the structure of a sentence, and therefore depend on knowledge of sentence boundaries. However, dividing a document into sentences is a processing step which, though it may seem simple on the surface, presents a wide variety of problems, especially when considering different languages. For example, written languages with punctuation systems which are relatively impoverished compared to English present a very difficult challenge in recognizing sentence boundaries. Thai, for one, does not use a period (or any other punctuation mark) to mark sentence boundaries. A space is sometimes used at sentence breaks, but very often there is no separation between sentences. Detecting sentence breaks in written Thai thus has a lot in common with segmenting a stream of spoken speech into sentences and words, in that the input is a continuous stream of characters (or phonemes) with few cues to indicate segments at any level.

Even languages with relatively rich punctuation systems like English present surprising problems. Recognizing boundaries in such a written language involves determining the roles of all punctuation marks which can denote sentence boundaries: periods, question marks, exclamation points, and sometimes semicolons, colons, and commas. In large document collections, each of these punctuation marks can serve several different purposes in addition to marking sentence boundaries. A period, for example, can denote a decimal point, an abbreviation, the end of a sentence, or even an abbreviation at the end of a sentence. Exclamation points and question marks can occur within quotation marks or parentheses (really!) as well as at the end of a sentence.[7] Disambiguating the various uses of punctuation is therefore necessary to recognize the sentence boundaries and allow further processing.

In the case of English, sentence boundary detection is an excellent example of both the discontinuities discussed previously and of the application of the corpus-based methodology to solving a practical problem. Simple techniques can achieve a rather high rate of success, but incrementally improving this initial rate and recognizing the difficult cases can require a significant amount of linguistic knowledge and intuition in addition to a thorough analysis of a large corpus of sentences.

The first step in the corpus-based methodology, obtaining and analyzing the data, is quite straightforward for this task; millions of sentences are readily available in many different languages. And while compiling and analyzing the data for some CL tasks involves linguistically sophisticated knowledge about transcribing or translation, the key for the sentence boundary detection task can be constructed with virtually no linguistic training.

The second step in the methodology, hypothesizing the procedure to solve the problem, may seem simple at first. When analyzing well-formed English documents such as works of literature, it is tempting to believe that sentence boundary detection is simply a matter of finding a period followed by one or more spaces followed by a word beginning with a capital letter; in addition, other sentences may begin or end with quotation marks. We could therefore propose the following simple rule as our entire sentence segmentation algorithm:

```
sentence boundary =
     period + space + capital letter
     OR period + quote + space + capital letter
     OR period + space + quote + capital letter
```

It is only through actually testing this rule on real data (Step 3 of the methodology), that we become aware of the range of possibilities. In some corpora (e.g., literary texts) the single pattern above indeed accounts for almost all sentence boundaries. In *The Call of the Wild* by Jack London, for example, which has 1640 periods as sentence boundaries, this single rule will correctly identify 1608 boundaries (recall of 98.1 per cent) while introducing just 5 false negatives (precision of 99.7 per cent). It is precisely these types of results that led many to dismiss sentence boundary disambiguation as a simple problem. However, the results are different in journalistic text such as the *Wall Street Journal*. In a small corpus of the WSJ which has 16,466 periods as sentence boundaries, the simple rule above would detect only 14,562 (recall of 88.4 per cent) while producing 2900 false positives (precision of 83.4 per cent).

We can use this knowledge to improve our hypothesis iteratively (Step 4 of the methodology) and attempt to produce a better solution which addresses the issues raised by the real data. Upon inspection of journalistic text, we see that our simple rule fails in cases such as "Mr. Rogers", "St. Peter", and "Prof. Thomopoulos." We therefore modify our rule to include the case of an abbreviation followed by a capitalized word:

```
sentence boundary =
        period + space + capital letter
        OR period + quote + space + capital letter
        OR period + space + quote + capital letter
        UNLESS abbreviation + period + space + capital
```

This new rule improves the performance on *The Call of the Wild* by eliminating false positives (previously introduced by the phrase "St. Bernard" within a sentence), and both recall and precision improve (to 98.4 per cent and 100 per cent, respectively). On the WSJ corpus, this new rule also eliminates all but 283 of the false positives introduced by the first rule. However, this rule introduces 713 false negatives because many abbreviations can also occur at the end of a sentence. Nevertheless, precision improves to 95.1 per cent because this augmentation produces a net reduction in false positives.

This last enhancement shows that recognizing an abbreviation is therefore not sufficient to disambiguate a period, because we also must determine if the abbreviation occurs at the end of a sentence. However, this problem ultimately illustrates the discontinuous nature of data in this area. An abbreviation like "St." is lexically ambiguous: it can mean "Saint", "street", or "state". Each of these interpretations has a different potential for ending a sentence, and disambiguation of these different interpretations is crucial for determining sentence boundaries. For instance, the current rule would correctly handle the use of "St." for "Saint" in the following example (from WSJ 11/14/91):

> The contemporary viewer may simply ogle the vast wooded
> vistas rising up from the Saguenay River and Lac St.
> Jean, standing in for the St. Lawrence River.

However, it would not correctly handle this use of "St." for "street" (from WSJ 1/2/87):

> The firm said it plans to sublease its current
> headquarters at 55 Water St. A spokesman declined to
> elaborate.

The simple techniques we've examined so far are not sophisticated enough to distinguish reliably among cases like these. Furthermore, these simple techniques rely on orthographic distinctions which are not always present. For text where case distinctions have been eliminated (as in e-mail, which is sometimes all lower case, or television closed captions, which is all upper case), the sentence task is noticeably more challenging. In the following example (also from the WSJ, 7/28/89), the status of the periods before "AND" and "IN" is not immediately clear, while in case-sensitive text their status would be unambiguous:

> ALASKA DROPPED ITS INVESTIGATION INTO POSSIBLE CRIMINAL
> WRONGDOING BY EXXON CORP. AND ALYESKA PIPELINE SERVICE
> CO. IN CONNECTION WITH THE VALDEZ OIL SPILL.

These cases, like the "St." case, require an analysis of the linguistic text which is more sophisticated than the simple orthographic rules we've seen so far. Useful information about the document may include part-of-speech information (Palmer and Hearst, 1997), morphological analysis (Müller *et al.*, 1980), and abbreviation classes (Riley, 1989).

8.6   EXAMPLE: PARSING

A second example of a practical application of this methodology can be seen in the recent history of parsing. Progress in corpus-based parsing began with the release of the **Penn Treebank** (Marcus *et al.*, 1993), developed at the University of Pennsylvania between 1989 and 1992. The Treebank consists of 4.5 million words of American English, tagged for part-of-speech information; in addition, roughly half of the Treebank is tagged with skeletal syntactic structure (hence the name "Treebank").

The annotation of syntactic structure consists of a bracketing of each sentence into constituents, as well as a non-terminal labeling of each constituent. The guidelines for bracketing, as well as the choice of non-terminal syntactic tags, were designed to be theory-neutral. Consequently, the degree of detail in the bracketing is relatively coarse, as compared to the analysis one might see in a complete parse. Again, this annotation design was strongly influenced by a desire for high accuracy and high inter-annotator reliability. The syntactic tag set consists of fourteen phrasal categories (including one for constituents of unknown or uncertain category), as well as four types of null elements.[8]

Here is an example sentence from Collins (1996), annotated for syntactic structure as in the Treebank:

```
[S [NP [NP John Smith]
       ,
       [NP [NP the president]
          [PP of IBM]]
       ,]
   [VP   announced
         [NP his resignation]
         [NP yesterday]]
    .]
```

The existence of the Treebank has been essential in enabling the direct comparison of many CL algorithms, and much recent progress in a number of areas of CL can be credited directly to the Treebank and similar resources. This has been particularly true in parsing, a task for which it has been notoriously difficult to compare systems directly.

Progress in parsing has also been greatly aided by the development of several evaluation metrics. These measures were developed in a community-sponsored effort known as PARSEVAL (Black *et al.*, 1991), with the goal of enabling the comparison of different approaches to syntactic analysis. All of these measures assume the existence of a reference corpus annotated for constituent structure with labeled brackets, as in the Treebank example above. This annotation is assumed to be correct, and is used as the key.

When a parser's hypothesis is compared to the key, several kinds of mismatches may occur:

- A bracketed constituent present in the key may not be present in the hypothesis.
- A constituent may occur in the hypothesis but not correspond to anything in the key.
- Two constituents from the key and the hypothesis may match in extent (that is, comprise the same words), but be labeled differently.

The measures defined by PARSEVAL attempt to separate these various kinds of errors, and include the following:

- **Labeled recall** is the percentage of constituents in the key that are realized in the parser's hypothesis, in both extent and non-terminal label
- **Labeled precision** is the percentage of constituents in the hypothesis that are present in the key, in both extent and non-terminal label

Labeled recall accounts for the first type of error above, while labeled precision accounts for the second. Both of these measures require the label as well as the extent to be correct; that is, the third error type above is both a recall and a precision error. There are also versions of these measures, referred to as *un*labeled precision and recall, in which the non-terminal labels need not match. This weaker definition of correctness allows the evaluation of a system with a different set of non-terminals than the key. There is also another PARSEVAL measure that disregards labels:

- **Crossing brackets** is the number of constituents in the hypothesis that have incompatible extent with some constituent in the key, i.e., which overlap with some key constituent, but not in a simple substring/superstring relationship. A typical crossing bracket violation arises if the key contains the bracketing

    ```
    [large [animal preserve]]
    ```

    but the hypothesis brackets the string as

    ```
    [[large animal] preserve]
    ```

Crossing brackets may be expressed as a percentage of the constituents in the hypothesis, similarly to precision and recall, but is more often a simple count averaged over all sentences in the test corpus. In particular, *zero crossing brackets* is the percentage of sentences with no such extent incompatibilities.

We can use our Treebank sentence from above to provide examples of each of these measures. The bracketed sentence is reproduced on p. 248, followed by a candidate parse hypothesis.[9]

The hypothesis has one crossing bracket error, due to the boundary violation between the hypothesis constituent [NP president of IBM] and the key's [NP president]. The key has eight constituents, the hypothesis nine. Six of the hypothesis' constituents match constituents in the key exactly, and thus labeled precision is 75 per cent (6/8), while labeled recall is 67 per cent (6/9).

A recent breakthrough in parsing that relied critically on resources such as the Penn Treebank and the evaluation mechanisms introduced by PARSEVAL was the work of David Magerman (1994). Magerman used probabilistic decision trees, automatically acquired from the Treebank and other annotated corpora, to model phenomena found in the corpus and his parser's accuracy was significantly higher than any previously reported, using any of the measures described above. Magerman's algorithm was, however, very complex and it was difficult to investigate the linguistics of the technique, since most of the workings were embedded in the decision tree algorithms.

```
Key:
[S [NP [NP John Smith]
       ′
       [NP [NP the president]
           [PP of IBM]]
       ,]
   [VP announced
       [NP his resignation]
       yesterday]
   .]
Hypothesis:
[S [S [NP [NP John Smith]
          ′
          [NP the
              [NP president
                  [PP of IBM]]]
          ,]
      [VP announced
          [NP his resignation]]
      yesterday]
   .]
```

Expanding on the surprising success of Magerman, Collins (1996) developed a corpus-based algorithm that achieved a parsing accuracy equaling or exceeding Magerman's results, yet was significantly simpler and easier to understand. Collins' approach offers a probabilistic parser that utilizes essential lexical information to model head-modifier relations between pairs of words.

Collins' success extended, in several ways, Magerman's linguistically-grounded insights. The crux of the approach is to reduce every parse tree to a set of (non-recursive) *base noun phrases* and corresponding dependency relationships. For these dependencies, all words internal to a base NP can be ignored, except for the head. Dependencies thus hold between base NP headwords and words in other kinds of constituents. The headword for each phrase is determined from a simple manually-constructed table while the dependency probabilities are estimated from a training corpus. The parsing algorithm itself is a bottom-up chart parser that uses dynamic programming to search the space of all dependencies seen in the training data.

In our example sentence, there are five base NPs, as indicated by the following bracketing:

```
[NP John Smith],[NP the president] of [NP IBM],announced
[NP his resignation] [NP yesterday].
```

The Treebank contains enough information to allow an approximation of a version annotated just with base NPs to be constructed automatically. From this, a simple statistical model is automatically constructed that is used to label new material with base NP bracketings. As noted above, each base NP is then reduced to its head for purposes of determining dependency probabilities between pairs of words in the sentence (punctuation is also ignored):

```
Smith president of IBM announced resignation yesterday
```

A dependent word may be either a modifier or an argument of the word it depends on; no distinctions are made among these dependencies here. Each dependency relationship is typed by the three non-terminal labels of the constituents involved in the dependency: the head constituent, the dependent, and the matrix or parent constituent. In our example sentence, the following six dependencies exist:

head	dependent	head label	dependent label	parent label
announced	Smith	<VP	NP	S>
Smith	president	<NP	NP	NP>
president	of	<NP	PP	NP>
of	IBM	<IN	NP	PP>
announced	resignation	<VBD	NP	VP>
announced	yesterday	<VBD	NP	VP>

Given this syntactic model, which is similar in many ways to dependency grammars, and link grammar in particular (Lafferty *et al.*, 1992), a parse is simply a set of such dependencies, as well as a set of base NPs. For each new sentence to be parsed, the most likely base NP bracketing is first determined, and then the parser estimates the likelihood of various sets of dependencies (parses), based on the probabilities gleaned from the training corpus. The most likely set of dependencies constitutes the parser's best guess as to the constituent structure of the sentence. The bracketing due to the base NPs is placed on the sentence, and then a labeled bracket can be mapped from each dependency[10] (for example, the last dependency listed above corresponds to the constituent [VP announced his resignation yesterday]). After this is done for every sentence in a test corpus, the result can be compared to a key, e.g., the Treebank, and metrics such as those described above can be computed.

The results reported by Collins show the power of such a simple parsing approach. On the *Wall Street Journal* portion of the Treebank, both labeled recall and precision were consistently greater than 84 per cent, matching or bettering Magerman's results in all experiments. The average crossing brackets per sentence was less than 1.5, while between 55 and 60 per cent of the test sentences had no crossing brackets at all, i.e., the constituent structure was completely correct on these sentences (although the labels on the constituents may have differed from the key). Notably, Collins' algorithm is significantly faster than Magerman's; it can parse over 200 sentences per minute, while Magerman's parsing algorithm could parse fewer than ten per minute.[11]

Both Magerman's and Collins' algorithms represented significant breakthroughs in parsing, and it is clear that these breakthroughs could not have taken place without large, annotated corpora such as the Treebank, as well as well-defined evaluation metrics. Nonetheless, it is equally clear that substantial linguistic insight was necessary in order to make good use of the information contained in the corpora.

8.7   BENEFITS

As we pointed out when we began, the motivation for adopting a good part of this methodology is that progress can be measured, in very broad and consistent terms. In this section, we review our two major themes with progress in mind.

8.7.1   The evaluation metric

One of the stated goals of theoretical linguistics has been to develop a complete grammar for a given language; the classic transformational grammar of English compiled by Stockwell, Schachter, and Partee (1973) was an attempt to approach just this goal. But a number of difficult problems present themselves almost immediately when we examine such a goal. The first is that although we may have a sense that progress is being made, without some stable paradigm of evaluation we cannot measure our progress toward our goal. No such paradigm has been proposed in theoretical linguistics, as far as we know.

The other problems manifest themselves as soon as we try to define an evaluation metric which is consistent with current theory. There is far more to reaching our goal than simply writing down all the rules a grammar requires. The reason is that any such reasonably large rule set turns out to induce massive ambiguity. In this situation, measuring how close we've come to our goal becomes quite complex. For the sake of simplicity, let us consider only the evaluation of the syntactic component, as outlined in Section 8.6 above. Instead of the strategies described there, let us assume that our goal is to evaluate any of the many syntactic theories currently being developed in theoretical linguistics. If this theory permits ambiguity, then we must address this fact in choosing our evaluation metric. One candidate might be that the analysis provided by the key must be one of the analyses permitted by the grammar. But this metric is far too weak; if one assumes a binary branching structure, as is common in linguistic theories, one's grammar could simply generate all possible labelings for all possible binary branchings of any given input and be judged perfect by the evaluation metric! This argument shows that the evaluation metric must be far more strict; in order to have any power, it must demand that the search space of analyses presented to it be narrowed in some substantial way, perhaps even to a single analysis. In other words, providing a set of rules is not enough; the means for choosing between the resulting analyses (that is, a disambiguation strategy) is required as well. Thus the appropriate evaluation metric for theoretical linguistics is how close the grammar and disambiguation strategy come to generating the most appropriate analysis, just as we have shown for CL.

8.7.2   Confronting the discontinuities

As we've seen, picking the right fundamental linguistic insights is crucial to this paradigm. The part-of-speech tag set used by the Penn Treebank is a distillation of the crucial lexical syntactic distinctions of English; Magerman (1994) and Collins (1996) exploit the notion of syntactic head to derive their syntactic bracketings; Yarowsky (1995) relies on the insight that word senses do not commonly shift within a single discourse to improve his word sense disambiguation algorithm; and Berger *et al.* (1994) identify sublanguages such as names and numbers, perform morphological analysis, and apply syntactic transformations in the course of their statistically-driven translation procedure. But eventually, the benefits of these initial insights are exhausted, and a noticeable error term still remains. In these cases, more expensive, less general insights must be brought to bear; these are the points of discontinuity we've emphasized throughout this article.

For instance, we can determine many syntactic bracketings based simply on part of speech, but additional accuracy can be gained only by referring to lexical subcategorization or semantic class. A good example is PP attachment. PP attachment is no less a problem for current CL than it has been for linguists throughout the ages; in any given sequence of [V N PP], the syntactic key provides an attachment, and the score assigned to our analyses (for example, in terms of crossing bracket measures) is dictated by how closely we conform to the attachments the key provides. This problem is a classic example, of course, of a situation where syntactic information is not particularly helpful. Although the subcategorization frame of the V in question may require a PP and thus provide input to the attachment algorithm, it provides no help when the PP turns out to be a modifier; that is, we cannot distinguish strictly on the basis of subcategorization frames or part-of-speech sequences whether a PP modifier modifies the N or the V. If we need semantic disambiguation, we need to model semantic information in our new paradigm.

At this point, one of the crucial differences between the human linguistic understanding task and the computational task manifests itself. In particular, the computer does not have access to the same sorts of semantic generalizations that humans do. In part, what we need to make PP attachment decisions is a ***domain model***: the knowledge of what objects there are in the world, how they can interact with each other, and how likely, prototypical, or frequent these interactions are. Humans acquire this information through many sources; in some cases, they read or hear the information, but in most cases (most likely), they acquire this information through direct experience and through the senses.[12] Needless to say, computers do not have access to these data sources, and as a result are at a tremendous disadvantage in semantic tasks. In effect, in attempting semantic analyses in the corpus-based paradigm, we are forced to imagine how a processor might approach such a task if its only source of information was what it reads.

It turns out that this problem is actually tractable under certain circumstances, as shown by Hindle and Rooth (1993). Their account assumes access to a suitably large set of reasonably correct bracketings, as produced by an algorithm verified by good performance against a bracketed key. This bracketing is incomplete; that is, the annotation procedure does not produce constituent structure annotations which it is not reasonably certain of. In terms of our evaluation metrics, the algorithm favors bracketing precision over bracketing recall. Hindle and Rooth take the head relationships corresponding to known instances of PP attachment and use those statistical distributions to predict the unknown cases.[13] In this approach, Hindle and Rooth use lexical heads as an approximation for semantic classes. This approximation is known to be unreliable, because of lexical sense ambiguity; and so others in the field have tackled this problem as well. Yarowsky (1995), for instance, provides a corpus-based algorithm for distinguishing between word senses, based on lists of senses provided from any of a number of sources, including machine-readable dictionaries and thesauri.

None of these analyses are perfect; in fact, some of them perform quite unacceptably in absolute terms. Yet at every step, the limits of simpler approaches are recognized, and the problem is analyzed in terms of identifying the next least complex, the next most powerful, the next most general step to take. And in many of the areas we've discussed here, the field has made substantial progress in the relatively short history of the application of this paradigm. It is safe to say, in fact, that the methodology reviewed here is the only methodology presented so far in theoretical or computational linguistics which can claim to provide ***quantifiable*** measurement of progress in the field.

8.8   CONCLUSION

In the preface to a recent influential dissertation, David Magerman wrote, "I would have liked nothing more than to declare in my dissertation that linguistics can be completely replaced by statistical analysis of corpora" (Magerman, 1994:iv). Magerman's wish hearkens back to other eras of CL research in which some practitioners in the field hoped to divorce themselves from theoretical linguistics. However, the difference between those periods and corpus-based CL today is that this wish is widely regarded as counterproductive; Magerman himself goes on to conclude that "linguistic input is crucial to natural language parsing, but in a way much different than it is currently being used" (*ibid*:v). We have attempted to emphasize this point throughout; while the details of current theory may not be relevant to current corpus-based tasks, the fundamental insights of the theoretical program are central. However, as we've also stressed, the demands of corpus analysis pose substantial theoretical challenges, some of which we've explored here: the nature of discontinuity among linguistic phenomena, the requirements of an evaluation metric for grammar coverage. We have only begun to explore these demands in this article, so by way of conclusion, we summarize two of the other substantial theoretical issues which corpus-based CL raises.

Coverage vs. depth: The goal of producing a complete grammar for a given language in theoretical linguistics has fallen from favor in recent years, perhaps due to its daunting intractability. In its place, researchers have focused on narrow, deep analyses of particular phenomena, in the hope that a range of such studies will elucidate the general nature of language. Whether or not this process will converge on an unskewed theory of language is an open question. Consider an analogy with geological research. The exhaustive examination of a single core sample cannot hope to document the geological history of the planet; whether the exhaustive examination of a selection of such samples will produce a fair account of that history depends entirely on whether these samples are representative, given our knowledge of surface topology and the general process of geologic change. It is not clear at all to us that we as linguists possess the knowledge to produce an analogous linguistic sample in an informed way.

The demands of corpus analysis imply a very different strategy. If a computational linguist chooses to parse a year's worth of the *Wall Street Journal*, she doesn't have the luxury of choosing the sentences she wants to examine; she must analyze *all* of them, in as much detail as the task requires and time and computational resources allow. The general strategy induced by such requirements is broad and shallow, rather than narrow and deep, with added complexity where required. The details of the corpus-based approach may not be appealing to theoretical linguists, but its progress is measurable, and the considerations used to craft these strategies are informed by the same fundamental linguistic insights as those that inform theoretical approaches.

The nature of data: Another important consequence of this paradigm is that we are severely constrained by the form of the data to be analyzed. Our analysis keys are pairs of raw data and analyses, where "raw" is defined differently for each problem to be evaluated. So for speech recognition, our keys are speech waveforms and their linguistic transcriptions; for part-of-speech tagging, our key is a document and its part-of-speech tags; for the information extraction tasks, the key is a document and its corresponding database entries. These tasks can be chained; so speech recognition feeds part-of-speech tagging, which in turn feeds information extraction.

There are two important observations to make about data constructed in this way. First, in most cases, the key presented to the system obeys the "no negative evidence" restriction frequently attributed to human language acquisition tasks;[14] second, the properties of the raw data present problems frequently overlooked or idealized away in theoretical linguistics. For instance, the problem of sentence and word segmentation is commonly overlooked, but is crucially relevant to the comprehension process, as demonstrated in Section 8.5 above. These two observations converge with statistical techniques in a recent article in the journal *Science*, which argues that young infants use probabilistic information about syllable distributions to determine word segmentation in speech (Saffran, Aslin, and Newport, 1996).

On one remaining significant issue, however, we are currently silent. Although we are convinced that the methodology outlined here ought to have a significant impact on linguistic theory, we do not know what form that impact might take. For instance, one of the primary motivations for examining linguistic questions is to test linguistic theories. However, from the corpus-based point of view, the data thus examined are seriously biased. Parasitic gap constructions, quantifier scope ambiguities, or any one of dozens of deeply-studied linguistic phenomena are infrequently represented in randomly-selected large corpora. Focusing on these examples could well constitute an examination of an unnatural subset of the data, and the resulting generalizations might not extend to the corpus as a whole. We are also aware that while "no negative evidence" is a property of language acquisition, it seems not to account for strong grammaticality judgments by adult speakers. Finally, we do not know what a theory which emphasizes broad coverage over deep analysis might look like. There is no *a priori* reason that the corpus-based methodology would not be applicable to fine-grained linguistic analysis (beyond the significantly larger amount of data which would be required to tease apart the subtleties in question), but the priorities dictated by broad-coverage analysis suggest that these concerns would necessarily be postponed.

In spite of these uncertainties, we believe, as linguists and computational linguists, that the paradigm we've outlined here is fundamental to genuine progress in language understanding. We also believe that it calls into question a number of common assumptions in mainstream linguistic theory, as a consequence of the demands of large corpus analysis. In this article, we've attempted to make the methodology accessible, to motivate its application, and to highlight its successes, with the hope that more linguists will incorporate this point of view into their daily work.

NOTES

1 Cf. Schank and Riesbeck 1981, for instance.

2 For a useful short summary of the history of structuralism, see Newmeyer (1986), chapter 1.

3 For a discussion, see the papers in Waibel and Lee (1990).

4 For a detailed discussion of an HMM-based part-of-speech tagger, see Cutting *et al.* (1991). For an application of this technique to higher-level language analysis, see Pieraccini and Levin (1995).

5 Some current speech-based telephone directory assistance, for example, uses this technology.

6 Some context-independent utterances were chosen because they represent the largest number of comparable data points. The error rate decreased steadily for all of the measures shown, by factors ranging from 4-fold to 9-fold in the period June 1990 to January 1995.

7 For a thorough discussion of the linguistics of English punctuation, see Nunberg (1990).

8 For some, the inclusion of null elements in the syntactic annotation may not qualify as "theory-neutral."

9 The observant reader will note that "yesterday" is unbracketed in the example here. This is because the PARSEVAL evaluation metric requires that singleton brackets be removed before scoring.

10 Note that many dependency grammar formalisms (as well as many syntactic theories) allow for discontinuous dependencies, while Collins' approach does not. Nor does the bracket-based evaluation framework described here allow for discontinuous constituents.

11 These parse rates were measured on different computer platforms, but it is clear that Collins' parser is at least an order of magnitude faster than Magerman's. Both approaches are substantially faster than a classical chart parsing algorithm.

12 In fact, there is a substantial body of recent work, typified by Lakoff (1987), that claims that a vast segment of human semantic and linguistic competence is directly inspired by such experiences.

13 Hindle uses this same strategy in an earlier paper (1990) to generate "concept" clusters and selectional restrictions of verbs.

14 The notable exception is speech recognition, where false starts and other disfluencies are frequently marked in the annotation.

Glossary

alias: A user-designated synonym for a Unix command or sequence of commands. Differs from a *variable* in that its value does not change: e.g., if you designate m to be your alias for `mailx`, then typing m will always run this mail program. Differs from a *script* in that scripts are normally stored in *executable* files, while aliases are loaded as part of the *shell* environment directly (and are thus simpler and faster). Aliases are a facility provided by the C-shell (`csh`) and its successors, like `tcsh`.

alphanumeric: Of ASCII characters, any string composed of only upper- or lower-case English letters or Arabic numerals.

anonymous ftp: Downloading files from a public-access Internet machine, i.e., one which allows a remote user to log in as "anonymous" and transfer files even if the user does not have an account on the machine. See *ftp*.

Archie: An Internet search facility that searches through directory and file names (and in some instances through file descriptions) in order to determine whether a particular string is present. If you ask an Archie server to find the string "phone" it will return the names of files that include this word, whether it refers to a sound or a telephone.

argument: As in mathematical or logical usage, a value to be operated on by a function or other command. By default, this is usually interpreted as a filename. In the command `cat message`, the argument is `message`, which is subcategorized as a file name by `cat`.

ARPA: See *DARPA*.

ASCII: The American Standard Code for Information Interchange is a standard *character set* that maps *character code*s 0 through 127 (*low ASCII*) onto control functions, punctuation marks, digits, upper case letters, lower case letters, and other symbols.

ASCII file: A data file, typically a text file with hard line breaks, that contains only character codes in the range 0 to 127 (*low ASCII*), and interprets them according to the *ASCII* standard.

ASCII, high: The unstandardized highest half (128–255) of the 256 characters in ASCII. While ***low ASCII*** is standard worldwide, ***high ASCII*** characters vary from one hardware platform to another, or even from one software program to another.

ATIS: The **A**ir **T**ravel **I**nformation **S**ystem evaluations were a series of evaluations of speech recognition and spoken language understanding systems sponsored by ***DARPA***. These evaluations began in 1990 and ended in 1995. They are responsible for the development of a ***corpus*** of approximately 20,000 utterances regarding air travel, grouped by speaker, session, and data collection site. The ATIS corpus is distributed by the ***Linguistic Data Consortium***.

attribute: [1] In ***SGML***, a qualifier within the opening ***tag*** for an ***element*** which specifies a value for some named property of that element.

[2] In an ***object-oriented database***, a named property of an object which not only holds information about a particular instance of an object, but also encapsulates behavior (such as integrity constraints and a default value) that is true of all instances of the class of objects.

backquote convention: A facility allowing indirect reference in Unix commands, by using the output of one command, enclosed within backquote characters (`, ASCII #96), as an argument to another command. For instance, in the command finger `whoami`, first the whoami program is run, returning the login id of the user; this is in turn used as the argument for the command finger, which returns information about a user.

base character: A ***character*** to which an overstriking ***diacritic*** is added.

batch processing: Running a computer program without any interaction with the process as it goes along. Sometimes called background processing.

binaries: See ***executable***.

binary, octal, decimal, hexadecimal: Four common arithmetic bases (2, 8, 10, and 16, respectively) widely used in computing. Computers use binary numbers internally, and octal and hexadecimal numbers are easily converted to binary (and vice versa). Decimal numbers are the norm in text, as usual; binary numbers, consisting of only 0 and 1, are easily recognized; octal numbers (now obsolete) use only the decimal digits [0–7]; hexadecimal (also called ***hex***) numbers contain the normal decimal digits [0–9], and add [A–F] to represent eleven through fifteen as single "digits". These "digits" are pronounced as letters, rather than extending conventional morphology; i.e., hex "A5" is pronounced "A-five," not "*eleventy-five."

binary transfer: A way of sending files by ***ftp***. The files are sent in binary code, not translated into ASCII, which would risk some information loss.

BinHex: More accurately BinHex 4.0. The standard Macintosh format used when a binary file must be converted into an ASCII file so that it may be safely transferred through a network. Do not confuse BinHex 4.0 with BinHex 5.0, which is not an ASCII format. All BinHex files should by convention carry the *extension* .hqx.

bit, byte: Related terms for small units of information. *Bit* is an acronym for **bi**nary dig**it**, the smallest possible unit of information: i.e., a single yes or no (1 or 0), in context. A *byte* is a unit consisting of eight bits, in order. There are 2^8 (= 256) possible bytes (combinations of 0 and 1), and thus 256 possible characters in *ASCII*, each with a unique byte value. Computer memory is normally specified in kilobytes, megabytes, and gigabytes.

black box evaluation: The evaluation of a complex system by examining only inputs to the system and outputs from the system, ignoring intermediate results and internal states.

browser, or *web browser:* A piece of software which retrieves and displays *World Wide Web* files. It acts as an interface to Internet protocols like *ftp* and *http*. Common browsers include Netscape, Internet Explorer, and Mosaic.

BSD, SysV: Two competing dialects of Unix. *BSD* is an acronym for **B**erkeley **S**ystem **D**istribution, an academic version developed at the University of California at Berkeley. *SysV* stands for **Sys**tem **V**, a commercial version originally developed by AT&T. The two systems are incompatible in some ways, though they are converging in the latest versions.

byte: See *bit*.

character: The minimal unit of *encoding* for text *file*s. A character usually corresponds to a single graphic sign, like a letter of the alphabet or a punctuation mark.

character code: A numerical code in a data *file* which represents a particular *character* in text.

character set: The full set of *character code*s used for *encoding* a particular language.

client: See *server*.

COCOA: A method of text *encoding* used by the *Oxford Concordance Program* and other software.

collating sequence: The sorting order for all the characters in a *character set*.

command: A linguistic (i.e., written-language-based) interface to a computer program or operating system; Unix and DOS have *command-line* interfaces, in which the user types commands which are then executed. Command-line systems are the earlier of the two principal user interfaces (the other is the **G**raphic **U**ser **I**nterface, or *GUI*). Command-line systems are powerful but complex; they can be added to and customized.

composite character: A single *character* which is a composite of two or more other characters. For instance, "à" is a composite of "a" (the *base character*) and "`" (a *diacritic*).

conceptual indexing: The automatic categorization and grouping of a set of short text objects according to what they are about. Sets of short text objects consist of items which are by nature just a paragraph or two in length (e.g., newswire stories and similar message streams) or which are the result of segmenting lengthy texts into short (presumably coherent) sets of items. In general, a conceptual indexing process categorizes (i.e. indexes) each item in the text set over multiple semantic dimensions and provides a measure of the relative semantic distance of all the members of the set from each other.

concordance: A list of words, normally in alphabetical order, where each occurrence of each word is shown with surrounding context and identified by a reference indicating where it occurs in the text.

control character, control-shift, Ctrl: The most common and most standard of the ASCII *metacharacter*s. ASCII keyboards contain a Shift key, which produces upper-case characters (# 41H through 5AH) when pressed, instead of lower-case (# 61H through 7AH). The Control-Shift key, by analogy, produces Control characters (# 01H through 2AH). These are non-printing and in principle have standard uses, though in practice they vary greatly. They are often represented by prefixing caret (^) to the appropriate alphabetic character; thus ^M represents CR or Carriage Return, sent by the **Return** key on all keyboards, and by the **Enter** key on most.

corpus: A body of linguistic data, either text or speech, intended to support the study of linguistic phenomena. This data may be compiled on a principled or systematic basis and it may be annotated in some way to enhance its usefulness. Examples of corpora include the Brown corpus, the LOB corpus, and the *Penn Treebank* and the *ATIS* corpus.

daemon (less commonly *demon*)*:* A pre-activated program that is always ready to perform its task (as opposed to one that must be called by the system activation software in response to a specific need). Web server programs are usually run as daemons.

DARPA: The **D**efense **A**dvanced **R**esearch **P**rojects **A**gency, a branch of the United States Department of Defense responsible for a wide range of research and applications development, and a long-time funder of research in language processing. For a number of years, in the late 1980s and early 1990s, this organization was known as **ARPA**. Its Web site is http://www.darpa.mil/

decimal: See *binary*.

diacritic: A small mark (such as an accent mark) added above, below, before, or after a *base character* to modify its pronunciation or significance.

digital image: An electronic representation of a page of text or other material which is a picture of the page, rather than a transcription of the text.

directory: A collection of files that are notionally "in" the same "place." Every Unix user has a **home directory**, in which one's files may be stored; it usually has the same name as the login id of the user, and may be referenced as $HOME or by the tilde convention (~ is $HOME, ~jlawler is jlawler's home directory). At any time in a Unix session, a user has a **current directory**, which may be changed with the cd command. Also called *folder*.

DNS: An Internet machine that knows the names and IP addresses of other machines in its subnet. When you attempt to connect to the Internet, your request goes to a **D**omain **N**ame **S**erver, which translates an address like emunix.emich.edu into an IP number like 35.1.1.42 and forwards your connection request to that IP address.

domain model: In computational linguistics and artificial intelligence, a symbolic representation of the objects and relationships in a particular segment (domain) of the world.

dot files: In Unix, special *ASCII* files placed in one's home *directory* to control various programs and set customized parameters. Their names begin with period ("dot," ASCII # 46) and are by default not shown by the ls program. Examples are .cshrc, which contains commands and definitions for the csh shell; .newsrc, for customizing newsreaders like trn; and .login, which contains commands executed once at the beginning of each Unix session.

DTD: **D**ocument **T**ype **D**efinition, the definition of the *markup* rules for an *SGML* document.

editor: A program that allows one to create, modify, and save text files. Virtually all popular editors (pico, emcas, vi) on Unix are screen editors, like wordprocessors. Early Unix line editors (ed, ex) operate with commands instead of direct typing; i.e., to correct a mistake like fase, you might enter the command replace s with t, rather than just overstriking the s with t.

element: In an *SGML* file, a single component of a document delimited by a start *tag* and an end tag. For instance, a title element might be delimited by <title> and </title>.

encoding: The manner in which information is represented in computer data files. Character encoding refers specifically to the codes used to represent characters. Text encoding refers specifically to the way in which the structural information in text is represented.

entity: In *SGML*, a named part of a *marked up* document. An entity can be used for a string of characters or a whole file of text. Non-standard characters (like "Ê") are normally represented by entities (like "Ê") in SGML.

escape (n): An *ASCII control* or *metacharacter* (#27, ^]) with its own key on most keyboards, intended originally to signify *escape (v)*. While it has been put to a number of different uses over the decades, it is still often used to pause or terminate a program or process. Frequently called **Meta** in some programs, notably emacs, where it is a common command prefix.

escape (v): [1] To pause a running program and return control temporarily to the operating system, usually in order to run some other program. In Unix, the exclamation point (ASCII #33, !, pronounced "bang") is an escape character that can be used in most programs to accomplish this.

[2] To cancel the default (meta-)interpretation of the following character in a string and interpret it literally instead. Thus, while the unescaped (meta)expression '.' matches any character, the regular expression '\.' matches a literal period or full stop character only, because it is *escaped* by the preceding '\'.

executable: A filename that can be used as a command, consisting either of a *script* of commands to be executed by typing the name, or of true compiled binary program code. In the latter sense (also called *binaries*), the executable(s) is/are sometimes used to distinguish compiled binary code from its human-readable programming-language source: "He gave me the executable, but I needed the source files."

extension: In a filename, the letters following the last dot. Often used to indicate type of file, e.g., .doc for Microsoft Word files, .txt for ASCII files, .c for C programs.

field: In a database, a subdivision of a *record* which stores information of a particular type.

file: A collection of information *encoded* in computer-readable form and associated with a single name by which the computer's operating system stores and retrieves it.

filter: A type of program especially common in Unix in which a file or other data stream (by default, the *standard input)* is read serially, modified in some regular way, and sent (in modified form) to some other file or stream (by default, the *standard output*), without any change to the original data source. There are many languages for creating simple text filters in Unix, like sed, awk, and perl.

folder: Synonym for *directory* (metaphorically, a place to put *files*), used in Macintosh, NeXT, Windows 95, and some other Graphic User Interfaces. See *GUI*.

font: A collection of bitmaps or outlines which supply the graphic *rendering* of every character in a *character set*.

font system: A subcomponent of an operating system which gives all programs and data files access to multiple *fonts* for *rendering* characters.

(file) format: The encoding scheme, often *proprietary*, in which the information in a file is *marked up*. Wordprocessing files created by different software are usually incompatible in format to some extent. To read one program's files using a different program requires format translation, which may be built into a full-featured wordprocessor, but is often a separate step requiring separate software. Many formats are in use; a frequent feature of upgrade versions of popular microcomputer software is a different (and usually incompatible) standard file format, and there are different standards and versions for different countries and languages.

frequency profile: In a concordance or similar program, a table showing how many words occur once, twice, three times, etc. up to the most frequent word.

ftp: Internet **F**ile **T**ransfer **P**rotocol, a way of sending files from one Internet machine to another.

full path: See *path*.

generalized markup: The discipline of using *markup* codes in a text to describe the function or purpose of the elements in the text, rather than their formating.

glyph: In character-encoding, the shape or form of a character, as opposed to a pairing of form and interpretation.

gopher: An Internet search facility, which allows the user to search through a hierarchically organized set of menus in order to find a particular file. Gopher menus categorize files according to content (e.g., "libraries," "phonebooks"), as determined by a human being, not a computer.

GUI: A **G**raphic **U**ser **I**nterface is one invoking visual rather than linguistic metaphors, often employing menus, non-text input devices like a mouse or trackball, and icons employing visual symbolism and metaphor, like a desktop with paper files on it.

hexadecimal: See *binary*.

Hidden Markov Model (HMM): A Hidden Markov Model is a statistical model of the distribution of "hidden" features, such as phonemes or *part-of-speech tags*, based on observable features, such as acoustic segments, or words. The computational models can be automatically trained from data samples, and then used to recognize the "hidden" layer, based on the statistical model derived from the *training* corpus.

high ASCII: See *ASCII, high*.

homograph: A word which has the same spelling but different meanings, e.g. "lead" as a verb "to lead" and as two different nouns "a leash" and the metal.

HTML: **H**ypertext **M**arkup **L**anguage is a method of marking a document that is to be displayed by a web *browser*. It consists primarily of formatting *tag*s, like `<b><i>boldface italic</i></b>` for *boldface italic*.

http: Hypertext Transfer Protocol. A way of sending hypertext documents over the Internet.

hypertext: A non-linear version of text presentation with embedded links to other information. The basis of the **World Wide Web** and of the Internet protocols employed on the Web.

hypothesis: In *corpus*-based linguistics, an annotation produced by an annotation procedure which can be checked against an annotation **key**.

index: An alphabetical or otherwise ordered list of words which is structured to facilitate rapid searching by an interactive retrieval program. Such an index is usually built by a special program module before any searches can be carried out. Concordance programs such as **OCP** may also produce printed indexes where the words are given in alphabetical order and where each word is accompanied by a list of references indicating where that word occurs in the text. Sometimes also called a **word index**.

information extraction: In computational linguistics, the process by which information in a form suitable for entry into a database is generated from documents.

input-output (I/O) redirection: Process (and capability) allowing a program (typically a *filter* program) to take its input from some other program, and/or send its output to another. A characteristic feature of Unix, much copied in other operating systems. The control structure implementing this is called a *pipe*, and the '|' symbol is used in the Unix command line to represent this.

inter-annotator agreement: The degree of agreement among human annotators on the tags assigned to a given corpus or for a given task. It is important because it sets an upper bound on the measurable accuracy of any automated procedure for performing the same task. A measure of inter-annotator agreement which is too low might be an indication that the annotation task being measured is too difficult or poorly defined.

interactive retrieval: The process of searching or querying a text and getting an instant response. The query is performed on an *index* which has been built previously.

IP number: A four-part number which uniquely identifies an Internet machine, giving the net and subnet to which it belongs. The IP number 35.1.1.42, for example, designates the Domain Name Server of the University of Michigan and tells us that it is part of net 35 and subnet 1. Part of the Internet *Protocol*.

key: [1] An individual button on a keyboard; by extension, the character(s) or command(s) it signals.

[2] In searching, a synonym for *search string*.

[3] In *indexing* or database management, the most important *field*, in the sense that it uniquely identifies an item (Chapter 4).

[4] In *corpus*-based linguistics, a benchmark against which the accuracy of an *annotation* procedure can be compared (Chapter 8).

Kleene closure: In ***regular expression***s, the use of asterisk (*, ASCII # 30) as a special character to indicate "any number of" the preceding character (including zero, or "none of"). Combined with the use of the special character ***dot*** (i.e., period, ASCII # 34) to represent "any character," the regular expression idiom '.*' represents "any string." Named after the logician Stephen Kleene.

lemmatization: The process of putting words under their dictionary headings, for example, "go," "going," "gone," "went," under "go."

line: A unit of organization in a text file including all the characters up to and including the line end character (either carriage return, line feed, or both, depending on operating system).

Linguistic Data Consortium: The ***LDC*** is an open consortium of universities, companies, and government research laboratories which creates, collects, and distributes speech and text databases, lexicons, and other resources for research and development in computational linguistics. It is hosted at the University of Pennsylvania. Its Web site is http://www.ldc.upenn.edu

link: Any mediated connection between pieces of information that allows them to be presented in the same context, for example, an embedded ***URL*** in a ***hypertext*** document. Links are created in ***HTML*** using the <a ... > "anchor" ***tag***, and are displayed in a ***browser*** as emphasized text (blue and underlined). When one clicks on a link, the ***browser*** requests the ***file*** and displays it.

loop: A programmed repetition of a set of instructions, typically with incrementation of some index value. The instructions will then be repeated on each member of the indexed set of values. Implemented by the **for**, **while**, or **do** structures in many computer languages.

low ASCII: See ***ASCII***.

machine learning: In computational linguistics and artificial intelligence, a set of techniques which allow a computer program to improve its performance iteratively on a chosen task.

markup: Codes added to the ***stream*** of an encoded text to signal structure, formatting, or processing commands.

metacharacter: A character or (shift-)key to be interpreted as modifying the value of the character (or key) following it in a string (or produced simultaneously in typing), either by prefixing a special character ("^x-Q terminates the program"), or by interpreting it literally, thus ***escaping*** the default special interpretation of the following character.

method: See ***object-oriented***.

MIME: **M**ulti-purpose **I**nternet **M**ail **E**xtensions. A way of sending files of different types (e.g., graphics, sound, or wordprocessor files) via e-mail without converting them into ASCII, or plain text. None of the original information will be lost, and, if the recipient has a MIME-compliant mailer program, it will call up the proper program needed to display or play the files.

Message Understanding Conference: *MUC* refers to a series of evaluations of text-based language processing systems sponsored by *DARPA*. These conferences are responsible for a series of corpora covering increasingly difficult information extraction tasks and subtasks.

multi-user, multi-tasking: Two independent characteristics of desirable operating systems, both found in Unix. A multi-user system is one that allows several users to run commands simultaneously without having to take turns. A multi-tasking system is one that allows any user to run several commands simultaneously without having to wait until each is done (**serial processing**). Multi-tasking is also called **parallel-processing**.

named entry: in corpus-based linguistics, a unique identifier of an organization, person, location, time or number.

news: An Internet utility that allows users to download (notionally, "read") "articles" posted to "newsgroups" by other users interested in the topic the newsgroup was formed to discuss. The newsgroup "sci.lang," for example, is dedicated to discussing the science of language. To read news, you need a news client like `trn` and access to a news server, such as those established at most universities.

normalization: The process of organizing a database in such a way that no piece of information occurs more than once in the database.

object: The fundamental unit of information modeling in the *object-oriented* paradigm. In principle, there is a one-to-one correspondence between objects in the data model and the entities in the real world which are being modeled. (This is not true, in general, of the data structures of conventional programming languages or database systems, and is less true in practice than in theory of official object-oriented languages and databases.) An object stores state information (like the *field* values of a database *record*; notionally nouns) and it stores behavioral information (called *methods*; notionally verbs) about what computations can be performed on an instance of the object. The information stored in an object is **encapsulated** in that it is not visible directly; it can only be seen by sending a message to the object which asks it to perform one of its methods.

object-oriented: A modern paradigm of programming which models information in terms of *objects*. Computation occurs when one object receives a message from another asking it to perform one of its **method**s, i.e., special subroutines subcategorized for each type of object. The object-oriented approach, in which the data and the program behavior are encapsulated in the objects, contrasts with the conventional approach to programming, in which a monolithic program operates on data which is completely separate. Object-oriented programming is more amenable to modeling parallel processing.

object-oriented database: A database system which models entities in the real world as *object*s and follows the *object-oriented* paradigm of programming.

octal: See *binary*.

open: Of software, especially an *operating system*, signifying that it conforms to a well-known internal architecture and set of standards, or that it is not restricted to use on a single brand of computer, or that it is manufactured and maintained by many vendors, or some combination of these. Contrasts with *proprietary*.

operating system (OS): The basic software that runs a computer, managing all other software and apportioning computing resources to avoid conflicts.

optical character recognition (OCR): A method of creating electronic text by automatically analyzing a *digital image* of a page of text and converting the characters on that page to *ASCII* text.

option: See *switch*.

Oxford Concordance Program (OCP): A flexible batch processing program for generating *concordance*s, *word list*s, and *index*es from many kinds of texts.

padding letter: A letter or other character that does not affect the sorting of words.

parallel corpus: A text *corpus* containing the same text in multiple languages. Such corpora are used for training corpus-based machine translation systems, for example. The Rosetta Stone is an example of a parallel corpus.

part-of-speech tagging: The process of assigning lexical categories (that is, part-of-speech tags) to words in linguistic data. This process can be performed automatically with a high degree of accuracy (above 95 per cent in English) without reference to higher-level linguistic information such as syntactic structure.

path: [1] A list of directories in which the operating system looks for files. To *put a directory in one's path* is to add the directory's name to this list; to *put a file in one's path* is to store the file in a directory that is on the list.

[2] Used also of the *full path* or *pathname* of a file, the sequential list of directories which locates the file on the disk; the reference is parsed recursively, like a linguistic tree, e.g., in Unix `/usr/jlawler/bin/aliases` specifies a file named `aliases`, which is further specified as being located in the subdirectory named `bin`, which is located in the subdirectory named `jlawler`, which is located in the subdirectory named `usr`, which is located under the top (root) directory (always called simply '/').

Penn Treebank: A **corpus** of *Wall Street Journal* documents annotated with **part-of-speech** and bracketing information, distributed by the **Linguistic Data Consortium**. Its web site is http://www.cis. upenn.edu/~treebank.

pipe: A notional conduit for the flow of information between programs in the **stream** metaphor. A pipe connects the output of one tool program as the input to another. Instantiated in Unix by the vertical bar '|', as in sort | uniq, in which sort sorts lines in a file alphabetically, then sends the sorted file to uniq, which removes contiguous identical lines.

PPP: **P**oint-to-**P**oint **Protocol**. A way of accessing the Internet which allows your home machine to act as if it were, itself, an Internet machine. PPP, for example, allows you to retrieve and display Internet graphics files. If you access the Internet through a serial line (formally the most common type of modem connection), you can not use a graphical browser.

precision: In information retrieval or **corpus**-based linguistics, the number of answers in an answer set hypothesis which are also in the answer key, divided by the size of the answer set hypothesis.

preference: See **switch**.

proprietary: Of software, especially an **operating system**, signifying that it is manufactured and maintained by only one vendor, or that it is the only type usable on a particular computer, or that it does not conform to a widely-accepted standard, or that its details are secret, or some combination of these. Contrasts with **open**.

protocol: An agreed-upon way of doing things. Internet protocols have been established for such actions as transmission of information packets (**TCP**), file transfer (**ftp**), and **hypertext** transfer (**http**). Any machine which does things according to these protocols can be a part of the Internet.

recall: In information retrieval or **corpus**-based linguistics, the number of answers in an answer set **hypothesis** which are also in the answer **key**, divided by the size of the answer key.

record (n): In a database, a collection of information about a single entity.

regular expression: A formal syntactic specification widely implemented in the Unix language family for reference to **strings**. For example, the regular expression denoting one or more **alphanumerics** (i.e., letters or numbers) is [A-Za-z0-9]*.

rendering: The process of converting a stream of **encoded characters** to their correct graphic appearance on a terminal or printer.

reverse alphabetical order: Sorting of words by their endings so that, for example, a **word list** in alphabetical order begins with words ending in -a. A wordlist in reverse alphabetic order is also called a **speculum**.

router: An Internet machine whose specialized job is finding paths for information packets. It looks for functional, uncongested paths to destinations and sends data along them.

RTF: **R**ich **T**ext **F**ormat is a special interchange file *format* that can be created and read by most popular wordprocessors. RTF preserves most formatting information, and graphics. Since they use only low *ASCII*, RTF documents can be usefully transmitted by e-mail.

*scanning***:** The process of creating a *digital image* of a page of text or other material. This term is sometimes also used for *optical character recognition*.

script: A collection of **command**s, often Unix commands, structured together as a program and stored as an *executable* file. The commands in a script are interpreted by the *shell* (normally sh) and treated as if they were entered in order by the user at the *command line*.

server: Software that forms part of a **server/client** pair. Typically, a server resides on a central machine and, when it is contacted by the client software on a user's machine, sends a particular type of information. Web servers, for example, send *hypertext* documents; news servers send articles posted to newsgroups.

SGML: **S**tandard **G**eneralized **M**arkup **L**anguage is a method for *generalized markup* that has been adopted by ISO (the International Organization for Standardization) and is consequently gaining widespread use in the world of computing.

sgmls: A shareware Unix and DOS program for validating SGML documents.

shell: A kind of *tool* program that parses, interprets, and executes **command**s, either interactively from the keyboard, or as a *script*. DOS uses a shell called COMMAND.COM; there are several shells available in Unix: the most common are the original Bourne shell (sh), used mostly for interpreting *script*s, and the C-shell (csh), the standard for interactive commands.

SLIP: **S**erial **L**ine **I**nternet **P**rotocol. This protocol allows a personal computer to interact across a serial line, i.e., via a modem and a phone line, as if it were a full Internet machine. Most systems now use *PPP* in preference to SLIP, which is an older, less flexible protocol.

special character: A *character* that is not available in one of the *character set*s already supported on a computer system.

speculum: See *reverse alphabetical order*.

standard input, standard output: The input and output *streams* for DOS or Unix *tool* programs. The *operating system* associates these streams with each program as it is run. The standard input defaults to the keyboard, and the standard output to the screen, though both are frequently redirected to other programs, or to files. See *I/O redirection*.

stream: A (long) string of *byte*s, which may come from any source, including a file. Streams are operated upon by *filter*s and other programs. *Stream* is often used as an alternative, active metaphor for *file*, when considered in terms of sequential (serial) throughput that can be redirected.

string: A sequence of *byte*s. Since bytes are used to code text, "string" is often used as a synonym for "word" or "phrase" in electronic text-processing environments. Special uses of the term include **search string** (the string to be matched in a searching operation) and **replacement string** (the string to be substituted for occurrences of the search string in a replacement operation).

style sheet: A separate *file* that is used with a document containing generalized markup to declare how each generalized text *element* is to be *format*ed for display.

subdirectory: A *directory* that is located inside another directory. There can be long chains of subdirectories in a *file*'s full *path* if it is deeply buried in the file system.

switch: One of a number of parameters that may be set for a program, each specifying special instructions (e.g., for the Unix `sort` program, a switch can specify reverse or numeric sort). Each program has its own unique array of possible switches, invoked on the *command line* before *argument*s, using a switch prefix (normally minus sign "-") before the individual letters indicating the switch settings, thus resembling clitics on the command verb. May be set by menu or checkbox in a *GUI*. Also called **option**s or **preference**s.

SysV: See *BSD*.

tag: [1] In *SGML*, a *string* of characters inserted into a text file to represent a *markup* code. Each text *element* of a given "type" is delimited by an opening tag of the form <type> and a closing tag of the form</type> (Chapter 1).
[2] In computational linguistics, an annotation associated with an element of a **corpus**. For instance, a *part-of-speech tag* is a lexical syntactic category associated with a word in a *corpus*; a coreference tag is an annotation indicating the referential dependency of the tagged phrase on other tagged phrases in the corpus (Chapter 8).

tag set: [1] In *SGML*, the set of tags defined for a particular application of the DTD (Chapter 4).
[2] In computational linguistics, a set of possible *tag*s for a given annotation task. For example, a **part-of-speech tag** set is a list of lexical syntactic categories which may be associated with lexical items (Chapter 8).

TCP, or *Transmission Control Protocol:* A way of transmitting information packets on the Internet so that those belonging to the same body of data can be identified and reassembled into their original order.

TEI: The Text Encoding Initiative is a joint effort of the Association for Computers and the Humanities, the Association for Literary and Linguistic Computing, and the Association for Computational Linguistics to develop *SGML*-based guidelines for the *encoding* of texts and the analysis of texts.

telnet: A way of logging in to a remote machine; also, the name of one of the more common programs that implement this facility.

test corpus: An annotated *corpus* set aside for evaluation of the annotation procedure. To ensure the accuracy of the evaluation process, there should be no overlap between training and test corpora.

tool: One of a generalized type of small useful modular programs, made to work together in a conceptually unified way so as to provide maximum flexibility, power, and ease of operation. Part of the Software Tools philosophy, instantiated most thoroughly in Unix.

training corpus: An annotated *corpus* whose contents are consulted in the process of developing a procedure to produce these annotations. To ensure the accuracy of the evaluation process, there should be no overlap between training and test corpora.

type/token ratio: A measure of the spread or richness of the vocabulary in a text, calculated by dividing the number of types (different words) by the number of tokens (instances of each word).

Unicode: A character set which attempts to include every character from all the major writing systems of the world. Version 1.0 contained 28,706 characters.

URL: Universal Resource Locator. A *World Wide Web* address.

uuencode: A file format which originated on Unix machine (though now commonly found elsewhere), and which is used for converting binary files to ASCII so that they may be safely transferred through a network. It is the default ASCII encoding for many mailers. By convention, such files should have the *extension* .uu

variable: A special name assigned to substitute for some term that may vary from user to user (and thus can not be supplied literally in documentation). For instance, in Unix, $HOME is a first-person indexical variable that refers to the *home directory* (see *directory*) of whatever user types it, while the variable bookmark might be assigned by one user to point to the full pathname of a file containing their Web bookmarks, and by another to a file containing a list of book reviews. $HOME is an example of a global, or system, variable, part of Unix and available to all users, while the various uses of bookmark are local, variables interpretable only in the environment of the particular user.

WAIS: Wide Area Information Service. An Internet search facility that retrieves filenames labeled with a score based on their probable relevance to the search criteria. Unlike Gopher, WAIS searches *index*es of the text inside the files rather than an index categorizing files by content.

web browser See *browser*.

wildcard: A simplified version of the *Kleene closure*, usually consisting only of '*' for "any string" and '?' for "any character," used to allow variable pattern specifications. Found in Unix shell dialects, DOS command syntax, and a large number of search languages based on *regular expression*s.

word list: A list of words, normally in alphabetical or frequency order, where each word is accompanied by a number indicating how many times that word occurs.

World Script: A subcomponent of the Macintosh operating system (version 7.1 and later) which gives programs access to script interface systems for multiple non-Roman writing systems.

WWW, or *World Wide Web:* The "web" is a metaphor for the multiplicity of links effected by Web *browser*s and Web *server*s, a notional place. It is not, itself, a piece of software or hardware.

Bibliography

Abney, Steven. 1996. Statistical Methods and Linguistics. In Klavans and Resnik, 1–26.

AECMA. 1989. *A Guide for the Preparation of Aircraft Maintenance Documentation in the Aerospace Maintenance Language, AECMA Simplified English*. AECMA Document: PSC-85–16598, Issue 1. Brussels.

Ansel, Bettina and Andreas H. Jucker. 1992. Learning Linguistics with Computers: Hypertext As A Key to Linguistic Networks. *Literary and Linguistic Computing* 7:124–31.

Antworth, Evan L. 1993. Glossing Text with the PC-KIMMO Morphological Parser. *Computers and the Humanities* 26:475–84.

Apple Computer. 1985. The Font Manager. In *Inside Macintosh* 1:215–40 (with updates in 4:27–48, 1986). Reading, MA: Addison Wesley.

—— 1988. The Script Manager. In *Inside Macintosh*, 5:293–322. Reading, MA: Addison Wesley.

Asher, Nicholas and Alex Lascarides. 1994. Intentions and Information in Discourse. In *Proceedings of the 32nd Annual Meeting of the Association for Computational Linguistics*: 34–41. Las Cruces, NM.

Bakker, Dik, Bieke Van der Korst, and Gerjan Van Schaaik. 1988. Building a Sentence Generator For Teaching Linguistics. In Michael Zock and Gerard Sabah (eds). *Advances in Natural Language Generation: An Interdisciplinary Perspective*. London: Pinter. 159–74.

Bantz, David A. *et al.* 1989. *Reviews of Instructional Software in Scholarly Journals: A Selected Bibliography*. Hanover: Dartmouth College.

Barwise, Jon. 1989. *The Situation in Logic*. CSLI Lecture Notes no. 17. Stanford: Center for the Study of Language and Information (distributed by the University of Chicago Press).

Barwise, Jon and John Perry. 1983. *Situations and Attitudes*. Cambridge, MA: MIT Press.

Becker, Joseph D. 1984. Multilingual Word Processing. *Scientific American* 251(1):96–107.

Beckwith, Richard and George A. Miller. 1990. Implementing a Lexical Network. *International Journal of Lexicography* 3(4):302–12.

Bell Laboratories. 1979. *Unix Programmer's Manual* Vol. 1. (Reprinted 1983, New York: Holt, Rinehart, and Winston.)

Bell System Technical Journal 1979. 57(6) part 2. (Reprinted 1987, Englewood Cliffs, NJ: Prentice-Hall.)

Berger, Adam *et al.* 1994. The Candide System for Machine Translation. In *Proceedings of the Human Language Technology Workshop*. March 8–11. Plainsboro, NJ.

Berry, Michael W., Susan T. Dumais, and Gavin W. O'Brien. 1995. Using Linear Algebra for Intelligent Information Retrieval. *SIAM Review* 37(4):573–95.

Bevan, David. 1993. What Can You Do with FindPhone? *Notes on Linguistics* 61:28–39.

Binns, Betty. 1989. *Better Type*. New York: Watson-Guptill.

Bird, Steven. 1995. *Computational Phonology: A Constraint-Based Approach*. Cambridge: Cambridge University Press.

Birner, Betty. 1994. Information Status and Word Order: An Analysis of English Inversion. *Language* 70:233–59.

Black, E., S. Abney, D. Flickenger, C. Gdaniec, R. Grishman, P. Harrison, D. Hindle, R. Ingria, F. Jelinek, J. Klavans, M. Liberman, M. Marcus, S. Roukos, B. Santorini, and T. Strzalkowski. 1991. A Procedure for Quantitatively Comparing the Syntactic Coverage of English Grammars. In *Proceedings of the Fourth DARPA Workshop on Speech and Natural Language*. San Mateo, CA: Morgan Kaufmann.

Bloomfield, Leonard. 1933. *Language*. Holt, Rinehart and Winston: New York.

—— 1962. *The Menomini Language*. Charles F. Hockett (ed.) New Haven: Yale University Press

Booch, Grady. 1994. *Object-oriented Analysis and Design with Applications*. 2nd edition. Redwood City, CA: Benjamin/Cummings Publishing Co.

Borgida, Alexander. 1985. Features of Languages for the Development of Information Systems at the Conceptual Level. *IEEE Software* 2(1):63–72.

Bresnan, Joan, Ronald Kaplan, Stanley Peters, and Annie Zaenen. 1982. Cross-serial Dependencies in Dutch. *Linguistic Inquiry* 13(4):613–35.

Brill, Eric. 1995. Transformation-Based Error-Driven Learning and Natural Language Processing: A Case Study in Part-of-Speech Tagging. *Computational Linguistics* 21(4):543–65.

Bringhurst, Robert. 1992. *The Elements of Typographic Style*. Vancouver: Hartley & Marks.

Brooks, Frederick P. 1995. *The Mythical Man-Month*. 20th Anniversary Edition. Reading, MA: Addison Wesley.

Brugman, Claudia. 1981. *Story of "Over"*. MA thesis. University of California, Berkeley. (Available from the University of Indiana Linguistics Club.)

Burnard, Lou D. 1991. An Introduction to the Text Encoding Initiative. In Daniel I. Greenstein (ed.). *Modeling Historical Data: Towards a Standard for Encoding and Exchanging Machine-Readable Texts*. (Halbgraue Reihe zur Historischen Fachinformatik, Serie A, Historische Quellenkunden, Band 1.) Max-Planck-Institut für Geschichte.

Burns, Hugh, James W. Parlett, and Carol Luckhardt Redfield. 1991. *Intelligent Tutoring Systems: Evaluations in Design*. Hillsdale, NJ: Lawrence Erlbaum Associates.

Butler, Christopher S. 1985. *Computers in Linguistics*. Oxford: Blackwell.

Charniak, Eugene. 1993. *Statistical Language Learning*. Cambridge, MA: MIT Press.

Chinchor, Nancy and Beth Sundheim. 1993. MUC-5 Evaluation Metrics. In *Proceedings of the Fifth Message Understanding Conference (MUC-5)*, 69–78.

Chinchor, Nancy, Lynette Hirschman, and David. D. Lewis. 1993. Evaluating Message Understanding Systems: An Analysis of the Third Message Understanding Conference (MUC-3). *Computational Linguistics* 19:409–49.

Chomsky, Noam. 1956. Three Models for the Description of Language. *IRE Transactions on Information Theory* IT-2:113–34.

—— 1963. Formal Properties of Grammars. In R. Duncan Luce *et al.* (eds). *Handbook of Mathematical Psychology* 2:328–428. New York: Wiley.

Church, Kenneth W. 1988. A Stochastic Parts Program and Noun Phrase Parser for Unrestricted Text. In *Proceedings of the Second Conference on Applied Natural Language Processing*. Austin, TX.

Church, Kenneth W. and Robert L. Mercer. 1993. Introduction to the Special Issue on Computational Linguistics Using Large Corpora. *Computational Linguistics* 19(1):1–24.

Coad, Peter, and Edward Yourdon. 1991. *Object-oriented analysis*. 2nd edition. Englewood Cliffs, NJ: Prentice-Hall.

Cole, P. (ed.). 1981. *Radical Pragmatics*. New York: Academic Press.

Cole, P. and J. Morgan (eds). 1975. *Syntax and Semantics 3: Speech Acts*. New York: Academic Press.

Collins, Michael. 1996. A New Statistical Parser Based on Bigram Lexical Dependencies. In *Proceedings of the 34th Annual Meeting of the Association for Computational Linguistics*.

Comrie, Bernard (ed.). 1987. *The World's Major Languages*. Oxford: Oxford University Press.

Comrie, Bernard and Norval Smith. 1977. Lingua Descriptive Studies: Questionnaire. *Lingua* 42:1.

Coombs, James H., Allen H. Renear, and Steven J. DeRose. 1987. Markup Systems and the Future of Scholarly Text Processing. *Communications of the ACM* 30:933–47.

Cover, Robin. 1992. Standard Generalized Markup Language: Annotated Bibliography and List of References. *<TAG>: The SGML newsletter</>* 5(3):4–12, 5(4):13–24, 5(5):25–36. (See http://www.sil.org/sgml for Cover's Web site which features an up-to-date version of this bibliography and a wealth of pointers to SGML resources.)

Craig, Collette (ed.). 1986. *Categorization and Noun Classification*. Philadelphia: Benjamins North America.

Culy, Christopher. 1985. The Complexity of the Vocabulary of Bambara. *Linguistics and Philosophy* 8(3):345–51.

Cutting, Doug, Julian Kupiec, Jan Pedersen, and Penelope Sibun. 1991. A Practical Part-of-Speech Tagger. In *Proceedings of the Third Conference on Applied Natural Language Processing*. Trento, Italy.

Davis, Daniel W. and John S. Wimbish. 1993. *The Linguist's Shoebox: An Integrated Data Management and Analysis Tool (version 2.0)*. Waxhaw, NC: Summer Institute of Linguistics.

Davis, Mark E. 1987. The Macintosh Script System. *Newsletter for Asian and Middle Eastern Languages on Computer* 2(1&2):9–24.

Dik, Simon C. 1989. *The Theory of Functional Grammar, Part I*. Dordrecht: Foris.

Dougherty, Dale. 1990. *sed & awk*. Sebastopol, CA: O'Reilly & Associates.

Dresher, B. Elan and Jonathan D. Kaye. 1990. A Computational Learning Model for Metrical Phonology. *Cognition* 34:137–95.

Ephratt, Michal. 1992. Developing and Evaluating Language Courseware. *Computers and the Humanities* 26:249–59.

Fellbaum, Christiane. 1990. English Verbs as a Semantic Net. *International Journal of Lexicography* 3(4):278–301.

Findler, Nicholas V. 1992. Automatic Rule Discovery for Field Work in Anthropology. *Computing in the Humanities* 26:285–92.

Ford, Ric, and Connie Guglielmo. 1992. Apple's New Technology and Publishing Strategies. *MacWeek* (September 28, 1992): 38–40.

Frantz, Donald G. 1970. A PL/I Program to Assist the Comparative Linguist. *Communications of the ACM* 13(6):353–56.

Fraser, Norman and Richard A. Hudson. 1992. Inheritance in Word Grammar. *Computational Linguistics* 18:133–58.

Friedl, Jeffrey. 1997. *Mastering Regular Expressions.* Sebastopol, CA: O'Reilly & Associates.

Fuchs, Ira. 1988. Research Networks and Acceptable Use. *EDUCOM Bulletin* Summer/Fall: 43–8.

Gazdar, Gerald, Ewan Klein, Geoffrey Pullum, and Ivan Sag. 1985. *Generalized Phrase Structure Grammar.* Cambridge, MA: Harvard University Press.

Goldfarb, Charles F. 1990. *The SGML Handbook.* Oxford: Oxford University Press.

Goodman, Danny. 1990. *The Complete HyperCard Handbook.* 3rd ed. New York: Bantam Books.

Grice, H. P. 1975. Logic and Conversation. In Cole and Morgan (eds), 1975: 41–58.

—— 1981. Presupposition and Conversational Implicature. In Cole (ed.), 1981: 183–198.

Grishman, Ralph and Beth Sundheim. 1996. Message Understanding Conference 6: A Brief History. In *Proceedings of the Sixteenth International Conference on Computational Linguistics (COLING-96).*

Gross, Derek and Katherine J. Miller. 1990. Adjectives in WordNet. *International Journal of Lexicography* 3(4):265–77.

Grosz, Barbara J. and Candace Sidner. 1986. Attention, Intentions, and the Structure of Discourse. *Computational Linguistics* 12:175–204.

Grosz, Barbara J., Aravind K. Joshi, and Scott Weinstein. 1995. Centering: A Framework for Modeling the Local Coherence of Discourse. *Computational Linguistics* 21:203–25.

Harris, Zellig. 1951. *Methods in Structural Linguistics.* Chicago: University of Chicago Press.

Harrison, Philip, Steven Abney, Ezra Black, Dan Flickenger, Claudia Gdaniec, Ralph Grishman, Donald Hindle, Robert Ingria, Mitch Marcus, Beatrice Santorini, and Tomek Strzalkowski. 1991. Evaluating Syntax Performance of Parser/Grammars of English. In Neal and Walter 1991:71–77.

Harrison, Philip. 1988. *A New Algorithm for Parsing Generalized Phrase Structure Grammar.* PhD dissertation. University of Washington, Seattle.

Heim, Michael. 1986. Humanistic Discussion and the Online Conference. *Philosophy Today* 30:278–88.

Herwijnen, Eric van. 1994. *Practical SGML.* 2nd ed. Dordrecht: Kluwer Academic Publishers.

Hindle, Donald and Mats Rooth. 1993. Structural Ambiguity and Lexical Relations. *Computational Linguistics* 19(1):103–20.

Hindle, Donald. 1990. Noun Classification from Predicate Argument Structures. In *Proceedings of the 28th Annual Meeting of the Association for Computational Linguistics*: 268–75.

Hirschberg, Julia and Diane Litman. 1993. Empirical Studies on the Disambiguation of Cue Phrases. *Computational Linguistics* 19:501–30.

Hirschman, Lynette, Madeleine Bates, Deborah Dahl, William Fisher, John Garofolo, David Pallett, Kate Hunicke-Smith, Patti Price, Alex Rudnicky, and Christine Pao. 1992. Multi-Site Data Collection for a Spoken Language Corpus. In *Proceedings of the International Conference on Spoken Language Processing.* Banff, Canada.

Hoard, James E. and Wolf Kohn. 1994. *A Synopsis of a Relational Logic Model of Natural Language Semantics.* Boeing Computer Services Technical Report, BCSTECH-94-037.

Hoard, James E., Richard Wojcik, and Katherina Holzhauser. 1992. An Automated Grammar and Style Checker for Writers of Simplified English. In Holt and Williams, 1992:278–96.

Hobbs, Jerry. 1978. Resolving Pronoun References. *Lingua* 44:311–38.

Hockey, Susan. 1989–92a. Chairman's Report. *Literary and Linguistics Computing* 4(4):300–02, 5(4):334–46, 6(4):299, 7(4):244–45.

—— 1992b. Some Perspectives on Teaching Computers and the Humanities. *Computing in the Humanities* 26:261–6.

Hofstadter, Douglas R. and Daniel C. Dennett. 1981. *The Mind's I*. New York: Basic Books.

Holt, Patrick O'Brian and Noel Williams (eds). 1992. *Computers and Writing: State of the Art*. Dordrecht: Kluwer.

Hudson, Richard. 1984. *Word Grammar*. Oxford: Blackwell.

—— 1990. *English Word Grammar*. Oxford: Blackwell.

Huls, Carla, Edwin Bos, and Wim Claasen. 1995. Automatic Referent Resolution of Deictic and Anaphoric Expressions. *Computational Linguistics* 21:59–79.

Hunt, Geoffrey R. 1988. Tone and Stress Analysis. *Notes on Linguistics* 41:14–18.

—— 1992. A Good Phonology Program. *Notes on Linguistics* 41:14–18.

Ide, Nancy. 1991. Computational Linguistics. In Lancashire, 1991:32–67.

Ingria, Robert J. P. and David Stallard. 1989. A Computational Mechanism for Pronominal Reference. In *Proceedings of the 27th Annual Meeting of the Association for Computational Linguistics*: 262–71. Vancouver, BC.

Irizarry, Estelle. 1992. Courseware in the Humanities: Expanded Horizons. *Computing in the Humanities* 26:275–84.

ISO. 1986. *Information Processing – Text and Office Systems – Standard Generalized Markup Language (SGML)*. ISO 8879–1986 (E). Geneva: International Organization for Standards, and New York: American National Standards Institute.

Johnson, Jeff and Richard J. Beach. 1988. Styles in Document Editing Systems. *IEEE Computer* 21(1):32–43.

Johnson, Mark. 1987. *The Body in the Mind: The Bodily Basis of Meaning, Imagination, and Reason*. Chicago: University of Chicago Press.

Kac, Michael. 1987. Surface Transitivity, *Respectively* Coordination and Context-Freeness. *Natural Language and Linguistic Theory* 5(3):441–52.

Kaliski, Terry. 1992. Computer-Assisted Language Learning (CALL). In Roach, 1992:97–110.

Kaplan, Ronald M. and Martin Kay. 1994. Regular Models of Phonological Rule Systems. *Computational Linguistics* 20:331–78.

Karttunen, Lauri. 1971. Implicative Verbs. *Language* 47:340–58.

—— 1983. KIMMO: A General Morphological Processor. *Texas Linguistic Forum* 22:163–86.

Kay, Martin, Jean Mark Gowron, and Peter Norvig. 1994. *Verbmobil: A Translation System for Face-to-Face Dialog*. CSLI Lecture Notes no. 33. Stanford, CA: Center for the Study of Language and Information.

Kehler, Andrew. 1994. Common Topics and Coherent Situations: Interpreting Ellipsis in the Context of Discourse Inference. In *Proceedings of the 32nd Annual Meeting of the Association for Computational Linguistics*: 50–7. Las Cruces, NM.

Kempson, Ruth M. (ed.). 1988a. *Mental Representations*. Cambridge: Cambridge University Press.

Kempson, Ruth M. 1988b. The Relation Between Language, Mind, and Reality. In Kempson, 1988a:3–25.

Kernighan, Brian, and Dennis Ritchie. 1978. (Second edition 1988.) *The C Programming Language*. Englewood Cliffs, NJ: Prentice-Hall.

Kernighan, Brian and P. J. Plauger. 1976. *The Elements of Programming Style*. Englewood Cliffs, NJ: Prentice-Hall.

—— 1976. *Software Tools*. New York: Addison Wesley.

—— 1981. *Software Tools in Pascal*. New York: Addison Wesley.

Kernighan, Brian and Rob Pike. 1984. *The Unix Programming Environment*. Englewood Cliffs, NJ: Prentice-Hall.

Kerr, Elaine B. 1986. Electronic Leadership: A Guide to Moderating Online Conferences. *IEEE Transactions on Professional Communication* 29(1):12–18.

Kew, Jonathan and Stephen McConnel. 1990. *Formatting Interlinear Text*. Occasional Publications in Academic Computing 17. Dallas, TX: Summer Institute of Linguistics.

Kew, Priscilla M. and Gary F. Simons (eds). 1989. *Laptop Publishing for the Field Linguist: An Approach Based on Microsoft Word*. Occasional Publications in Academic Computing 14. Dallas, TX: Summer Institute of Linguistics.

Kidder, Tracy. 1981. *The Soul of a New Machine*. New York: Little, Brown.

Kiraz, George A. 1996. SEMHE: A Generalized Two-Level System. In *Proceedings of the 34th Annual Meeting of the Association for Computational Linguistics*: 159–66. Santa Cruz, CA.

Klavans, Judith and Martin S. Chodorow. 1991. Using a Morphological Analyzer to Teach Theoretical Morphology. In *Computers and the Humanities* 5:281–87.

Klavans, Judith and Philip Resnik. 1996. *The Balancing Act*. Cambridge, MA: MIT Press.

Kleene, Stephen C. 1956. Representation of Events in Nerve Nets and Finite Automata. In Claude Shannon and John McCarthy (eds). *Automata Studies*. Princeton, NJ: Princeton University Press. 3–42.

Knowles, Gerald. 1986. The Role of the Computer in the Teaching of Phonetics. *CELTR* 133–48.

—— 1990. The Use of Spoken and Written Corpora in the Teaching of Language and Linguistics. *Literary and Linguistic Computing* 5:45–8.

Knuth, Donald E. 1986. *The T$_e$Xbook*. Reading, MA: Addison Wesley.

Koskenniemi, Kimmo. 1983. *Two-level Morphology: A General Computational Model for Word-Form Recognition and Production*. Publication No. 11. University of Helsinki: Department of General Linguistics.

—— 1984. A General Computational Model for Word-Form Recognition and Production. In *Proceedings of the 10th International Conference on Computational Linguistics / 22nd Annual Meeting of the Association for Computational Linguistics*: 178–181. Stanford, CA.

Krol, Ed. 1994. *The Whole Internet*. Sebastopol, CA: O'Reilly & Associates.

Kučera, Henry and W. Nelson Francis. 1967. *Computational Analysis of Present-Day American English*. Providence, RI: Brown University Press.

Kupiec, Julian. 1992. Robust Part-of-Speech Tagging Using a Hidden Markov Model. *Computer Speech and Language* 6:226–242.

Ladefoged, Peter. 1992. *A Course in Linguistics*. New York: Harcourt Brace Jovanovitch.

Ladefoged, Peter. 1993. *A Course in Phonetics*. 3rd edition. Fort Worth London: Harcourt Brace College.

Lafferty, J., D. Sleator, and D. Temperley. 1992. Grammatical Trigrams: A Probabilistic Model Of Link Grammar. In *Probabilistic Approaches to Natural Language*. AAAI Technical Report FS-92-04.

Lakoff, George and Mark Johnson. 1980. *Metaphors We Live By*. Chicago: University of Chicago Press.

Lakoff, George. 1987. *Women, Fire, and Dangerous Things: What Categories Reveal About the Mind*. Chicago: University of Chicago Press.

Lamport, Leslie. 1986. *LaT$_e$X: a Document Preparation System*. Reading, MA: Addison Wesley.

Lancashire, Ian. 1991. *The Humanities Computing Yearbook 1989–90*. Oxford: Clarendon Press.

Lancashire, Ian, John Bradley, Michael Stairs, Willard McCarty, and T. R. Wooldridge. 1996. *Using TACT with Electronic Texts: A Guide to Text-Analysis Computing Tools*. Modern Language Association (Book and CD-ROM).

Langacker, Ronald W. 1987. *Foundations of Cognitive Grammar. Vol. 1: Theoretical Prerequisites*. Stanford: Stanford University Press.

Langendoen, D. Terence and Gary F. Simons. 1995. A Rationale for the TEI Recommendations for Feature Structure Markup. *Computers and the Humanities* 29:191–209.

Lappin, Shalom and Herbert J. Leass. 1994. An Algorithm for Pronominal Anaphora Resolution. *Computational Linguistics* 20:535–61.

Levy, Steven. 1984. *Hackers: Heroes of the Computer Revolution*. New York: Doubleday/Anchor.

Libes, Don. 1989. *Life With Unix*. Englewood Cliffs, NJ: Prentice-Hall.

Liu, Cricket, Jerry Peek, Russ Jones, Bryan Buus, and Adrian Nye. 1994. *Managing Internet Information Services*. Sebastopol, CA: O'Reilly & Associates.

London, Jack. *The Call of the Wild*. Available from Project Gutenberg at ftp://ftp.cdrom.com/.22/gutenberg/etext95/callw10.txt

MacCormac, Earl R. 1985. A Cognitive Theory of Metaphor. Cambridge, MA: Bradford Books, MIT Press.

Macfarland, Talke. 1997. Introspection versus Corpus Data: The Case of the Passive Cognate Object Construction. Paper presented at the 1997 LSA meeting, Chicago, IL.

Mackay, Wendy E. 1988. Diversity in the Use of Electronic Mail: A Preliminary Inquiry. *ACM Transactions on Office Information Systems* 6(4):380–97.

Magerman, David. 1994. *Natural Language Parsing As Statistical Pattern Recognition*. PhD dissertation. Department of Computer Science, Stanford University.

Marcus, Mitchell P., Beatrice Santorini, and Mary Ann Marcinkiewicz. 1993. Building a Large Annotated Corpus of English: the Penn Treebank. *Computational Linguistics* 19. Reprinted in Susan Armstrong (ed.) 1994. *Using Large Corpora*. Cambridge, MA: MIT Press.

Martin, James H. 1992. Computer Understanding of Conventional Metaphoric Language. *Cognitive Science* 16:233–70.

Maxwell, Michael. 1994. Parsing Using Linearly Ordered Phonological Rules. In *Proceedings of the Workshop of the First Meeting of the ACL Special Interest Group in Computational Phonology*: 59–70.

McLean, Ruari. 1980. *The Thames and Hudson Manual of Typography*. London: Thames and Hudson.

Merialdo, Bernard. 1994. Tagging English Text with a Probabilistic Model. *Computational Linguistics* 20(5):155–171.

Michaelis, Laura. 1996. On the Use and Meaning of "Already". *Linguistics and Philosophy* 19(5):477–502.

Mikheev, Andrei. 1996. Unsupervised Learning of Word-Category Guessing Rules. In *Proceedings of the 34th Annual Meeting of the Association for Computational Linguistics*: 327–33.

Miller, George A. 1990. Nouns in WordNet: A Lexical Inheritance System. *International Journal of Lexicography* 3(4):245–64.

Miller, George A., Richard Beckwith, Christiane Fellbaum, Derek Gross, and Katherine A. Miller. 1990. Introduction to WordNet: An On-line Lexical Database. *International Journal of Lexicography* 3(4):235–44.

Monmonier, Mark. 1993. *Mapping It Out: Expository Cartography for the Humanities and Social Science*. Chicago: University of Chicago Press.

Müller, Hans, V. Amerl, and G. Natalis. 1980. Worterkennungsverfahren als Grundlage einer Universalmethode zur automatischen Segmentierung von Texten in Sätze. Ein Verfahren zur maschinellen Satzgrenzenbestimmung im Englischen. *Sprache und Datenverarbeitung* 1.

Neal, Jeannette G. and Sharon M. Walter (eds). 1991. *Natural Language Processing Systems Evaluation Workshop*. Rome Laboratory, Technical Report, RL-TR-91-362.

Neal, Jeannette G., Elissa L. Feit, Douglas J. Funke, and Christine A. Montgomery. 1992. *An Evaluation Methodology for Natural Language Processing Systems*. Rome Laboratory, Technical Report, RL-TR-92-308.

Newmeyer, Frederick J. 1986. *Linguistic Theory in America*. 2nd edition. Orlando, FL: Academic Press.

Nicolino, Thomas A. 1994. A Natural Language Processing Based Situation Display. In *Proceedings of the 1994 Symposium on Command and Control Research and Decision Aids*: 575–80. Monterey, CA: Naval Postgraduate School.

Nunberg, Geoffrey. 1990. *The Linguistics of Punctuation*. CSLI Lecture Notes, no. 18. Stanford, CA: Center for the Study of Language and Information.

Oflazer, K. 1994. Two-level Description of Turkish Morphology. *Literary and Linguistic Computing* 9:137–48.

Palmer, David D. and Marti A. Hearst. 1997. Multilingual Adaptive Sentence Boundary Disambiguation. *Computational Linguistics* 23(2):241–67.

Parker, Rogers C. 1988. *Looking Good in Print: A Guide to Basic Design for Desktop Publishing*. Chapel Hill, NC: Ventana.

—— 1989. *The Make-Over Book*. Chapel Hill, NC: Ventana.

Parunak, H. Van Dyke. 1982. Database Design for Biblical Texts. In Richard W. Bailey (ed.). *Computing in the Humanities*. Amsterdam, NY: North Holland Publishing Company. 149–61.

Passonneau, Rebecca J. 1989. Getting at Discourse Referents. In *Proceedings of the 27th Annual Meeting of the Association for Computational Linguistics*: 51–9. Vancouver, BC.

Perfect, Christopher and Jeremy Austin. 1992. *The Complete Typographer*. Englewood Cliffs, NJ: Prentice-Hall.

Pieraccini, Roberto and Esther Levin. 1995. Spontaneous-Speech Understanding System for Database Query Applications. In *Proceedings of the ESCA Workshop on Spoken Dialogue Systems*. Vigso, Denmark.

Pollard, Carl and Ivan A. Sag. 1987. *Information-based Syntax and Semantics, Volume 1: Fundamentals*. CSLI Lecture Notes no. 13. Stanford, CA: Center for the Study of Language and Information.

—— 1994. *Head-driven Phrase Structure Grammar*. CSLI: Stanford, CA. Chicago: University of Chicago Press.

Price, Patti. 1996. Combining Linguistic with Statistical Methods in Automatic Speech Understanding. In Klavans and Resnik, 1996:119–34.

Proceedings of the Fifth Message Understanding Conference (MUC-5). 1993. Sponsored by the Advanced Research Projects Agency (ARPA), Software and Intelligent Systems Technology Office. San Francisco: Morgan Kaufmann Publishers.

Psotka, Joseph, L. Dan Massey, and Sharon A. Mutter. 1988. *Intelligent Tutoring Systems: Lessons Learned*. Hillsdale, NJ: Lawrence Erlbaum Associates.

Pullum, Geoffrey K. and William A. Ladusaw. 1996. *Phonetic Symbol Guide*. Choicago: University of Chicago Press.

Pustejovsky, James, Sabine Bergler, and Peter Anick. 1993. Lexical Semantic Techniques for Corpus Analysis. *Computational Linguistics* 19(2):331–358.

Quarterman, John S. 1995. *The Matrix: Computer Networks and Conferencing Systems Worldwide*. Bedford, MA: Digital Press.

Rabiner, Lawrence R. 1989. A Tutorial on Hidden Markov Models and Selected Applications in Speech Recognition. In *Proceedings of the IEEE*, reprinted in Waibel and Lee, 1990:267–96.

Raymond, Eric S. 1996. *The New Hacker's Dictionary*. 3rd edition. Cambridge, MA: MIT Press.

Reichman, Rachel. 1985. *Getting Computers to Talk Like You and Me*. Cambridge, MA: Bradford Books, MIT Press.

Rettig, Marc, Gary F. Simons, and John V. Thomson. 1993. Extended Objects. *Communications of the ACM* 36(8):19–24.

Rettig, Marc. 1992. Practical Programmer: A Succotash of Projections and Insights. *Communications of the ACM* 35(10):25–30.

Riley, Michael D. 1989. Some Applications of Tree-based Modelling to Speech and Language Indexing. In *Proceedings of the DARPA Speech and Natural Language Workshop*: 339–52. Morgan Kaufmann: San Mateo, CA.

Roach, Peter (ed.). 1992. *Computing in Linguistics and Phonetics: Introductory Readings*. London: Academic Press.

Roche, Emmanuel and Yves Schabes. 1995. Deterministic Part-of-Speech Tagging with Finite-State Transducers. *Computational Linguistics* 21(2):227–53.

Rosch, Eleanor. 1978. Principles of Categorization. In Rosch and Lloyd, 1978:27–48.

—— 1983. Prototype Classification and Logical Classification: The Two Systems. In Scholnick, 1983:73–86.

Rosch, Eleanor and B. B. Lloyd (eds). 1978. *Cognition and Categorization*. Hillsdale, NJ: Lawrence Erlaum Associates.

Saffran, Jenny R., Richard N. Aslin, and Elissa L. Newport. 1996. Statistical Learning by 8-Month-Old Infants. *Science* 274(5294):1926–8.

Salus, Peter 1994. *A Quarter Century of Unix*. Reading, MA: Addison Wesley.

Sanders, Ted J. M., Wilbert P. M. Spooren, and Leo G. M. Noordman. 1993. Coherence Relations in a Cognitive Theory of Discourse Representation. *Cognitive Linguistics* 4(2):93–133.

Schank, Roger and Christopher Riesbeck. 1981. *Inside Computer Understanding*. Hillsdale, NJ: Lawrence Erlbaum Associates.

Schneiderman, Ben. 1987. *Designing the User Interface*. Reading, MA: Addison Wesley.

Scholnick, E. (ed.). 1983. *New Trends in Cognitive Representation: Challenges to Piaget's Theory*. Hillsdale, NJ: Lawrence Erlbaum Associates.

Selfridge, A. 1958. Pandemonium: A Paradigm for Learning. In J.A. Anderson and E. Rosenfeld (eds). 1989. *Neurocomputing: Foundations of Research*. Cambridge, MA: MIT Press.

Sgarbas, K., N. Fakotakis, and G. Kokkinakis. 1995. A PC-KIMMO-based Morphological Description. *Literary and Linguistic Computing* 10:189–201.

Shieber, Stuart. 1986. Evidence Against the Context-Freeness of Natural Language. *Linguistics and Philosophy* 8(3):333–43.

Simons, Gary F. 1980. The Impact of On-site Computing on Field Linguistics. *Notes on Linguistics* 16:7–26.

—— 1987. Multidimensional Text Glossing and Annotation. *Notes on Linguistics* 39:53–60.

—— 1989a. The Computational Complexity of Writing Systems. In Ruth M. Brend and David G. Lockwood (eds) *The Fifteenth LACUS Forum*: 538–53. Lake Bluff, IL: Linguistic Association of Canada and the United States.

—— 1989b. Working with Special Characters. In Priscilla M. Kew and Gary F. Simons (eds). *Laptop Publishing for the Field Linguist: An Approach Based on Microsoft Word*. Occasional Publications in Academic Computing 14. Dallas, TX: Summer Institute of Linguistics, 109–18.

—— 1992. What Computer Should I Buy? *Notes on Computing* 11(5):45–7.

—— 1997. Conceptual Modeling Versus Visual Modeling: A Technological Key To Building Consensus. *Computers and the Humanities* 30(4):303–19.

Simons, Gary F. and John V. Thomson. 1988. *How to Use IT: Interlinear Text Processing on the Macintosh*. Edmonds, WA: Linguist's Software.

—— (forthcoming). Multilingual Data Processing in the CELLAR Environment. To appear in John Nerbonne (ed.). *Linguistic Databases*. Stanford, CA: Center for the Study of Language and Information. (The original working paper is available at http://www.sil.org/cellar/mlingdp/mlingdp.html)

Simons, Gary F. and Larry Versaw. 1987. *How to use IT: A Guide to Interlinear Text Processing*. Dallas, TX: Summer Institute of Linguistics. (3rd edition 1992.)

Smith, Henry C. 1985. Database Design: Composing Fully Normalized Tables from a Rigorous Dependency Diagram. *Communications of the ACM* 28(8):826–38.

Smith, J. Jerome. 1987. LEXISTAT: A Pascal Program for Creating Lexico-statistical Exercises. *Innovations in Linguistics Education* 5:71–83.

Sobin, Nicholas. 1991. An AI Approach to Teaching Linguistics. *Innovations in Linguistics Education* 5:21–34.

Sperber, Dan and Dierdre Wilson. 1986. *Relevance: Communication and Cognition*. Oxford: Blackwell.

—— 1988. Representation and Relevance. In Kempson, 1988:133–53.

Sperberg-McQueen, C. M. and Lou Burnard. 1994. *Guidelines for the Encoding and Interchange of Machine-Readable Texts*. Chicago and Oxford: Text Encoding Initiative. (See also http://www.uic.edu/orgs/tei)

Stallman, Richard M. 1993. *GNU Emacs Manual*. 9th edition, Version 19. Cambridge, MA: Free Software Foundation.

Stockwell, Robert, Paul Schachter, and Barbara Hall Partee. 1973. *The Major Syntactic Structures of English*. New York: Holt, Rinehart and Winston.

Stoll, Cliff. 1989. *The Cuckoo's Egg*. New York: Pocket Books.

Stonebraker, Michael, Heidi Stettner, Nadene Lynn, Joseph Kalash, and Antonin Guttman. 1983. Document Processing in a Relational Database System. *ACM Transactions on Office Information Systems* 1(2):143–88.

Tufte, Edward R. 1983. *Visual Display of Quantitative Information*. Cheshire, CT: Graphics Press.

—— 1990. *Envisioning Information*. Cheshire, CT: Graphics Press.

Turing, A. M. 1950. Computing Machinery and Intelligence. *Mind* 59(236): 433–60. Excerpted in Hofstadter and Dennett, 1981:53–67.

Tversky, Barbara. 1986. Components and Categorization. In Craig, 1986: 63–76.

Unicode Consortium. 1996. *The Unicode Standard: Version 2.0*. Reading, MA: Addison Wesley. (See also http://www.unicode.org)

Updegrove, Daniel. 1990. Electronic Mail and Networks: New Tools for University Administrators. *Cause/Effect* 13:41–8.

Waibel, Alex and Kai-Fu Lee. 1990. *Readings in Speech Recognition*. San Mateo, CA: Morgan Kaufmann.

Webber, Bonnie. 1988. Discourse Deixis: Reference to Discourse Segments. In *Proceedings of the 26th Annual Meeting of the Association for Computational Linguistics*: 113–21. Buffalo, NY.

Weber, David J. 1986. Reference Grammars for the Computational Age. *Notes on Linguistics* 33:28–38.

Whorf, Benjamin Lee. 1956. *Language, Thought, and Reality: Selected Writings of Benjamin Lee Whorf*. In John B. Carroll (ed.). Cambridge, MA: MIT Press.

Wiebe, Janyce M. 1994. Tracking Point of View in Narrative. *Computational Linguistics* 20:233–87.

Williams, Robin. 1990. *The Mac Is Not a Typewriter*. Berkeley, CA: Peachpit Press.

Winkler, Dan and Scot Kamins. 1990. *HyperTalk 2.0: The Book*. New York: Bantam Books.

Wojcik, Richard H., Philip Harrison, and John Bremer. 1993. Using Bracketed Parses to Evaluate a Grammar Checking Application. In *Proceedings of the 31st Annual Meeting of the Association for Computational Linguistics*: 38–45.

Yarowsky, David. 1995. Unsupervised Word Sense Disambiguation Rivaling Supervised Methods. In *Proceedings of the 33rd Annual Meeting of the Association for Computational Linguistics*: 189–96.

Zdonik, Stanley B. and David Maier (eds). 1990. *Readings in Object-oriented Database Systems*. San Mateo, CA: Morgan Kaufmann.

Index